Mentoring in early childhood education: A compilation of thinking, pedagogy and practice

Mentoring in early childhood education: A compilation of thinking, pedagogy and practice

Edited by Caterina Murphy and Kate Thornton

NZCER PRESS

NZCER PRESS
New Zealand Council for Educational Research
PO Box 3237
Wellington
New Zealand

© Authors, 2015

ISBN 978-1-927231-65-4

This book is not a photocopiable master.
No part of the publication may be copied, stored or communicated in any form by any means (paper or digital), including recording or storing in an electronic retrieval system, without the written permission of the publisher. Education institutions that hold a current licence with Copyright Licensing New Zealand may copy from this book in strict accordance with the terms of the CLNZ Licence.

A catalogue record for this book is available from the National Library of New Zealand

Designed by Smartwork Creative, www.smartworkcreative.co.nz

Cover: A photograph of a beautiful old tree in Cambridge taken by Leah Murphy. For the context of this book, this organic image represents growth, learning, wisdom, complexity and enlightenment.

Dedication

This book is dedicated to:

- all who work within the early childhood sector, and who actively mentor others and/or aspire to develop their mentoring potential
- Caterina's children and grandchildren—hold your Greek Cypriot ancestors deep within your hearts, and may someone always be there to guide you wisely, and may you, in return, guide others wisely
- Kate's mentors, past and present—for your willingness to support and challenge her.

Contents

About the contributors	viii
Foreword	xix
Preface	xxv
Acknowledgements	xxx

Part One: Mentoring and professional learning

Chapter 1: The impact of mentoring on leadership capacity and professional learning — 1
　Kate Thornton

Chapter 2: Becoming an effective mentor in early childhood settings: One programme in action — 14
　Barbara Watson

Chapter 3: Mentoring and reflective practice: Transforming practice through reflexive thinking — 25
　Elizabeth Rouse

Chapter 4: Te Whāriki: A socio-cultural framework for mentoring — 39
　Viv Shearsby

Chapter 5: Fostering pedagogical leadership through peer mentoring groups — 51
　Raewyn Penman and Kathryn O'Connell-Sutherland

Part Two: Māori perspectives

Chapter 6: Applying te ao Māori considerations within mentoring relationships — 67
　Jenny Ritchie and Carol Smith

Chapter 7: A Māori perspective of mentoring for early childhood settings — 77
　Kuni Jenkins, Meremaihi Williams, Emily Sinclair, Paeakau Harris, Heeni Jenkins and Pearl Waaka

Chapter 8: Kia tīaho Tamanuiterā: A metaphor for mentoring — 89
　Jacqui Brouwer, Gail Pierce, Julie Treweek and Tristan Wallace

Part Three: Mentoring student teachers

Chapter 9: Dual roles: Mentoring and assessment in the early childhood practicum — 105
　Karyn Aspden

Chapter 10: Contextual factors that affect the mentor–mentee relationship — 119
　Cheryl McConnell

Chapter 11: 21st century mentoring for 21st century teachers — 132
　Nicole Downie

Chapter 12: Ka puta ki te ao mārama: Te huarahi o ngā kaiārahi piri—Into the world of light: Mentoring teachers' journeys — 144
　Margaret Kempton, Rosemilly Piasi Teaheniu, Arapera Witehira, Susana Smith, Margarette Cantwell and Winnie Korina

Part Four: Mentoring through appraisal and registration

Chapter 13: Mentoring with integrity: A story of teacher registration 159
  Diti Hill and Mele Vete

Chapter 14: Mentoring provisionally registered teachers in neoliberal times 167
  Bradley Hannigan

Chapter 15: Awakening beginning teachers' passion through mentoring 178
  Celeste Harrington

Chapter 16: Mentoring through the appraisal cycle: How our team became intrinsically motivated professional learners 187
  Vicky Wilson

Chapter 17: Who's learning here? Mentee or mentor? 198
  Janet Dixon and Emma Stanic

Part Five: Mentoring complexities and future directions

Chapter 18: Politics and practices: Critical provocations for meaningful early mentoring 211
  Andrew Gibbons, Sandy Farquhar and Marek Tesar

Chapter 19: Supporting and strengthening practice with teachers of priority learners: Mentoring and managing change 223
  Claire McLachlan, Chrissy Lepper, Karen Mackay, Alison Arrow and Tara McLaughlin

Chapter 20: Mentoring Australian early childhood teachers: Belonging, being and becoming 237
  Andrea Nolan and Anne-Marie Morrissey

Chapter 21: Relational-cultural theory: Future possibilities for mentoring in early childhood education? 250
  Shirley Harris and Kaye Kara

Chapter 22: Mentoring as a navigational change compass: Attending to the personal transition process 263
  Michele Morrison and Jenny Ferrier-Kerr

Index 279

About the contributors

Alison Arrow (PhD) is a senior lecturer in literacy at Massey University. One of Alison's research areas is professional development in literacy with early childhood education teachers. She has also published on the nature of literacy in early childhood, and a current research area is looking at how young children use digital technology at home and school for literacy. Alison is currently co-principal investigator on a Ministry of Education-funded longitudinal intervention project examining the effectiveness of providing teachers with more targeted literacy teaching strategies for improving child literacy outcomes.

Karyn Aspden (PhD) is a lecturer in early-years education at the Institute of Education, Massey University. She began her career as a teacher and leader in a range of early childhood services, before moving into initial teacher education. Her teaching and research interests include practicum, professional practice, effective teaching practice, early intervention, and infant and toddler pedagogy. The importance of meaningful relationships is the thread that weaves through each of these areas. Karyn has recently completed her doctorate, with a focus on the assessment of practicum in early childhood initial teacher education.

Jacqui Brouwer (PGDipEd) is a professional leader for Central Kids Kindergartens. Currently she is pausing from her master's and focusing on te reo rangatira to build her puna mātauranga. She is of Ngāti Porou and English descent, a wife, and a mother of two amazing children. She has been a part of the early childhood education whānau for 28 years.

Margarette Cantwell (PGDip) found her passion teaching infants, toddlers and young children after some years' teaching in primary schools and having a family. She spent 18 years teaching and managing early childhood education and care centres, and continued to study and gain qualifications. Margarette wanted to make a difference in more children's lives by educating teachers, so she began her next path—lecturing in a tertiary institution. Margarette is currently leader, education delivery, at the Manukau base of Te Rito Maioha Early Childhood New Zealand.

Janet Dixon (MEd) has been involved in early childhood for over 40 years. She has worked in kindergartens, private day care, university and community settings. Janet is currently an adviser/facilitator and has been mentoring provisionally registered teachers for 5 years.

Nicole Downie (MEdLdrshp) is a principal academic staff member at Waikato Institute of Technology, Hamilton. Nicole lectures on the Bachelor of Teaching (ECE), is the co-ordinator of practicum, and is a key member of the early childhood education leadership team within the School of Education. She has taught in the early childhood education sector for the past 20 years. Her experience includes child care, kindergarten, and hospital-based early childhood education. Nicole lives in Te Awamutu, with her 3-year-old son and husband.

Sandy Farquhar (PhD) began her teaching career as a kindergarten teacher. She is currently a senior lecturer, early childhood education, in the Faculty of Education at the University of Auckland. Her research interests focus on teachers' work, professionalism, narrative and identity politics. She is a member of the Philosophy of Education Society of Australasia, and has published and presented nationally and internationally in philosophy and early childhood education. She is also a co-convenor of the Narrative and Metaphor Special Interest Network.

Jenny Ferrier-Kerr (MEd) is a senior lecturer in initial teacher education and educational leadership at the Faculty of Education, University of Waikato, Hamilton. Jenny's research spans a range of topics, from the teaching practicum, professional development and inter-university partnerships, to tertiary educators' experiences of being mentored for teaching pedagogy. She has also developed and teaches postgraduate coaching and mentoring qualifications. Jenny is currently a member of the editorial board for *The International Journal of Evidence-Based Coaching and Mentoring*. Recently published papers focus on sustainable e-mentoring programmes in schools, and enhancing educational leaders' practice through coaching conversations.

Andrew Gibbons (PhD) is an early childhood teacher educator and associate professor at the School of Education at AUT University. He has worked as a journalist, in the social services in England, and in early childhood education in Auckland. Andrew's research draws together a wide range of contexts associated with the work of early childhood teachers and the philosophy of education, with a particular interest in the role of new media and the construction of the early childhood teaching profession. He is associate editor of *The Encyclopaedia of Educational Philosophy and Theory*, and a member of the Philosophy of Education Society of Australasia.

Bradley Hannigan (PhD) is a senior education advisor at Nelson Tasman Kindergartens, where he works with kaiako to enhance outcomes for tamariki, kaiako and whānau. His research interests include curriculum development, critical education theory, philosophy of education, and strategic organisational management.

Celeste Harrington (MEd) has been involved in mentoring for most of her career. However, it has been in the last 15 years, as an early childhood educator, that mentoring has become central to the work she does with and alongside others. As a lecturer visiting students, and as a professional leader working with provisionally registered teachers, Celeste has mentored many teachers from varied backgrounds, and the parallel learning this has offered continues to be rewarding. Celeste is currently working as the manager of the University of Auckland Childcare Centres.

Paeakau Harris (MIS) is the Acting Programme Coordinator for the Bachelor of Education at Te Whare Wānanga o Awanuiārangi as well as being a lecturer in the Education courses. She completed research in the Induction and Mentoring Pilot for NZTC project 2008–2011. She is enrolled in Te Whare Wānanga o Awanuiārangi's Professional Doctorate programme.

Shirley Harris (PhD) is currently the curriculum adviser (research) at the New Zealand Tertiary College. As part of this role she oversees research for the Christchurch campus. Previously she led research and degree content development at the New Zealand College of Early Childhood Education. Shirley has extensive experience working across all sectors in the education system, including working as a private educational consultant and contract researcher in community-based projects at both local and national levels. Her research interests include leadership, mentoring, change management, pedagogy and research methodologies.

Diti Hill (MA Hons) has worked in the early childhood education sector for over 40 years as parent, teacher and teacher educator. She has recently retired as senior lecturer in the Faculty of Education and Social Work at the University of Auckland. Diti has always been passionate about inspiring early childhood teachers to continually explore and debate the nature of the learning–teaching process and to consider the political and ethical aspects of their practice.

Heeni Jenkins (MEd Hons) is a Lecturer in Undergraduate Studies at Te Whare Wānanga o Awanuiārangi. She is completing her PhD at Awanuiārangi. The topic of her research is 'The changing education landscape of Wānanga'.

Kuni Jenkins (PhD) is a Professor, Senior Researcher and Lecturer in Undergraduate and Post Graduate Studies at Te Whare Wānanga o Awanuiārangi. She completed research in the Induction and Mentoring Pilot for Mentoring Pilot for NZTC project 2008–2011, and a Marsden Fund Research project 2005–2008 on the history of Māori–Pākehā Relationships through First Schools in New Zealand.

Kaye Kara (MEd) is a qualified primary teacher and has extensive experience working with both early childhood and primary pre-service teachers: firstly with the University of Canterbury, and then in her current role as a lecturer at the New Zealand Tertiary College. She is working on a PhD in the area of assessment. Her main research interests are mentoring, leadership, assessment, the history and philosophy of education, and the politics of education.

Margaret Kempton (PhD) is currently a lecturer and programme developer for Te Rito Maioha Early Childhood New Zealand. She has also worked for many years as a researcher and evaluator in both community and formal educational contexts. Her current research interests include literacy learning across a range of socio-cultural contexts, as well as reducing bullying and the development of respectful relationships across contexts. She is a graduate of the University of Auckland.

Winnie Korina (BEd [ECE]) is from Kiribati/Ngāpuhi descent and has been in early childhood education for 17 years, working in various education and care centres before moving on to professional development with Pasifika centres. Winnie is currently a lecturer at Te

Rito Maioha Early Childhood New Zealand and is passionate about infants and toddler education and care, as well as how to use information and communication technology in effective ways in her teaching and in the centres.

Chrissy Lepper (BEd) is the director of early childhood development for the Massey Centre for Educational Development. She has considerable experience of both early childhood teaching and professional learning and development for the early childhood sector. In 2014 she was the recipient of the Margaret Blackwell Trust Award and travelled to Italy, Canada and the UK researching matters associated with early childhood teaching. She has led several Ministry of Education contracts in recent years and is well recognised for her leadership in the early childhood sector.

Karen Mackay (BEd) is an early childhood facilitator for the Massey Centre for Educational Development. She is an experienced early childhood teacher and in recent years has made a strong contribution to professional learning and development. Like her colleague, Chrissy Lepper, she has worked on a number of Ministry of Education contracts and is a passionate advocate for quality in early childhood education.

Cheryl McConnell (MPET) has been in early childhood education for 31 years and is a principal academic lecturer at the Eastern Institute of Technology in Hawke's Bay. Over this time she has mentored student teachers in both their field-based context (12 hours per week voluntary or paid practicum) and their teaching practicum. The opportunity to research the field-based practicum component as partial fulfilment of her Master's contributed to a growing knowledge base about this option for teacher education. Other research interests include investigating pedagogical practice where student teachers are involved in project-based learning.

Claire McLachlan (PhD) is professor of childhood education at Massey University Institute of Education. She teaches a range of papers on research methods, language and literacy, and on young children's thinking in the BA, BEd, MEd and EdD programmes, as well as providing significant postgraduate supervision. Her primary research interests include early literacy, physical activity, early childhood curriculum, assessment and evaluation, and teachers' beliefs about practice.

Her current research focuses on physical activity and nutrition in early childhood education, and the effectiveness of family literacy programmes. In 2012 Claire was awarded a Massey University Research Award for distinction in educational research.

Tara McLaughlin (PhD) is a senior lecturer in the Institute of Education at Massey University. She is an experienced teacher, teacher educator and researcher. Her current research interests relate to teaching practices that support children's learning and social-emotional competence within natural environments; professional learning opportunities for early childhood teachers and teams; family-support practices that promote home–school partnerships; and examining ways to characterise and examine childhood disability in terms of functioning and participation. She has worked with young children and children with disabilities and their families in the United States and New Zealand for over 15 years.

Michele Morrison (MEdL) is a senior lecturer in educational leadership and initial teacher education at the Faculty of Education, University of Waikato, Hamilton. Informed by extensive practitioner experience, Michele's research and teaching focus on the professional formation of educational leaders through dialogic praxis. Michele prioritises educative processes that privilege lived experience and a concern for the humanity of leadership. This has led her to develop and teach postgraduate coaching and mentoring qualifications, to research tertiary pedagogies for leadership formation, and to explore the centrality of context in change leadership, leadership for social justice and educational governance.

Anne-Marie Morrissey (PhD) is a lecturer and researcher in early childhood education at Deakin University, Australia, teaching on undergraduate and postgraduate teacher preparation programmes. She was a chief investigator for the Victorian State Wide Mentoring Programme for Early Childhood Teachers. As well as the professional development and identity of early childhood teachers, Anne-Marie's research interests include play-based pedagogy, quality in child-care programmes, early gifted development, and the role of natural outdoor spaces in children's learning, development and wellbeing.

Caterina Murphy (PhD) has been involved in early childhood education for 29 years and in tertiary education since 1999 across a range of academic roles. She is currently freelancing her academic leadership services through AcademicExpressNZ to tertiary institutions, individuals, schools and businesses. She has an MEd (Hons) from Massey University and a PhD (Indigenous Studies) from Te Whare Wānanga o Awanuiārangi. Her professional and research interests include early years education, teaching practice, mentoring, qualitative research, gifted education and oral history methodology. This is her third edited book with NZCER Press.

Andrea Nolan (PhD) is professor of education (early childhood) at Deakin University, Australia. She has had extensive experience teaching in the university sector and supervising Higher Degree Research students. Andrea has conducted research at the state, national and international level. The overarching focus of her research is on workforce development, with a specific focus on professionalisation and practice. Andrea has researched the impact of the current Australian reform agenda on professional identities and educator practice, professional work, and reflective practice as a way to better understand practice. Andrea was a chief investigator on the Victorian State Wide Mentoring Programme for Early Childhood Teachers.

Kathryn O'Connell-Sutherland (MEd) is an education services manager at Kidsfirst Kindergartens, based in Christchurch. Prior to Kidsfirst, she worked as lecturer for Te Tari Puna Ora o Aotearoa / New Zealand Childcare Association. Kathryn is passionate about supporting teachers in their professional learning and development, especially concerning bicultural practice as a Pākehā teacher and fellow learner. She has had various leadership and development roles, and a highlight was as a member of a writing team in the development of a degree programme. Kathryn is interested in the practice and learning of leadership, relational teaching and engaging in future-focused pedagogy.

Raewyn Penman (MBA) has been working for the last 5 years as an education services manager at Kidsfirst Kindergartens in the Christchurch and West Coast areas of New Zealand. Prior to joining Kidsfirst, Raewyn had extensive experience as a teacher in kindergarten and early childhood centres, a professional development facilitator, a pre-service lecturer, and an early childhood centre owner. In addition, she has held management positions in education, the disability sector and the sports sector. Raewyn combines her teaching/business administration qualifications with her practical experience to support, coach and mentor early childhood teachers in their leadership roles.

Rosemilly Piasi-Teaheniu (PGDip) is from Ndugore, Kolombangara Island, in the Solomon Islands. She has a background of primary teaching and is currently a lecturer at Te Rito Maioha Early Childhood New Zealand. Rosemilly is passionate about enhancing the knowledge and skills of indigenous educators to be able to make a difference in students' knowledge.

Gail Pierce (MEd Ldrship) is a professional leader for Central Kids Kindergartens. She has recently completed her dissertation which focused on leading from a distance. She has worked within the early childhood community for the past 30 years.

Jenny Ritchie (PhD) has a background as a child-care educator and kindergarten teacher, followed by 25 years' experience in early childhood teacher education. Her teaching, research and writing have focused on supporting early childhood educators and teacher educators to enhance their praxis in terms of cultural, environmental and social justice issues.

Elizabeth Rouse (EdD) has had many years working in the early childhood sector in Australia and is currently a lecturer and researcher in early childhood education at Deakin University. She has a strong research focus on mentoring, specifically with early childhood teachers, and has been one of a team involved in a government pilot project examining mentoring with newly graduated early childhood teachers across Victoria. Elizabeth has published a number of books and academic articles on educator professional practice, particularly in the area of educational leadership, reflective practice, and infants and toddler programmes.

Viv Shearsby (PGCertEd) has been involved in early childhood education for 25 years. The majority of her work in the last 15 years has been lecturing in early childhood teacher education and facilitating professional learning and development with teachers across Aotearoa New Zealand. Much of Viv's professional practice is currently focused on aspects of governance, management, leadership and mentoring. During the last 5 years Viv has engaged increasingly in investigating approaches to early childhood leadership, with a specific interest in transformational learning and mentoring. She also has a particular interest in teaching/learning environments, advocating the role of the environment in learning, and challenging institutionalism.

Emily Sinclair (BEd ECE) is a lecturer in early childhood education at Te Whare Wānanga o Awanuiārangi. She completed research in the Induction and Mentoring Pilot for NZTC project 2008–2011. She is curently enrolled at Waikato University to complete her Master of Education degree.

Carol Smith (BTch) has been an educator for the past 40 years in the field of early childhood education and is committed in this role to ensuring that issues relating to Te Tiriti o Waitangi and its relevance to society in Aotearoa New Zealand are embodied in all levels of education. She is passionate about social justice and challenging the powers responsible to ensure equity is addressed.

Susana Feogoaki Smith (MEd Hons) is a Niue descendant and currently a lecturer at Te Rito Maioha Early Childhood New Zealand, and teaches on the Bachelor of Early Childhood Teaching programme. She has 25 years' experience within Pasifika and mainstream early childhood educational settings and teacher education, holding both academic and leadership roles. Her research interests are in Pacific and arts education, indigenous epistemologies, infant and toddler pedagogy, mentoring, professional development and advocacy.

Emma Stanić (Grad Dip ECE) has worked with young children for the past 17 years. This is her 5th year teaching. She is currently head teacher of a community child-care centre and she has started her own journey as a mentor. She worked with Janet Dixon (co-author) for 2 years (2011–2013) towards full registration.

Marek Tesar (PhD) is a lecturer in childhood studies and early childhood education at the Faculty of Education at the University of Auckland. His focus is on the history, philosophy and sociology of childhood, and early career teachers. He has published numerous journal articles and book chapters in this area, and his doctorate on this topic received prestigious national and international awards.

Kate Thornton (PhD) is a senior lecturer and head of school (education) in the Faculty of Education at Victoria University of Wellington. Her research is primarily focused on educational leadership and leadership development. Other research interests include the use of mentoring and coaching to support leadership development, professional learning communities in early childhood education, and online professional learning. Kate is currently involved in research projects related to the educational leadership role of mentors and the sustainability of professional learning communities.

Julie Treweek (PG Dip ED Ldrshp) is a senior professional leader for Central Kids Kindergartens. She is completing her Master of Educational Leadership and is about to embark on her thesis, which will have a social justice lens and focus on the voice of children as leaders. She has been involved in early childhood education for 34 years and also has a Diploma in Early Intervention.

Mele Vete (GradDipTch ECE) began working in the early childhood sector 8 years ago and with her husband, Penisimani, owns Our Space ECE Centre in Whangaparaoa, Auckland. Mele manages the centre and is a lead teacher. She holds full teacher registration and values mentoring experiences. She thrives on open-ended dialogue with tentative outcomes; these enrich and enliven her capacity for learning and teaching.

Pearl Waaka (BEd) is a lecturer in Student Support. Her research activity was with Te Wānanga o Aotearoa in 2005 where she completed an education study in the curriculum. She is currently enrolled at Te Whare Wānanga o Awanuiārangi in a Masters in Matauranga Māori.

Tristan Wallace (BTchLn) is a professional leader for Central Kids Kindergartens. With 34 years of experience in early childhood education, he has mentored students, registering teachers, teachers and leaders. The focus of his professional life is building capacity in teachers and leaders to provide the best possible positive outcomes for children and their whānau.

Barbara Watson (MEd Admin (Hons)) is a professional learning facilitator for early childhood teachers and a director of inspirED ECE, independent professional learning and development providers based in Auckland. She previously worked in the professional learning and development team at the University of Auckland. Barbara is a qualified early childhood and primary teacher and has owned and managed early childhood centres. She graduated with a Master of Educational Administration (Hons) from Massey University in 2008, focusing on leadership and adult education, and is currently studying towards a PhD researching mentoring in education and care services

Meremaihi Williams (MIS) is the Head of School in Education at Te Whare Wānanga o Awanuiārangi where she also is a Senior Lecturer. She completed research in the Induction and Mentoring Pilot for NZTC project 2008–2011. She is currently enrolled in PhD studies at Te Whare Wānanga o Awanuiārangi.

Vicky Wilson (MTchLn) is an early childhood teacher, mentor and leader living in the Bay of Plenty. She has been a head teacher for 4 years at a kindergarten. Her Master's research, completed in 2011, had a focus on using information and communication technology in assessment to support the involvement of children, families and whānau. More recently her focus has been on supporting others to become leaders through mentoring and empowerment. She is passionate about leadership and believes in the power of self-motivation and goal setting, along with feedback for learning and positive encouragement.

Arapera Witehira (BchTch Early Years) is a pouako/lecturer at Te Rito Maioha Early Childhood New Zealand in the Manukau–Auckland teaching base. Arapera was the subject group leader and curriculum advisor for the mātauranga Māori papers of the degree programme, working alongside the academic leader. Arapera has also been part of the Early Childhood Professional Development team with the Ministry of Education offices in the Northern region, and the Early Childhood Development Unit office in the Waikato region, where she has supported centres to develop their bicultural curriculum programme.

Foreword
Mentoring in ECE: A compilation of thinking, pedagogy and practice
Anne Meade

This book explores mentoring concepts and practices, as well as research on mentoring, in early childhood education in Aotearoa New Zealand. It fills a gap in the literature not only for mentors, leaders and teachers involved in early education in this country, but also for mentors overseas and in schools. The number of chapters (22) indicates the size of the gap. Filling such a significant gap would have posed a challenge from the outset for Caterina Murphy, the instigator of the publication: How to do justice to the diversity of sub-topics, such as mentoring education as well as mentoring approaches, relationships, roles, contexts and purposes revealed in the research? How to encompass varying viewpoints on mentoring, both pragmatic and theoretical? The editors (Caterina Murphy and Kate Thornton) have managed these challenges by working with writers, both individuals and groups, who have undertaken recent research on mentoring and/or are experienced in mentoring in the early childhood sector here in Aotearoa and Australia. This publication is a wide-ranging compilation focusing on thinking, pedagogy and practice in relation to mentoring in early childhood education.

The book covers Māori perspectives, different frameworks and mentoring approaches, and mentoring for a range of types of educator, including student teachers. Many of us tend to assume it is all about mentoring individuals, because of the isolated experiences of mentoring provisionally registered teachers or student teachers in an early education setting, typically one or two at a time. The Māori perspectives chapters and the chapter by a team from a kindergarten association about peer group mentoring challenge this individualistic assumption. New Zealanders also tend to think mentoring only applies some of the time, and only to some settings. However, the chapter by Elizabeth Rouse makes us aware that mentoring is becoming far more widespread across the Tasman after the government in Australia mandated that the role of education leader is to be included in all early childhood education and care settings there.

The release of *Mentoring in Early Childhood Education* is also remarkably well timed. As one chapter in Part Five highlights, there is a connection between politics and early childhood practices, and mentoring practices are no exception. The growth in professionalism in the early childhood education sector, and critiques of the effectiveness of education more generally, has coincided with changes in the professional body for teachers in Aotearoa New Zealand, the New Zealand Teachers Council. It broadened its activities in publishing *Professional Learning Journeys: Guidelines for Induction and Mentoring and Mentor Teachers* (Teachers Council, 2011) and has provided workshops on mentoring provisionally registered teachers since 2012. More recently, it has added workshops and tools for connecting registration processes with appraisal systems for teachers. The Teachers Council's courses and tools for leaders in early childhood services and schools were designed to strengthen teachers as professionals. Coaching and mentoring for adults are core learning processes linked to these changes.

In 2015 the Teachers Council was reconstituted in law and given a new name, Education Council of Aotearoa New Zealand (EDUCANZ). Two interconnected changes for EDUCANZ in the Education Amendment Act 2015 are relevant to mentoring practices:

- EDUCANZ will grant practising certificates for 3-year periods
- at least 10 percent of appraisals for practising certificates each year will be audited by the Education Review Office.

I advise leaders in early childhood services who are responsible for teachers' appraisals to continue mentoring teachers after they become fully registered to ensure all teachers meet the Practising Teacher Criteria for renewal of their practising certificate now that the Education Review Office is involved, by law.

These policy developments have been a significant factor in a 'seismic shift' in approaches to ongoing professional learning and development for teachers, which has occurred during the last decade in Aotearoa New Zealand. Before the turn of the century individual teachers going out to 1-day courses was the norm, along with specialist professional development advisers providing research-based information and guidance in centres. Differentiation of professional development services according to the amount of experience of the teacher was seldom factored in. Evaluations of the effectiveness of courses generally showed minimal impact on learning outcomes for children.

Syntheses of research on professional development approaches, such as the best-evidence synthesis by Mitchell and Cubey (2003), pointed to the need for changes to be made in approaches to professional learning. Mitchell and Cubey found that teacher inquiry is very effective. Teacher inquiry involves teachers analysing data from their own settings, challenging existing assumptions, and thereby becoming more aware of their actions and influence. Effective approaches involve critical reflection to help teachers change unhelpful beliefs, attitudes and interactions with children and parents. Professional learning by gaining knowledge of alternative practices was found to be another effective approach for reaching the goal of all children benefiting from their early education. These conclusions were based on research where professional development advisers were involved.

In response to the report by Mitchell and Cubey (2003), and related best-evidence syntheses in New Zealand and literature reviews overseas, more whole-centre options involving teacher inquiry were established, such as the early childhood education Centres of Innovation programme, which ran from 2003 to 2009, funded by the Ministry of Education. One of the features of this programme was the use of academic research associates to mentor practitioner–researchers in the designated centres. The design of the programme attracted and grew agentic early childhood education leaders; the mentoring component strengthened the practitioner–researchers' inquiry mind set. As a consequence, the programme spawned a cohort of remarkable educational leaders, many of whom are still influencing the quality of early education in Aotearoa New Zealand today through their ongoing research and dissemination, their articulate advocacy for the best possible early education for all children, and, for some, their mentoring of other early education services and schools.

In the same decade, the Ministry of Education contracts for whole-centre professional development often included teacher-inquiry processes, with expert professional development advisers who understood best practice in adult education providing mentoring to leaders and teachers. These advisers were typically employed by tertiary institutions and were research literate and research active in their field. Within their universities there was collegial dialogue and joint projects involving the professional development advisers and early childhood education lecturers, which deepened their expertise in facilitating best practice. These collaborators added to their impact by being vocal and visible in the sector.

When the global financial crisis led to a reduction in Ministry expenditure, most of these professional learning and development programmes were stopped or reduced. It was convenient timing for policy makers, given the economic climate, that mentoring was shown to be effective. It provided a rationale for tilting responsibility for organising professional learning, including mentoring, towards early childhood education services. Individual services—or umbrella organisations, where they exist—now have to shoulder the responsibility of developing communities of learners in their workforce and finding mentors. The availability, use and visibility of expert adult educators as mentors to professional leaders in early childhood education services has waned. The seismic shift has meant that former professional development advisers have moved to other jobs and the majority of mentors at the centre level have no access to them. The loss of expertise is significant. I think the changes in the macrosystem have created gaps in New Zealand's ecology of human development (to use Bronfenbrenner's terminology)—both in the exosystem and in the mesosystem (Bronfenbrenner, 1979).

Many of the writers in this publication have responded to the shift—and the gap—through their work as mentors and their associated research and development in mentoring. It is very helpful to have their work gathered into a single volume like this. Notwithstanding the worth of this publication, there need to be more mentors with expertise in mentoring, and equitable access to them.

Most of those who have become mentors in recent years are knowledgeable and experienced educators of infants, toddlers and young children but have minimal expertise as adult educators. Yet the system expects hundreds (possibly thousands) of them to demonstrate expertise in mentoring. As several authors in this volume note, mentors now typically learn from one role model, quite possibly the person who was their own mentor and who probably lacked advanced skills, knowledge and confidence in relation to the demanding professional role of mentor.

I agree with the writers in this book who express their concern that support for professional leaders (positional leaders and mentors) to develop their capabilities to mentor adults is sparse, especially in the early childhood education sector. Some initial teacher education providers offer postgraduate papers on mentoring for educational leadership, and EDUCANZ offers day-long workshops, as described above. To my knowledge only one university has developed a full qualification on mentoring, while a few others offer a mentoring paper. But professional leaders in many locations won't be able to access any of this. Other initiatives to help educators study and gain appropriate knowledge and skills for mentoring are described in Part One of this book.

I am adding my voice to those of many writers in this book who advocate for more programmes to help professional leaders become effective mentors. Evidence points to the need for these programmes to foster 'educative mentoring':

> Educative mentoring is an approach that fosters an inquiry mindset in both mentor and mentee … educative approaches to mentoring are focused on developing reflective, agential teachers who positively affect learner outcomes. (Watson, 2015, citing Feiman-Nemser, 1998).

The educative mentoring approach is implicit in the tools that EDUCANZ has developed for its appraisal workshops for professional leaders in schools and early childhood services. They reflect the findings in best-evidence syntheses that focus on learner outcomes (Mitchell & Cubey, 2003; Timperley, Wilson, Barrar, & Fung, 2007), which have influenced the Government's increased emphasis on high-quality leadership and teaching for positive learning outcomes for all children. At the centre of the EDUCANZ evidence analysis tool for appraisals are learner outcomes, the Registered Teacher Criteria and *Tātaiko* (Ministry of Education & New Zealand Teachers Council, 2011). I applaud the inclusion of learner outcomes and *Tātaiko*.

The purposes of mentoring have been expanded in recent years by teachers and leaders developing professional learning communities, and by changes in the policy context influenced by EDUCANZ. The breadth of content in *Mentoring in Early Childhood Education* indicates the complexity of mentoring in education and the range of aspects that warrant further research and scholarship on the topic.

Filling the yawning gap in the provision of further education for mentors to give them the professional skills, knowledge and confidence they need in that role is an urgent priority. The book has set the scene well. Its arrival is a provocative reversal of what typically happens, where a tertiary programme is established and then its facilitators scramble to locate and publish relevant literature. The editors and chapter authors are to be congratulated for crafting this publication and filling gaps in the literature now.

References

Bronfenbrenner, U. (1979). *The ecology of human development: Experiments by nature.* Cambridge, Mass: Harvard University Press.

Ministry of Education and New Zealand Teachers Council (2011). *Tātaiako, cultural competencies for teachers of Māori learners.* Wellington: Ministry of Education.

Mitchell, L., & Cubey, P. (2003). *Characteristics of professional development linked to enhanced pedagogy and children's learning in early childhood settings: Best evidence synthesis.* Wellington: Ministry of Education.

New Zealand Teachers Council (2011). *Professional Learning Journeys: Guidelines for Induction and Mentoring and Mentor Teachers.* Wellington: Author.

Timperley, H., Wilson, A., Barrar, H., & Fung, I. (2007). *Teacher Professional Learning and Development: Best vidence Synthesis.* Wellington: Ministry of Education.

Watson, B. (2015). Becoming an effective mentor in early childhood settings: One programme in action. In C. Murphy & K. Thornton (Eds.). *Mentoring in early childhood education: A compilation of thinking, pedagogy and practice.* Wellington: NZCER Press.

Preface

It seems only natural that because of my Greek Cypriot heritage I would draw on early Greek history to introduce a book about mentoring. Not just because there once lived an ancient Greek, Mentor, whose name became well known when people wanted to emulate him, but also because of the influence of Socrates across the centuries. Mentor, a character in Homer's epic poem *The Odyssey*, became adviser to the son of Odysseus, the human form the gods took when they sought to intervene with the gifts of their own wisdom (Buckley, 2010). And Socrates—how did his insight come to be, his great wisdom, his ability to guide, influence, assure and uplift the identity, the most inner source of another? He most certainly believed that he was guided by God, and perhaps it was this belief that underpinned his confidence to mentor Plato, who in turn mentored Aristotle, who mentored Alexander the Great. What a global influence that mentoring process came to have: Alexander became the King of Macedonia and conqueror of the Persian Empire!

It is fair to say that it is my own passion for helping others realise and fulfil their potential that spurred the desire to produce a book of this nature. This book is by no means a 'flight of fancy'. I have been conscious of the gap in the sector of such a publication for quite some time. Mentoring has been an understated and under-discussed element of teaching, leading learning and change in the early childhood sector and, in my view, in the wider education sector also. I know only too well the very real questions, issues, dilemmas, needs and aspirations within the early childhood sector—whether from student teachers, beginning teachers or postgraduate students—where effective mentoring (or coaching) might have made someone's road to travel a little less 'bumpy' in places, a little more guided (Butcher & Murphy, 2012; McMaster & Murphy, 2014; Murphy, 2001, 2004; Murphy & Butcher, 2009a, 2009b, 2011, 2013a, 2013b, 2015). I have listened to those voices and heard them. Those voices have been in my mind during the development of this book.

Mentoring in Early Childhood Education: A Compilation of Thinking, Pedagogy and Practice is the first of its kind. *Leadership in Early Childhood* by Jillian Rodd (first published in 1994, and with subsequent editions to 2013) has been a classic text for early childhood teachers and those in teacher education relating to leadership. She suggested that

> leaders also benefit by acting as mentors. New understanding and insight can be achieved, better relationships can be developed, professional competence and careers can be enhanced and professional renewal and re-energisation can be experienced. (Rodd, 2006, p. 173)

With this assertion in mind, what sets this book apart from others is its focus on mentoring from historical, theoretical, cultural, political and practical perspectives. Its innovation also lies in the fact that it is grounded in the context of early childhood education in Aotearoa New Zealand and Australia. Aside from internet-based, blog-formatted information, this book has no equivalent.

I hope this book will empower those working in the early childhood sector to consider what the role of educative mentor (Education Council, 2015) might entail in their own context and to reflect on what knowledge, skills, talents and dispositions are required to undertake a mentoring role. The Education Council (2015) clearly indicates the importance of pedagogical expertise development and the provision of effective support "so the new teacher thrives" (p. 27). For many, mentoring has a dimension of spiritual and collective consciousness that enables them to take a 'mentoring from the heart' perspective. It still gives me real joy to see someone have a light-bulb moment, when they realise they have what it takes within them to pursue or achieve anything they want to do in life, and that they can mentor someone else along the way. They just have to find the right person for them—one who doesn't give them the answers to all their questions, but empowers them to seek out the answers themselves, to authentically delve within and truly listen to their 'inner voice' or 'self-talk'.

I hope this book challenges current, habitual ways of seeing and doing in early childhood and brings to people's attention the importance of mentoring. I also hope this book supports the many positive shifts that have started within the sector already. Mentoring is a collective process—something that can be seen by reading many of the chapters in this book. It is humbling to have such a committed group of authors for this book, who have provided the compilation of thinking, pedagogy and practice I envisioned.

The book is divided into five parts, each covering key aspects of mentoring pertaining to the early childhood context. Part 1 introduces mentoring in the context of evolving leadership capacity, providing essential information about the impact of mentoring on professional learning. Of course it includes *Te Whāriki* as a social-cultural framework through which early childhood teachers can build their own mentoring capacity.

Part 2 celebrates indigenous epistemology by examining Māori perspectives of mentoring and associated considerations.

Part 3 discusses practice issues, specifically those related to mentoring the student teacher during their teacher education practicum. Quality mentoring is essential to support and guide student teachers to make wise decisions about their teaching and to be able to further strengthen their own pedagogies.

Part 4 focuses on the mechanics of the teaching profession: the appraisal and teacher registration processes. It shares important stories of what has been occurring in the early childhood sector and highlights the attributes and dispositions required to remain motivated and strengthen relationships.

The final part presents some of the complexities and future directions for mentoring within the early childhood sector and offers provocations that should be read by all teachers, but especially those outside the immediate teaching environment, such as policy makers and those in decision-making positions. This final part concerns finding and voicing some of the powerful questions that must be asked if our sector is to progress further in the areas of quality practice, driving pedagogy and leading change.

Not all the ideas within each chapter are viewpoints endorsed in full by the editors, but that does not matter. What matters is that this book, *Mentoring in Early Childhood: A Compilation of Thinking, Pedagogy and Practice*, contains a diverse range of perspectives which represent the early childhood sector of Aotearoa New Zealand in 2015. It will be interesting over the next 10 years to see how these views will be reflected on, reconceptualised perhaps, and celebrated to have contributed to early childhood teachers strengthening their leadership and mentoring capacity. I hope you enjoy it.

Dr Caterina Murphy
AcademicExpressNZ

References

Buckley, T.A. (2010). Introduction. In Homer's *The Odyssey* (trans. Alexander Pope). Boston, MA: mobilereference.com.

Butcher, J., & Murphy, C. (2012). "It pushes you beyond the boundaries": The paradox of setting teaching goals in a field-based early childhood teacher education programme. *New Zealand Research in Early Childhood Education, 15*, 176–185.

Education Council. (2015). *Professional learning journeys: Guidelines for induction and mentoring and mentor teachers.* Retrieved from, www.educationcouncil.org.nz

McMaster, C., & Murphy, C. (Eds). (2014). *Postgraduate study in Aotearoa New Zealand: Surviving and succeeding.* Wellington: NZCER Press.

Murphy, C. (2001). Survey of early childhood postgraduate students. In S.-E. Farquhar (Ed.), *Proceedings of the fifth early childhood research symposium* (pp. 47–52). Christchurch: New Zealand Early Childhood Research Network.

Murphy, C. (2004). Steady and committed: Early childhood postgraduate students in New Zealand. *New Zealand Research in Early Childhood Education, 7*, 197–203.

Murphy, C., & Butcher, J. (2009a, January). *Stories about teaching practice: Perceptions of first year student teachers in a field-based programme.* Paper presented at NZ EC Research Symposium, Wellington.

Murphy, C., & Butcher, J. (2009b). *Teaching practice experiences of year one early childhood student teachers in a field based teacher education programme.* Retrieved from http://akoaotearoa.ac.nz/ako-hub/ako-aotearoa-northern-hub/resources/pages/teaching.

Murphy, C., & Butcher, J. (2011). The intricacies of mentoring and teaching assessment in field-based early childhood teacher education. *New Zealand Research in Early Childhood Education, 14*, 53–56.

Murphy, C. & Butcher, J. (2013a, November) *"I want to be like her": Stories of early childhood teachers concerning mentoring and leadership.* Paper presented to the NZARE conference and annual meeting, Dunedin.

Murphy, C., & Butcher, J. (2013b). They took an interest: Student teachers' perceptions of mentoring relationships in field-based early childhood teacher education. *New Zealand Research in Early Childhood Education Journal, 16*, 45–62.

Murphy, C., & Butcher, J. (2015). "It made me argue more confidently and I can stand by my words": Beginning teachers' perspectives about mentoring, goal setting, and leadership during teacher registration. *New Zealand Research in Early Childhood Education Journal, 18*, 1–19.

Rodd, J. (2006). *Leadership in early childhood* (3rd ed.). Crows Nest, NSW: Allen & Unwin.

Acknowledgements

We wish to pay tribute to:

- all the contributing authors, without whom this book would not have eventuated, and those who have supported and guided them throughout their careers and with their writing
- our husbands, for supporting us working long hours to bring this much-needed book to fruition
- Dr Richard Smith, for his assistance with proposal development and abstract selection.

PART 1: MENTORING AND PROFESSIONAL LEARNING

Chapter 1

The impact of mentoring on leadership capacity and professional learning

Kate Thornton

Introduction

Mentoring is an important strategy for supporting new and aspiring teachers, as well as experienced leaders. It is also an effective leadership approach that enhances professional learning and practice. This chapter will begin by considering definitions of mentoring and the differences and similarities between mentoring and coaching. Mentoring and coaching practices and the mentoring role of leaders from both within and outside of early childhood education (ECE) services will then be discussed.

I will be drawing on research from both the school and ECE sectors, and in particular my research over the last decade into approaches to leadership practice, leadership development, and leadership in professional learning communities. The chapter will conclude with a discussion of the lack of support for leaders to develop their mentoring and coaching capacity, and suggestions for future professional learning. This discussion provides an opportunity for teachers to reflect on how mentoring and coaching are enacted in their contexts.

Defining mentoring

Mentoring has been described as a relationship that involves supporting, motivating, shaping, guiding and encouraging, with the purpose of helping a mentee to reach their potential (Varney, 2012). While there is general agreement about these key mentoring strategies, there are different interpretations of the nature of mentoring relationships and the balance of influence within these relationships. Traditionally mentoring has referred to a more experienced person passing on their skills and knowledge to a less experienced person (Craft, 2000), but several authors advocate a less top-down, more collaborative relationship involving mutual learning (Asada, 2012; Bollinger, 2009).

The voluntary nature of mentoring relationships is also a source of debate. Traditionally, mentoring relationships are informal, and it is up to the mentee to select their own mentor. However, mentoring has increasingly become associated with formal preparation programmes, and mentors are assigned because of their expertise rather than being chosen because of their compatibility with mentees.

Mentoring or coaching?

There appears to be confusion between the terms 'mentoring' and 'coaching', with some authors suggesting there is little difference (Brockbank & McGill, 2006; Pask & Joy, 2007), while others see them as quite distinct activities (Fletcher, 2012). There seems to be broad agreement that mentoring is a more holistic term that suggests an ongoing supportive relationship, whereas coaching involves more specific actions such as listening, questioning and goal setting (Fletcher, 2012). Coaching has been described as "the process used to help people reflect, find power and courage within themselves, and think and act in new ways in order to bring about positive change" (Wise & Jacobo, 2010, p. 163). Ives (2008) considers that the purpose of coaching is to help the person being coached "to focus on and achieve their clearly defined goals" (p. 103).

It has been suggested that coaching is an essential aspect of mentoring, along with relating, assessing and guiding (Rowley, 2006). Solansky (2010) sees the two roles as complementary and advocates for mentors to engage in coaching behaviours that increase the likelihood of leadership learning. The importance of coaches using "open-ended questions to provide thought, raise awareness, and to inspire motivation and commitment" (Ives, 2008, p. 103) could also apply to mentors. Both concepts are relevant to teachers working in ECE services, whether they are in formal leadership roles or not.

There are different views on the specific expertise and skills required by mentors and coaches. Rodd (2013) suggests that mentors need to have specific knowledge and experience of the work of the mentee, while seeing coaches as taking a more specific time-bound role in helping individuals move forward, and so do not need specific expertise. However, Waniganayake, Cheeseman, Fenech, Hadley and Shepherd (2012) propose an alternative distinction, suggesting that coaches have specific expertise and focus on skill development, whereas mentoring is a process of sharing knowledge and skills and does not require technical expertise. A different perspective again is offered by Brockbank and McGill (2006), who have suggested that the most useful way of distinguishing between mentoring and coaching is by looking at the purpose and practices involved in each activity. In line with this idea, the purpose of each term was discussed above, and the practice will be explored in the following section.

Mentoring and coaching practices

Mentoring in the education sector in Aotearoa New Zealand has typically focused on supporting beginning teachers by providing access to a mentor teacher, who enables them to gain full teacher registration. The term 'mentor teacher' was introduced with the release of the *Guidelines for Induction and Mentoring and Mentor Teachers* (New Zealand Teachers Council [NZTC], 2011). The change in terminology from the previous term 'tutor teacher' to 'mentor' in these guidelines signalled a shift in the way that beginning teachers are supported, with the focus being on educative mentoring, which involves support, provision of feedback and the facilitation of "evidence-informed reflective learning conversations" (NZTC, 2011, p. 10), rather than advice and guidance that may have limited benefits.

The benefits of induction and mentoring programmes are well established. Effective mentoring of beginning teachers within schools and ECE services has been shown to have a positive effect on the retention of teachers, the quality of teaching and learning, and the achievement of students (Hobson, Ashby, Malderez, & Tomlinson, 2009; Ingersoll & Strong, 2011; Pavia, Nissen, Hawkins, Monroe, & Filimon-Demeyen, 2003).

Mentoring is also employed in many leadership development programmes because it is viewed as an effective leadership development strategy. It is one of six approaches discussed by Day (2000), who argues that mentoring can be either formal or informal, and has the potential to support leadership development if it is aimed at growing leadership in the whole organisation rather than in individual leaders. The use of mentoring to support leadership development is also discussed by Solansky (2010), who suggests that a useful purpose of mentoring is for mentees to develop security in their leadership roles. Rhodes and Fletcher (2013) highlight mentoring as an effective leadership development approach that builds self-efficacy and has the potential to reduce the attrition rate of those in leadership positions. Ongoing mentoring for leaders in ECE is promoted by Waniganayake et al. (2012), who suggest that mentoring benefits both experienced and new leaders, because mentors can act as sounding boards and critical friends. Critical friends have been described as those who offer a different perspective on one's practice (Costa & Kallick, 1995). The inherent tension between the roles of critic and friend has been discussed, with the conclusion drawn that the concept is "more complex than the simple balance between the two potentially contrasting roles, as it is the combination of these roles that provides richness" (Thornton, 2009, p. 170).

Coaching has been referred to as a key tool in programmes focused on developing school leaders (Burley & Pomphrey, 2011). Such programmes involve goal setting to support the professional learning of individual leaders, with the purpose of achieving learning and personal growth (Blackman, 2010). Coaching not only supports the professional learning of those in leadership positions, but also encourages leadership in others. Fletcher (2012) has suggested that school leaders who have been coached are likely to go on to "identify and coach aspiring leaders in their institutions" (p. 36). A leader who uses coaching as a strategy is likely to be perceived as more collaborative than directive, and more of a listener and facilitator than a teller and decision maker (Bloom & Krovetz, 2009). Coaching leaders assist those they work with to "identify their unique strengths and weaknesses and tie them to their personal and career aspirations" (Goleman, 2000, p. 87). They are less worried about short-term task completion than ongoing learning. This coaching approach to leadership is seen to have a positive impact on organisational climate and performance (Goleman, 2000).

Mentoring and coaching for leadership in early childhood education

Mentoring and coaching are both seen as important strategies for supporting leadership and professional learning in ECE settings. A study exploring the definitions and perceptions of leadership in the UK early years' sector (Aubrey, Godfrey, & Harris, 2013) identified leading others by mentoring and coaching as a common theme, along with being a role model and having a clear vision. Rodd (2013) has suggested that both mentoring and coaching are important leadership strategies for supporting the professional learning of both individuals and teams. She also likened the role of the mentor to that of a critical friend, and suggested that the relationship should be based on trust, honesty and mutual respect, and should also be supportive and non-judgemental. A recent study by Murphy and Butcher (2015) found that beginning teachers are more likely to develop confidence in their own leadership capacity if they have experienced positive mentoring relationships.

Mentoring and coaching have been promoted as strategies for both leadership development and effective leadership practice in the New Zealand ECE sector. I identified mentoring as an important leadership development strategy in a study exploring notions of leadership in the Centres of Innovation programme (Thornton, 2005). This research, which explored how leadership was defined and enacted in several of the first-round Centres of Innovation, identified a lack of support for leadership development in both teacher preparation and professional development programmes, and suggested strategies that would encourage the development of distributed leadership. Distributed leadership has been defined as leadership that is dispersed across group members and is characterised by interdependence and co-operation (Thornton, 2009). Mentoring approaches recommended in this study included developing relationships based on professionalism, mutual trust and respect. A study carried out by Clarkin-Phillips (2007) explored a particular model of professional development and identified coaching as an aspect of professional development that supports distributed leadership, along with networking and collaboration. The results of this research included the finding that distributed leadership is "a significant factor in empowering teachers and affording them opportunities for ongoing learning and leadership" (p. 132).

More recently, I have been involved in research on professional learning communities in the ECE sector. Professional learning communities are groups of "professional educators working collectively and purposefully to create and sustain a culture of learning for all students and adults" (Hipp & Huffman, 2010, p. 12). Among the indicators of effective professional learning communities are shared and supported leadership and shared personal practice, including opportunities for mentoring and coaching. Professional learning communities are relevant to the New Zealand ECE sector because there is an expectation that all registered teachers will "contribute to the professional learning community" as an indicator of "showing leadership that contributes to effective teaching and learning" (NZTC, 2011, p. 11). A national survey revealed that "opportunities for coaching and mentoring were not as prevalent as some other aspects of shared personal practice and were mainly available for provisionally registered teachers" (Thornton & Wansbrough, 2012, p. 57). This research also highlighted the importance of mentoring and coaching as leadership actions that "support the collective learning of all teachers" (p. 59). Subsequent research focused on the factors that contribute to effective professional learning communities, particularly organisational and structural factors (Cherrington & Thornton, 2015). This study involved case studies of different models of professional learning communities, and the role of the researchers/facilitators will be discussed later in the chapter.

In an article offering a vision of effective ECE leadership practice (Thornton, 2009), I suggested that relationships within and between services should include aspects of both mentoring and coaching. These relationships "may involve the professional leader mentoring less experienced teachers or they may take the form of critical friend relationships where teachers both support and challenge each other's practice" (p. 5). The lack of leadership development opportunities for those working in the New Zealand ECE sector was emphasised in this article, and there seems little evidence that anything has changed over the past 6 years.

Access to professional learning and/or tertiary qualifications for mentoring teachers was also highlighted in another New Zealand study focusing on the relationships and experiences of ECE student teachers working with their associates while on practicum (Murphy & Butcher, 2013).

Inside and outside mentoring roles

The mentoring and coaching roles taken by leaders, both within ECE services and from outside of ECE services, have been discussed in the literature. Waniganayake et al. (2012) have suggested that ECE leaders have a responsibility to mentor others in order to promote professional learning, leading to positive learning outcomes for children. Mentoring may take the form of modelling and encouraging "a culture of continual growth and professional responsibility" (Waniganayake et al., 2012, p. 100). Those who mentor or coach others can benefit just as much from the relationship as those they mentor or coach, and leaders who engage in mentoring may be encouraged to reflect on their own practice. Rodd (2013) has discussed the benefits for mentors from an ECE perspective, including the development of insight and new understanding, the enhancement of professional competence, and increased self-awareness and reflection.

The importance of trusted professionals from outside ECE services providing mentoring and coaching has been discussed in New Zealand research. My study, involving three of the first-round Centres of Innovation, identified several mentoring roles. One of these was the role taken by the programme co-ordinator, Dr Anne Meade, who provided support and encouragement to the Centres of Innovation. Also, one of the services in this study mentored a nearby service; the relationship between these services was described as collegial and ongoing (Feltham, 2004). It was not so much a relationship of dependence as one that was characterised by "trust and reciprocity" (Feltham, 2004, p.1), and involved mutual learning. Both these roles had positive impacts on the effectiveness of the programme and the sector as a whole (Thornton, 2005).

I coined the term 'trusted inquisitor' for the role I took as an action learning facilitator in my doctoral research into blended action learning for leadership learning in ECE (Thornton, 2009). As the researcher/

facilitator, I worked with small groups of leaders over a period of 6 to 8 months to support their leadership learning, both in face-to-face sessions and through online interactions—hence the term 'blended learning'. Action learning involves a questioning and reflective listening process in response to a problem or issue, and in the context of a small group of learners. This role involved coaching in the practice of "forming and encouraging trusting relationships characterised by empathy and support; and also questioning and challenging participants to encourage reflective practice and leadership learning" (Thornton, 2009, p. 169). This coaching role also involved providing participants with options for how they might proceed in their leadership journeys. As a result of being coached, participants in this study began to use coaching strategies with their teaching teams and several commented on how empowering their teachers found this approach.

The recent research exploring the relevance of professional learning communities to the New Zealand ECE sector (referred to earlier) discusses the roles taken by the facilitators/researchers and their similarity to critical friends. These roles involved facilitating face-to-face meetings and responding to the online postings of the study participants. Among the elements of the role commented on by the participants were the provision of resources, non-judgemental listening, and questioning to encourage reflection (Thornton & Cherrington, 2014), actions similar to those taken by mentors or coaches. In the more effectively functioning professional learning communities in this study, where there was a high level of relational trust and the participants were willing to be challenged, "deeper level questioning encouraged reflection and led to shifts in practice" (p. 101).

All the mentoring and coaching relationships described above promote professional learning and encourage leadership in different ways. Although leaders who coach and mentor teachers within their service provide support, someone from outside the service is able to provide a different perspective on service practice and/or leadership and can encourage critical reflection. The importance of outside facilitation to effective professional learning has been emphasised in a review of continuing professional development in the New Zealand ECE sector (Cherrington & Thornton, 2013). This outsider role was discussed in Mitchell and Cubey's (2003) best evidence synthesis on professional development in early childhood settings, which concluded that expert facilitators have an important role in challenging practice and providing alternative perspectives. The value of a trusted but impartial person from outside the service supporting a mentoring relationship was promoted by Pavia et al. (2003). These authors suggested that such third parties have the potential to contribute to the effectiveness of the relationship "by assessing the ongoing needs of both and collaborating with mentors to devise strategies for more effective interactions" (p. 259).

Future mentoring/coaching practice in the New Zealand ECE sector

The provision of support for leadership development programmes involving elements of mentoring and coaching in the New Zealand school sector contrasts with the lack of support for leadership development in the ECE sector and the lack of opportunities for those in leadership roles to develop their mentoring and coaching skills. First-time principals in Ministry of Education-funded programmes are assigned a mentor for the course of their 1-year programme, and aspiring principals involved in the National Aspiring Principals programme (also nationally funded) receive coaching. There are no equivalent Ministry of Education-funded programmes to support leadership development in the ECE sector, with the only financial support available for more generic professional development. There is clear evidence in the research literature that mentoring and coaching are important strategies for supporting beginning teachers (Murphy & Butcher, 2013), for aspiring leaders (Waniganayake et al., 2012), and for building and sustaining professional learning communities (Thornton & Cherrington, 2014). There are, however, very few opportunities for professional leaders to develop the necessary skills, or to learn about and reflect on their role as mentors and coaches.

The model of professional learning communities offers a useful framework for reflecting on the way shared and supportive leadership, collective learning, shared personal practice and supportive relationships are enacted in ECE services. Professional leaders wanting to develop collaborative leadership practices and to distribute leadership across the teaching team need to focus on effective mentoring and coaching strategies. These include listening, giving non-judgemental feedback, effective questioning, and goal setting, and their effective implementation requires specific and ongoing opportunities for professional learning.

Becoming an effective mentor requires specialist preparation and support (Patterson & Thornton, 2014). Such opportunities should be a priority for the Ministry of Education to ensure that not only are ECE teachers able to demonstrate professional leadership and participate in professional learning communities, as required in the Registered Teacher Criteria (NZTC, 2011), but can also contribute to a stronger, critically reflective ECE sector (Cherrington & Thornton, 2015).

Conclusion

Effective ECE leaders mentor and coach their colleagues and encourage them to become involved in leadership. This approach supports the development of professional learning communities, characterised by shared and supportive leadership, collective learning, shared personal practice and supportive relationships. Mentoring and coaching both require complex skills, but there are very few opportunities for leaders or teachers in the New Zealand ECE sector to develop these skills. The provision of professional learning programmes for leaders in the sector that include aspects of mentoring and coaching would provide support for effective leadership practice and for participating in professional learning communities. This provision is long overdue and should be a priority for the sector.

References

Asada, T. (2012). Mentoring: Apprenticeship or co-inquiry. In S. Fletcher & S. Mullen (Eds), *Mentoring and coaching in education* (pp. 139–154). London, UK: Sage.

Aubrey, C., Godfrey, R., & Harris, A. (2013). How do they manage?: An investigation of early childhood leadership. *Educational Management Administration & Leadership, 41*(5), 5–29.

Blackman, A. (2010). Coaching as a leadership development tool for teachers. *Professional Development in Education, 36*(3), 421–441.

Bloom, G., & Krovetz, M. (2009). *Powerful partnerships: A handbook for principals mentoring assistant principals*. Thousand Oaks, CA: Corwin Press.

Bollinger, K. (2009). Mentoring: A two way street. *Adult Learning, 20*(1/2), 39–40.

Brockbank, A., & McGill, I. (2006). *Facilitating reflective learning through mentoring and coaching.* London, UK: Kogan Page.

Burley, S., & Pomphrey, C. (2011). *Mentoring and coaching in schools.* Abingon, Oxon: Routledge.

Cherrington, S., & Thornton, K. (2013). Continuing professional development in early childhood education in New Zealand. *Early Years: An International Research Journal, 33*(2), 119–132.

Cherrington, S., & Thornton, K. (2015). The nature of professional learning communities in New Zealand early childhood education. *Professional Development in Education, 41*(2), 310–328.

Clarkin-Phillips, J. (2007). *Distributing the leadership: A case study of professional development.* Unpublished master's thesis, University of Waikato.

Costa, A., & Kallick, B. (1995). Through the lens of a critical friend. In A. Coster & B. Kallick (Eds), *Assessment in the learning organization: Shifting the paradigm* (pp. 153–156). Alexandria, VA: ASCD.

Craft, A. (2000). *Continuing professional development: A practical guide for teachers and schools.* London, UK: RoutledgeFalmer.

Day, D. (2000). Leadership development: A review in context. *Leadership Quarterly, 11*(4), 581–613.

Feltham, S. (2004). More than neighbours. *New Zealand Education Gazette, 83*(8), 1, 4, 5.

Fletcher, S. (2012). Coaching: An overview. In S. Fletcher & C. Mullen (Eds), *Mentoring and coaching in education* (pp. 24–40). London, UK: Sage.

Goleman, D. (2000). Leadership that gets results. *Harvard Business Review, 78*(2), 78–90.

Hipp, K., & Huffman, J.B. (2010). *Demystifying professional learning communities: School leadership at its best.* Plymouth, UK: Rowman & Littlefield Education.

Hobson, A., Ashby, P., Malderez, A., & Tomlinson, P. (2009). Mentoring beginning teachers: What we know and what we don't. *Teaching and Teacher Education, 25,* 207–216.

Ingersoll, R., & Strong, M. (2011). The impact of induction and mentoring programs for beginning teachers: A critical review of the research. *Review of Educational Research, 82*(2), 201–233.

Ives, Y. (2008). What is 'coaching'?: An exploration of conflicting paradigms. *International Journal of Evidence Based Coaching and Mentoring, 6*(2), 100–113.

Mitchell, L., & Cubey, P. (2003). *Professional development in early childhood settings: Best evidence synthesis iteration.* Wellington: Ministry of Education.

Murphy, C., & Butcher, J. (2013). They took an interest: Student teachers' perceptions of mentoring relationships in field-based early childhood teacher education. *New Zealand Research in Early Childhood Education Journal, 16,* 45–62.

Murphy, C., & Butcher, J. (2015). "It made me argue more confidently and I can stand by my words": Beginning teachers' perspectives about mentoring, goal setting, and leadership during teacher registration. *New Zealand Research in Early Childhood Education Journal, 18,* 1–19.

Pask, R., & Joy, B. (2007). *Mentoring-coaching.* Maidenhead, UK: Open University Press.

Patterson, S., & Thornton, K. (2014). Challenging New Zealand mentor practice. *Journal of Educational Leadership, Policy and Practice, 29*(1), 41–57.

Pavia, L., Nissen, H., Hawkins, C., Monroe, M., & Filimon-Demyen, D. (2003). Mentoring early childhood professionals. *Journal of Research in Childhood Education, 17*(2), 250–260.

NZTC. (2011). *Professional learning journeys: Guidelines for induction and mentoring and mentor teachers.* Wellington: Author.

Rhodes, C., & Fletcher, S. (2013). Coaching and mentoring for self-efficacious leadership in schools. *International Journal of Mentoring and Coaching, 2*(1), 47–63.

Rodd, J. (Ed.). (2013). *Leadership in early childhood.* Crows Nest, NSW: Allen & Unwin.

Rowley, J. (2006). *Becoming a high performance mentor.* Thousand Oaks, CA: Corwin Press.

Solansky, S. (2010). The evaluation of two key leadership development program components: Leadership skills assessment and leadership mentoring. *The Leadership Quarterly, 21*(4), 675–681.

Thornton, K. (2005). *Courage, commitment and collaboration: Notions of leadership in the New Zealand ECE centres of innovation.* Unpublished master's thesis, Victoria University of Wellington.

Thornton, K. (2009). *Blended action learning: Supporting leadership learning in the New Zealand ECE sector.* Unpublished doctoral thesis, Victoria University of Wellington.

Thornton, K., & Wansbrough, D. (2012). Professional learning communities in early childhood education. *Journal of Educational Leadership, Policy and Practice, 27*(2), 51–64.

Varney, J. (2012). Humanistic mentoring. *Kappa Delta Pi Record, 45*(3), 127–131.

Waniganayake, M., Cheeseman, S., Fenech, M., Hadley, F., & Shepherd, W. (2012). *Leadership: Context and complexities in early childhood education.* Melbourne, VIC: Open University Press.

Wise, D., & Jacobo, A. (2010). Towards a framework for leadership coaching. *School Leadership and Management, 30*(2), 159–169.

Chapter 2

Becoming an effective mentor in early childhood settings: One programme in action

Barbara Watson

Introduction

Mentoring newly qualified teachers to support them to become more effective in their roles has continued to gain importance in New Zealand and internationally over recent years. Yet, while individuals may be effective teachers of children, this does not necessarily mean they have the knowledge, skills and dispositions to be effective mentors.

In her book outlining the challenges associated with mentoring new teachers, Cameron (2009) stated that New Zealand is considered to be an international front-runner in terms of funding provided to support teachers as they make the transition into the profession. Despite this reputation, the provision of induction and mentoring programmes for those new to the profession, and the development of effective mentors to work with them, is not without its challenges. This may be particularly so for teachers in the early childhood sector, where a lack of funding support, lack of time for professional discussion, inconsistencies in the valuing and resourcing of induction and mentoring, and a scarcity of professional learning opportunities for mentors are potential constraints.

This chapter begins with an outline of what it means to be an effective mentor, including the key skills, knowledge and dispositions required. It then describes one programme in the Aotearoa New Zealand early childhood sector providing professional learning and development (PLD) for mentors. The chapter concludes with how, after reflection on the design and outcomes, we have refined the programme to better support the transfer of learning into mentor practice.

The expectation for educative mentoring

The expectations of the New Zealand Teachers Council (NZTC) with regard to the attributes of a high-quality mentor explicitly include a focus on educative mentoring. These expectations, along with requirements of induction and mentoring programmes, are outlined in *Professional Learning Journeys: Guidelines for Induction and Mentoring and Mentor Teachers* (NZTC, 2011). This publication was primarily developed to clarify expectations of what should occur in the period of provisional registration—typically, the first 2 years after graduation. However, it is also relevant for those acting as professional leaders and experienced teachers who act as mentors for others, including those who are fully registered.

Feiman-Nemser (1998) describes educative mentoring as an approach to mentoring that fosters an inquiry mind set in both the mentor and mentee. It requires mentors both to address the day-to-day issues and concerns of teachers and to have a long-term view of mentee development (Feiman-Nemser, 2001a), while viewing themselves as co-learners within the mentoring relationship. Educative approaches to mentoring are focused on developing reflective, agential teachers who positively affect learner outcomes.

By contrast, Langdon, Flint, Kromer, Ryde and Karl (2011) have described other mentoring approaches as 'limited' because they have less of a focus on mentees problematising, reflecting on and refining their practice in order to effect better learner outcomes. For example, the key purpose of the humanistic approach is to ensure the emotional wellbeing and pastoral care of the mentee (Wang & Odell, 2002). In the 'situated apprentice' approach, the primary purpose is to provide technical support and advice, passing on strategies that have been successful for the mentor in their own teaching practice (Wang & Odell,

2002). Another difference between educative and limited approaches to mentoring lies in how the relationship between mentor and provisionally registered teacher (PRT) is conceptualised. In humanistic and advice-based approaches, the mentor is viewed as an expert, guide, supporter and/or adviser, whereas an educative mentor is a co-learner and co-constructor of knowledge about teaching, alongside the PRT.

Key skills, knowledge and dispositions of an educative mentor

The characteristics of high-quality induction and mentoring programmes and the skills, knowledge and dispositions needed to be an effective educative mentor are detailed in *Professional Learning Journeys: Guidelines for Induction and Mentoring and Mentor Teachers* (Education Council, 2015). The list in Table 1 is derived primarily from this document, which was informed by an extensive literature review. In addition, it has been expanded with ideas from Feiman-Nemser (2001b) as the recognised seminal writer on educative mentoring.

Table 1: Key knowledge, skills and dispositions of an educative mentor

Knowledge	Skills	Dispositions
Contextual knowledge (about the PRT, the teaching context, the children)	Initiating and facilitating learning conversations with PRTs	Inquiry/growth mind set
		Critically reflective (of teaching and mentoring practice)
Current theoretical and philosophical approaches	Using effective observation strategies	Open-minded / non-judgemental
Pedagogy of teaching and mentoring	Giving effective, evidence-based feedback	Collaborative
Requirements of induction and mentoring programmes	Keeping learner outcomes as the focus	Perceptive and insightful
Managing change	Culturally competent	Empathetic and supportive
Analysis and interpretation of assessment data	Facilitative questioning	
	Setting goals	
	Articulating own practice and justifying teaching decisions	
	Negotiating on behalf of and advocating for the PRT	

The development of educative mentors

Langdon's (2013) work in the primary sector has shown that educative mentoring does not come naturally to many mentors, perhaps because of an unconscious focus on survival and perpetuating the status quo.

In a recent ECE study, Williams (2015) investigated the mentoring approaches revealed in mentoring conversations and found that the most prevalent approach used by participants was one based on advice and guidance rather than one consistent with an educative approach.

Historically, there have been very few opportunities in New Zealand for those stepping into a mentoring role to learn about what effective mentoring involves and how to develop and refine the necessary skills. With the exception of a small number of postgraduate papers at some tertiary institutions, there are still very limited professional learning opportunities for aspiring or active mentor teachers to learn and develop their craft (Watson, 2014). This lack of mentor development opportunities often results in mentors relying on trial and error to build their effectiveness, or in adopting the approach of the mentor who supported them as a PRT. While trial and error is a legitimate and valuable method of learning, it needs to occur within an informed and critically reflective framework or it may be to the detriment of the PRT.

There is a strong body of research that emphasises the need for mentors to undertake training and ongoing professional learning in order to develop and refine the skills, characteristics and attributes of effective mentoring (Achinstein & Athanases, 2006b; Carver & Feiman-Nemser, 2009; Schwille & Dynak, 2000). The scarcity of mentor training available in New Zealand and the personal and professional feedback I have received about the lack of skill, knowledge and confidence mentors have in their role raises serious concerns, given the importance of mentor training highlighted in the literature.

Mentors in my own doctoral research study have all stated that they have modelled their mentoring style and expectations on their own mentor and PRT experience (Watson, in progress). Without professional learning opportunities to keep abreast of new initiatives and research, I suggest that many PRTs may be at risk of receiving less than adequate mentoring. If this is the case, they miss the opportunity to develop the practice and professional habits of effective teachers through educative approaches during the period of provisional registration.

Following the introduction of the *Guidelines for Induction and Mentoring Programmes and Mentor Teachers*, the NZTC provided a number of 1-day workshops that gave an introduction to educative mentoring and some of its associated skills. However, there has not been ongoing support to integrate this learning into practice. There is currently only one mentor development programme for ECE teachers listed on the Council website, and it is with this programme that I am involved.

A mentor development programme

As a team of PLD providers based at a university in Auckland, my colleagues and I worked in a range of ECE services providing customised PLD to centres and organisations. We initially developed a mentor development programme in 2010 in response to demand and a lack of professional learning opportunities for mentors and aspiring mentors working with PRTs and student teachers. The programme design drew on the frameworks of two well-established mentoring/leadership programmes.

Firstly, the programme at the New Teachers Centre in Santa Cruz, California, was selected because it is considered by many internationally to be the 'gold-standard' of mentor training (Bullough, 2012). Secondly, the First Time Principals Programme, run by the University of Auckland Centre for Educational Leadership, was chosen because of its strong curriculum which has successfully built pedagogical leaders over a number of years. These sources provided the conceptual underpinning and key curriculum components of the programme. They were used along with the indicators of high-quality induction and mentoring programmes and mentoring outlined by the NZTC (2011) to develop both the content and the approach of the programme.

The intention was to provide a research-informed professional learning programme for those mentoring, or wishing to mentor, other teachers. We designed the programme with the aim that participants would develop the knowledge and skills necessary to mentor effectively, in alignment with the expectations of the NZTC. Although many participants were mentors of PRTs, they also included those mentoring student teachers on practicum and those leading teaching teams.

The ability to mentor in an educative way is developed over time, through engagement in professional learning focused on their role, and by having the opportunity to gain and apply the new skills and knowledge in mentoring experiences (Earl & Timperley, 2008; Langdon, 2013; Robinson & Lai, 2006). Therefore, the programme consisted of a series of full- and half-day workshops spread over a 6-month period. Content focused on the development of the key knowledge, skills and dispositions outlined in Table 1. Because many of the mentors were responsible for the induction and mentoring of PRTs, it was important to ensure that participants understood the components of a high-quality induction and mentoring programme and the qualities of an effective mentor, as defined by the NZTC. The programme also assisted mentors to develop knowledge about adult learning theory, current pedagogical theory and managing change.

A large proportion of the programme was dedicated to skill building: undertaking quality observations, analysing practice and having quality conversations (Cameron, 2009); keeping improved outcomes for children to the fore (Achinstein & Athanases, 2006b); and analysing assessment data and using the findings to plan future teaching practice. In programme sessions, participants saw skills such as observation, feedback and facilitative questioning modelled, then had the opportunity to discuss and problematise what they had experienced. Facilitated practice sessions were carried out in groups, and participants received feedback from the facilitator and their peers. Interim tasks completed between the sessions provided mentors with opportunities to practise skills and contextualise their learning before returning and debriefing as a group. In this way, participants were able to learn from others' experiences as well as their own.

Supporting mentors to overcome contextual challenges
Early childhood centres—particularly those outside of umbrella organisations—are faced with some particular challenges with regard to mentoring. These challenges include: no dedicated funding to support induction and mentoring; difficulty finding shared non-contact time in which to have quality professional discussions; and the complexity of contexts where qualified teachers often work alongside non-qualified adults. A further constraint may be centre management structures that do not value or adequately resource mentoring (Watson, 2014). Since the support grant for PRTs was stopped in 2011, increasing numbers of PRTs and mentors working with my team fund their own induction and mentoring programmes and professional development. Another common occurrence is that experienced teachers find themselves in the

role of mentor without a particular interest or the requisite skills to carry it out effectively because of a lack of fully registered teachers in the centre.

Due to the complexities of providing induction and mentoring programmes in ECE, part of the mentor development programme was dedicated to discussion and collaborative problem solving around the particular contextual challenges the participants were dealing with in their own centres. The solutions developed together varied depending on the exact nature of the problem and the context of the mentors' work, but several points of interest are worth noting.

One key issue that frequently arose was the perceived under-valuing and subsequent under-resourcing of mentoring by some centre owners and managers. Some owners without a background in education appeared not to prioritise the importance of professional discussion and mentoring support, or if they did value it, found it difficult to allocate sufficient resources in fiscally tight circumstances. Some participants said that they had successfully used the induction and mentoring guidelines (NZTC, 2011) to advocate for programme provision with centre management. Many considered this to be a useful strategy and one that they had not previously thought of using.

In addition, mentors actively sought opportunities and found creative ways to have professional discussions in addition to full team meetings. These included scheduling common non-contact time for mentors and PRTs to carry out assessment and planning collaboratively, and the use of online discussions such as blogs, forums and graffiti boards for communication, assessment and planning. In order to reach common understanding within the diverse beliefs and values of teaching teams, participants developed strategies to revisit centre philosophy and unpack the Registered Teacher Criteria (NZTC, 2010) in order to reach shared understanding about what 'good teaching' looks like.

Realising the need for programme review and refinement

Participant evaluations of the programme have been consistently positive, with many mentors able to describe significant shifts in their thinking and practice. Many said that they had moved beyond humanistic and situated apprentice models to more educative ways of working. Participants talked about what had changed in their mentoring practice, but did not provide verification that this was the case from the teachers with whom they worked. Therefore, as facilitators we had some reservations about the extent to which the programme was making a difference for PRTs and the children with whom they worked.

This doubt was supported by the findings of a small-scale research study conducted by one of our team, in which mentors, some of whom had been through one of our programmes, recorded mentoring conversations (Williams, 2015). When analysed, the transcripts showed that educative approaches were not prevalent. As a team we considered this finding and concluded that it was a reflection of our programme design rather than participant capability. As a result, we have significantly restructured our programme for delivery in 2015.

In particular, we realised that our design ran the risk of mentors espousing the knowledge and skills of educative mentoring but not fully integrating them into their practice, due to bypassing the necessary critical reflection on their own mentoring practice. This may be a result of mentors not viewing their mentoring role as part of their teaching practice and therefore not a focus for reflection. Achinstein and Athanases (2006a) proposed that mentoring conversations take a bifocal view, focusing on the learning of both the PRT and the children. Langdon (2013) has suggested that mentors need to be tri-focal, also attending to their own learning about mentoring, reflecting on and inquiring into their mentoring practice in the same way as they do of their teaching practice. Our programme needed the strengthening of this tri-focal approach Langdon advocates.

Therefore, while still focusing on the programme content we have used and developed over the past 5 years, we are now making more explicit the mentor's professional inquiry into their mentoring practice. It is our belief that unless mentors have a well-grounded understanding of teaching as inquiry (Education Review Office, 2012; Ministry of Education, 2007), they are not well positioned to evaluate the effectiveness of their work with PRTs, or to work productively to refine and develop it. In addition, mentors need to actively inquire into their practice—both teaching and mentoring— in order to provide strong models of inquiry-mindedness for others (Fowler, 2012). If mentors are not reflecting deeply on their mentoring practice and analysing its effects on the learning of both PRTs and children, they may not be confident in their effectiveness as mentors.

The strengthened emphasis in our programme on taking an analytical and inquiry stance (Feiman-Nemser, 2001a; Langdon, 2013) to teaching and learning is consistent with messages in international literature (for example, Bradbury, 2010; Langdon, 2013). It is also aligns with the expectations of the NZTC as expressed in RTC12 (NZTC, 2010) and the Appraisal for Teachers workshops (NZTC, 2014) delivered for them across New Zealand during 2013 to 2015.

Conclusion

This chapter has argued that in order to be an effective mentor of PRTs (and other teachers) in New Zealand, an educative approach is necessary. This requires the acquisition and application of a specific range of skills and knowledge in addition to those used in more traditional mentoring approaches based on the provision of affective support or advice and guidance alone. International literature supports the need for mentors to undertake ongoing professional learning in order to effectively enact their role.

One mentor development programme currently available to early childhood teachers has been outlined, as have the planned refinements of the programme in response to recent research findings. It is expected that through engagement in the programme, mentors will critically examine their own mentoring practice and be able to identify areas for improvement that will enhance learning outcomes for PRTs. If, through quality mentoring, PRTs are supported to become high-quality, reflective practitioners, then outcomes for children's learning will also be enhanced.

References

Achinstein, B., & Athanases, S. Z. (2006a). Mentors' knowledge of equity and diversity: Maintaining a bifocal perspective on new teachers and their students. In B. Achinstein & S.Z. Athanases (Eds), *Mentors in the making: Developing new leaders for new teachers* (pp. 38–54). New York, NY: Teachers College Press.

Achinstein, B., & Athanases, S.Z. (2006b). New visions for mentoring new teachers. In B. Achinstein & S.Z. Athanases (Eds), *Mentors in the making:*

Developing new leaders for new teachers (pp. 1–22.). New York, NY: Teachers College Press.

Bradbury, L.U. (2010). Educative mentoring: Promoting reform-based science teaching through mentoring relationships. *Science Education, 94*(6), 1049–1071.

Bullough, R.V. (2012). Mentoring and new teacher induction in the United States: A review and analysis of current practices. *Mentoring & Tutoring: Partnership in Learning, 20*(1), 57–74. doi:10.1080/13611267.2012.645600

Cameron, M. (2009). *Lessons from beginning teachers: Challenges for school leaders.* Wellington: NZCER Press.

Carver, C.L., & Feiman-Nemser, S. (2009). Using policy to improve teacher induction: Critical elements and missing pieces. *Educational Policy, 23*, 295–328. doi:10.1177/0895904807310036

Earl, L., & Timperley, H. (Eds). (2008). *Professional learning conversations: Challenges in using evidence for improvement.* London, UK: Springer.

Education Council. (2015). *Professional learning journeys: Guidelines for induction and mentoring and mentor teachers.* Retrieved from, www.educationcouncil.org.nz

Education Review Office. (2012). *Teaching as inquiry: Responding to learners.* Wellington: Author.

Feiman-Nemser, S. (1998). Teachers as teacher educators. *European Journal of Teacher Education, 21*(1), 63–74.

Feiman-Nemser, S. (2001a). From preparation to practice: Designing a continuum to strengthen and sustain teaching. *Teachers College Record, 103*(6), 1013–1055.

Feiman-Nemser, S. (2001b). Helping novices learn to teach. *Journal of Teacher Education, 52*(1), 17–30.

Fowler, M. (2012). Leading inquiry at teacher level: It's all about mentorship. *set: Research Information for Teachers, 3,* 2–7.

Langdon, F.J. (2013). Evidence of mentor learning and development: An analysis of New Zealand mentor/mentee professional conversations. *Professional Development in Education, 40*(1), 36–55. doi:10.1080/19415257.2013.833131

Langdon, F.J., Flint, A., Kromer, G., Ryde, A., & Karl, D. (2011). *Induction and mentoring pilot: Primary: Leading learning in induction and mentoring.* Wellington: NZTC.

Ministry of Education. (2007). *The New Zealand curriculum*. Wellington: Learning Media.

NZTC. (2010). *Registered teacher criteria handbook*. Wellington: Author.

NZTC. (2011). *Professional learning journeys: Guidelines for induction and mentoring and mentor teachers*. Wellington: Author.

NZTC. (2014). *Workshop one powerpoint: Strengthening understanding of appraisal processes*. Retrieved from http://www.teacherscouncil.govt.nz/content/appraisal-teachers-project

Robinson, V.M.J., & Lai, M.K. (2006). *Practitioner research for educators: A guide to improving classrooms and schools*. Thousand Oaks, CA: Corwin Press.

Schwille, S.A., & Dynak, J. (2000). Mentor preparation and development (mentoring framework: Dimension IV). In S. Odell & L. Huling (Eds), *Quality mentoring for novice teachers* (pp. 67-76; 7). Indianapolis, IN: Kappa Delta Pi.

Wang, J., & Odell, S. (2002). Mentored learning to teach according to standards-based reform: A critical review. *Review of Educational Research, 72*(3), 481-546.

Watson, B. (2014). Mentoring provision in education and care settings: Policy and professional issues. In H. Hedges & V.N. Podmore (Eds), *Early childhood education: Pedagogy, professionalism and philosophy* (pp. 123-138). Auckland: Edify.

Watson, B. (in progress). *Induction and mentoring in education and care: A bioecological perspective*. Unpublished doctoral thesis, University of Auckland.

Williams, B. (2015). *What mentoring approaches are revealed in mentoring conversations between early childhood mentors and provisionally registered early childhood teachers?* Unpublished master's thesis, University of Auckland.

Chapter 3
Mentoring and reflective practice: Transforming practice through reflexive thinking
Elizabeth Rouse

Introduction

The Australian National Quality Framework for Early Childhood Education and Care [NQF] (Australian Children's Education & Care Quality Authority, 2012) provides a platform for early childhood educators to become strong leaders and mentors in meeting the needs and aspirations of children, families and the community through building capability and practice in educators across the sector. Mentoring is a reciprocal professional relationship which not only helps to improve the professional practice of new teachers but also provides opportunities for more experienced teachers to gain fresh perspectives. The inclusion of the role of an educational leader in all early childhood education and care settings in Australia has created a new role for experienced educators in mentoring and developing the practice of others in their teams. Building the professional practice of new teachers through mentoring has also been a key component of teacher development programmes. The role mentors play in supporting beginning teachers to become active agents in building their own practice has long been recognised as influential in developing teacher identity in graduate teachers.

This chapter explores the relationship between mentoring and reflective practice, and raises a number of questions for mentors to consider when undertaking this role with graduate teachers. Exploring reflective practice from a theoretical perspective will help mentors to better understand their own capabilities as reflective mentors, and will also help mentors to build the reflective capabilities of those they mentor. The chapter will also provide a context for exploring the mentor's personal capabilities, behaviours and understanding of their own practice by introducing the notion of reflexivity—an exploration of personal values, assumptions, attitudes, thought processes, prejudices and actions. In mentoring there is a strong relationship between the ability to act reflexively and building reflective practice in others, as it is this reflexive capability that will support the mentor to better build reflective practices in those they are mentoring.

Mentoring and reflective practice

The NQS (Quality Standard 1.2) directs educators to be intentional, purposeful and thoughtful in their decisions and actions, and requires them to engage in reflective practice as a form of ongoing learning that involves engaging with questions of philosophy, ethics and practice (Australian Children's Education & Care Quality Authority, 2013). Across the early childhood education and care sector, mentors are increasingly taking on the role of supporting and developing educators as reflective practitioners. However, to build this practice in others, unless a mentor is able to reflect on their own behaviours, values and assumptions as both mentor and early childhood educator, their capacity to effectively build this skill in others is inhibited.

How prepared and capable emerging mentors and leaders are to take up the challenge of leadership and mentoring in many ways relies on their capacity to engage in reflective practice. Reflective practice is a form of ongoing learning that involves engaging with questions of philosophy, ethics and practice. It is a critical component of effective professional practice and underpins teacher efficacy and growth. Reflection and reflective practice are held internationally to be important aspirations for teachers and educators. More recently, reflective practice has been embedded in the standards for teacher practice across all sectors of education (Australian Institute for Teaching and School Leadership, 2011; Department of Education, Employment and Workplace Relations, 2009).

A reflective practitioner is someone who is able to critically examine their own practice, experiences, values and beliefs to gain insights that support, inform and enrich decision making and enhance their understanding of their own skills, knowledge and learning needs (Rouse, 2012). In order to get mentees to engage in meaningful reflective practice, it is essential that the mentor be able to explore and reflect on their own capabilities as a reflective practitioner—to critically examine their own practice and the beliefs and values that guide their practice first, before they can shape the practice of others.

What is reflective practice?

When most people think of reflective practice they usually think of the work of Donald Schön (1987). However, reflective practice has its origins in the works of Dewey much earlier, where he identified reflective thinking as being purposeful and active, a conscious approach to consider beliefs and the grounds and reasons for these beliefs (Dewey, 1910, cited in Rouse, 2012). In other words, reflective thinking is thinking with a purpose and consciously challenging what has been accepted. Dewey's work acknowledged that there is not necessarily one way of thinking, nor one correct way of responding to situations. In fact, as educators we need to be able to think and do, using alternative approaches, if we are to be build professional capability.

However, reflective practice is more than just about knowledge. There also needs to be an acknowledgement that the knowledge gained will be applied in some way. It is all well and good to know that by evaluating your engagement with your mentee you do not really feel that you made any headway in getting her (or him) to think differently, but the next step as mentor is to examine why you have not made the inroads you wanted and what role you played in this. What will you do differently next time? At your next meeting you might gauge this by asking how successful the mentee felt the previous meeting was. What inroads were made, why, what affected the outcome? This leads to a never-ending cycle of plan, do, reflect, plan, do …

Schön (1987) framed reflective practice as using two separate but related processes, which he described as "reflection-on-action" and "reflection-in-action". Mentors must consciously and unconsciously engage in both these processes regularly in their relationship with the mentee, and mentees also need to approach their role as both building their relationship with the mentor and their own practice. Schön (1987) recognised that professionals face unique and challenging situations on a daily basis; he argued that using previous experiences to better understand how and why things happen will lead to greater effectiveness. In this respect, educators are encouraged to take responsibility for improvements in their own practice.

Reflection-on-action is the typical self-evaluation that mentors and leaders engage in at the end of the day, or at the end of a meeting with the mentee. It is a deliberate and conscious attempt to evaluate and learn about a past experience in order to reshape the future. Reflection-on-action is most often a conscious and deliberate process, where the mentor might document thinking and possible modifications for the next meeting with the mentee, or as a partnership might openly share and discuss events and outcomes together to arrive at a mutual way of thinking and to modify the way you approach your interactions and engagement. Schön (1983) argues that the most effective professionals use their previous experiences to better understand how and why things happen.

Reflection-in-action occurs on the run, when a mentor might stop in the middle of something to analyse what is happening. It is the conscious response to a situation or event, which leads to an understanding of why things are occurring and immediately building on this understanding. Reflection-in-action can be likened to an 'Ah ha!' moment, when we realise something and then take action. Reflection-in-action is an intuitive process and involves responding to the here and now, and relying on having the cognitive capacity to be able to think on your feet and make an immediate response. This might occur when a mentor realises that the mentee does not have the practical experience and understanding to fully make meaning of their thinking—the mentor will stop and reframe the idea by using an example from their own experience to make the thinking more tangible.

Although Schön (1987) identified two reflective actions—reflection-on-action and reflection-in-action—there is a third way to examine reflective practice, which is 'reflection-for-action'. Reflection-for-action is about recognising and acknowledging that we *want* to learn and develop and taking active steps to embark on the journey (Wright, 2008). It requires a high level of emotional intelligence: the ability to recognise and monitor our own feelings and emotions, as well as those of others (Goleman, 2001). This awareness and understanding guides our thinking and actions.

People who are high in emotional intelligence are able to see constructive feedback as positive and build on it, rather than see it as criticism. These people are also able to recognise and acknowledge their own contribution to events and experiences that may not have gone as planned, and can learn from them to build their own personal self-efficacy. In interactions with others, an individual with high emotional intelligence is able to gain awareness of the emotions expressed by others and reframe their own behaviour in response. It is this component of reflective practice that, for a mentor, is the most critical when building the practice of the mentee. The mentor–mentee relationship is built on trust, mutual respect and open and honest interactions. The ability to recognise and acknowledge their own contribution to events and experiences will lead the mentor to create a space where a mentee feels safe to share and acknowledge their own practice, thus sharing their reflections on their own contribution to the situation.

The role of the mentor

The decision to seek out a mentor, or to take on the role of a mentor, requires a high level of emotional commitment because it involves a willingness to be open to criticism, and to acknowledge and share imperfections and be open to change. For this to occur, there have to be high levels of trust, respect and mutuality. The effectiveness of the relationship is in some ways reliant on a goodness of fit between the mentor and the mentee, but it also requires highly reflective skills on the part of the mentor to be able to recognise their own contribution to the mentor–mentee relationship.

Harrison, Lawson and Wortley (2005) discuss three types of mentor relationship:
- a procedural relationship, where the mentor is quite procedural and unresponsive to the particular strengths and concerns of the mentee

- a power relationship, bounded by an expert–apprentice approach
- a personal type, which creates a genuine working partnership because it recognises a mentee's strengths while acknowledging an apprentice–expert relationship (p. 424).

In the personal type of mentor relationship, Harrison et al. argue that it is the nature and type of feedback given and the overall approachability of the mentor that create the goodness of fit and the effective working partnership. Mentors need to reflect on the mentor–mentee relationship they have created. Engaging in reflection-for-action on the part of the mentor creates a way of examining the nature of the relationship between them and their mentee with a view to building a more effective relationship. How might the relationship be defined? Is it one based on power? As a mentor are you—consciously or unconsciously—enacting a master–apprentice way of viewing the mentee? Or is it one based on a more mutual collaborative understanding of your mentee and your own strengths and needs? Why? What underpins this? How do you know? To what extent do your own personal beliefs, prejudices and past experiences influence the nature of the interactions with the mentee?

Reflexivity: different from reflective practice?

Past experiences and subjective understanding influence the nature of the relationships and interactions between the mentor and the mentee. Reflexivity builds on the concept of reflective practice by exploring the notion of how we know what we know, and is positioned within a theory of social constructivism (Warwick & Board, 2013), which views individuals as creating their sense of reality through the social interactions they have with others. In a mentoring relationship, reflexivity enables the mentor to question their level of objectivity in how they are interacting with and shaping the thinking of their mentee. Reflexivity presupposes that each individual has a differently constructed reality, because each individual has a unique set of experiences that have shaped them. It is how these experiences are then interpreted that influences the construction of their knowing and understanding. Reflexivity creates a platform from which an individual can think more critically about themselves—their assumptions, actions, and the situations they encounter—to see that there may be multiple interpretations and multiple realities. Reflexivity therefore involves examining one's own realities and ways of being, knowing and doing, to understand how one knows what one knows, and recognising that these are subjective realities, and that these realities may not be the same for others because they have not had the same lived experiences.

Reflexivity is about finding strategies to question one's own attitudes, thought processes, values, assumptions, prejudices and habitual actions. A reflexive mentor is one who is trying to understand and make sense of their role in relation to others, particularly those they are mentoring. They are able to reflect on how their own behaviour, past experiences and subjectivity influence the way others develop their own sense of reality. In a mentoring relationship, reflexivity involves being aware of the limits of our knowledge, and the limits of our own experiences in creating and forming our knowledge and understanding. In essence, reflexivity involves an active and conscious development and transformation, leading to self-understanding, exploring and examining biases—conscious or unconscious biases—and reflecting on the ways in which our own values, experiences, interests, beliefs, political commitments, and broader life aims have influenced the ways and thinking of others (Bolton, 2010; Ryan & Bourke, 2013; Warwick & Broad, 2013). This is true for both the mentor and the mentee

If reflective thinking is thinking with a purpose and consciously challenging what has been accepted, reflexivity is a conscious self-examination of why we think what we do and why we know what we know, and how we have created this knowledge and understanding. In order to challenge what has been accepted, it is important to know why it has been accepted—the ingrained assumptions—and why it needs to change, and how you have come to know this. Assumptions are the taken-for-granted beliefs about the world and our place within it, and, as Brookfield (1995) suggests, in many ways it is our assumptions that drive us: assumptions give meaning and purpose to who we are and what we do.

In early childhood education it is important to question our practices in line with this thinking about assumptions. The role of mentors is to work with their mentees in exploring the thinking that underpins practice. The mentor can challenge the mentee to examine the extent to which their practice and teaching are based on assumptions, past practices, or sound pedagogical thinking as it relates to the children in the context of their programme. Using the existing mentor–mentee relationship enables this exploration to unfold in a collaborative, trusting dialogue. This sharing of thinking builds not only the practice of the newly graduated mentee, but also enables the mentor to explore their own assumptions and practices, building their reflexivity through self-examination.

Developing reflexivity in mentoring

It could be argued that in order to be an effective mentor, the mentor needs to be both reflective and reflexive. Being reflexive can be challenging. In order to develop this skill the mentor needs to be prepared to step out of their comfort zone and to stand back from their often ingrained belief and value systems, their habitual ways of thinking and relating to others, their structures of understanding themselves and their relationship to the world, and their assumptions about the way the world impinges upon them, to look at themselves as if from the outside. This is not always an easy thing to do. Challenging our assumptions and ways of knowing involves an element of risk, because we are challenging our own constructed realities, and in doing so, creating new realities.

However, in keeping with the notion of reflexivity, in order to challenge our own reality we need to become aware of what we perceive as reality and what has shaped this understanding. Is this reality the same as that of everyone else? Have you ever had a meeting with a colleague which you thought was a waste of time, or sat an exam that you thought was really hard, only to chat with your peer and find that they felt completely differently? Each of us has our own version of reality. Therefore we need to find lenses through which to examine our assumptions and through which to reflect back a different picture of who we are and what we do (Brookfield, 1998).

Rogoff (1995) presents a way of understanding 'knowing' that is framed across three planes: the personal plane, the interpersonal plane and the community plane. When exploring how to become more reflexive in our reflections, examining our assumptions and realities through these lenses can provide an insight into ourselves. These planes are useful for mentors and mentees in early childhood education to consider because they provide a way to examine the underpinning influences on practice. Reflecting on practice using the lens of the personal plane allows for introspective examination of the past beliefs, experiences and values that teachers bring to their practice. The interpersonal plane allows for an examination of the way knowledge and practice have been built and influenced through interactions with others, while the community plane explores practices as guided by a collective community understanding of what is effective practice.

The personal plane is a personal exploration of our ways of knowing, usually undertaken through a personal journal, which Bolton (2010) refers to as 'through-the-mirror writing'—an intuitive, spontaneous personal narrative written for self-illumination and exploration. This form or narrative is more than just a reflective diary: it is written to provide personal insight and to explore assumptions, which challenge the perceived realities. It creates a platform for self-examination—not as you see yourself but by 'looking through the mirror' at not only what others might be seeing, but also reflecting on why and how they may be seeing this. The mentoring process provides an opportunity for this personal exploration, because it enables the mentor to provide a different perspective to the mentee in terms of what they as the mentor are seeing and hearing when practice is shared. This allows the mentee to explore their own practice by seeing what others might be seeing and why, drawing from the introverted self-examination to a deeper, insightful examination based on the interpretation of others, and examining why this alternative perspective might have arisen, thus looking at themselves 'through the mirror'. Using Rogoff's (1995) notion of the interpersonal plane builds on this notion of reflection because it creates an opportunity to explore more deeply the assumptions and ways of knowing that have influenced a perception of reality by exploring, with others, how this perception has been formed.

Exploring assumptions and ways of knowing with another creates an avenue for a third space where a new shared reality is formed together, one in which there is reciprocal understanding, realised through joint sharing of assumptions, beliefs, values and experiences. This interpersonal shared reflectivity is what underpins the mentoring process. It enables both the mentor and the mentee to share and explore their own lived experiences in the context of others, and as a result build new, shared understanding. The interpersonal plane also enables both mentors and mentees to explore practice by examining where the practice has come from, examining in a collaborative and trusting discussion how these assumptions have been formed and how they have been perpetuated and embedded in practice through interactions with peers and colleagues. Sharing these reflections in the mentoring process will lead to new practice created through shared understanding.

The community plane brings in the notion of the social construction of learning, where personal assumptions and beliefs are examined using a community of practice approach (Wenger, McDermott, & Snyder, 2002). Based on the concepts of trust, respect and being non-judgemental, in communities of practice, peers and colleagues are used as 'critical friends' (Bambino, 2002) to bounce ideas off and seek support through reflective conversations, where assumptions and constructed realities are explored in a wider context. It is these reflective conversations that build the practice across the group as the participants share issues and ideas about their own assumptions, engaging in conversations in a non-judgemental, collaborative and supportive environment (Cook & Rouse, 2014). Mentors who are working with more than one mentee can build a community of practice with their team of mentees in which they come together, connected through a shared passion for their role as early childhood teachers and a collective desire not only to build their practice but to support the development of others. Within this community of practice the mentees will develop enduring and collaborative relationship with others, who can act as critical friends who are used to share issues and concerns, as there is a shared practice among the group. Mentors can also form a community of practice with each other to explore the nature and concerns in their own role as mentors, supporting each other to build shared practice and understanding, which they can then take to their individual relationships with their own mentees.

Developing reflective practice in others
Being a reflective or a reflexive practitioner is a key practice principle for early childhood teachers, and teachers have regular opportunities to engage in reflection on their practice. However, for newly graduated teachers, engaging in reflection on practice can be a challenge if this

concept is new to them. Harrison et al. (2005) suggest that, for newly qualified teachers especially, learning to reflect requires a degree of nurturing and professional example. Mentors play an important role in supporting their mentees to make this journey. Van Manen (1997, cited in Killen, 2007) suggests three levels of reflecting: technical, practical and critical. It can be argued that a newly graduated teacher, or one not as experienced in engaging in reflective practice, begins by reflecting using a technical frame, which focuses on examining practice as it reflects the day-to-day tasks and how they might apply the knowledge learnt to their practice.

The role of the mentor is to move the mentee from this technical way of thinking through to more critically reflective practice, whereby they are beginning to examine the influence in their practice and behaviours of their own biases, values and beliefs, and exploring the ethical, moral and broader societal issues that might have an impact on educator practice (Rouse, 2012). Critically reflective practice is most effective when a mentor is involved. In order to assist their mentee in moving along this continuum, mentors and mentees together, through a reflective partnership, need first to examine those individual assumptions that are influencing their ways of knowing, and how their lived experiences, beliefs, understanding and values are guiding these assumptions. However, if the mentor has not been able to engage reflexively in a practice of self-examination, then supporting others to move from a more technical reflection to be critically reflective, and on towards their own reflexivity, will be hindered.

In developing others to be a reflective practitioner, a mentor first needs to understand where the mentee is on the reflection journey and why this might be. The mentor also needs to understand where they are themselves on the reflection journey. When exploring your interactions and the reflective discussions that have occurred in the interactions, ask yourself what realities and assumptions you were drawing on. How did your behaviour and interactions influence the development of a reciprocal third space, where shared understanding has been formed? How effectively have you created an environment of trust, security and openness to enable reciprocal ways of knowing to develop? In using Rogoff's (1995) lenses, how have you explored the nature of your relationship with the mentee—the way the relationship is defined—and whose reality is this?

Reflective journaling (Rouse, 2012) creates a vehicle for socialising the mentee into the reflective practice space by supporting them to develop their thinking, as described by van Manen (cited in Killen, 2007). Reciprocal journaling builds on this by creating a vehicle for further developing the reflective skills in the mentee, and assists in moving them along the reflective practice journey. In reciprocal journaling, the mentee shares their reflective journaling with their mentor, who then builds on this through reflecting on the reflection, creating a cyclical approach to building reflection reflexivity. The intrapersonal nature of reflective journaling enables the shift from the technical reflective practices to more critical thinking, through the feedback loop provided in the reciprocal reflections that both mentor and mentee are engaging in. This process also provides a vehicle for the mentor to develop their own understanding and challenge their assumptions on the nature of their own practice—both as an educator and as a mentor—and to build a third space where a shared reality is created.

Conclusion

This chapter has positioned mentoring within a broader notion of encouraging and supporting reflective and reflexive practice in early childhood education contexts. Exploring mentoring through this frame can support mentors to better understand their own capabilities as reflective mentors and to help them build the reflective capabilities of their mentees. Encouraging exploration of the mentor's personal beliefs, understanding and perceived realities through reflexivity can better support the mentor to more effectively take those they are mentoring further along the journey of reflective practice.

References

Australian Children's Education & Care Quality Authority. (2012). *Introducing the national quality framework*. Retrieved from http://acecqa.gov.au/national-quality-framework/introducing-the-national-quality-framework

Australian Children's Education & Care Quality Authority. (2013). *Guide to the national quality standards*. Retrieved from http://files.acecqa.gov.au/files/National-Quality-Framework-Resources-Kit/NQF03-Guide-to-NQS-130902.pdf

Australian Institute for Teaching and School Leadership. (2011). *Professional standards for teachers*. Retrieved from http://www.aitsl.edu.au/docs/default-source/apst-resources/australian_professional_standard_for_teachers_final.pdf

Bambino, D. (2002). Critical friends. *Educational Leadership*, *59*(6), 25.

Bolton, G. (2010). *Reflective practice–writing and professional development*. Thousand Oaks, CA: Sage.

Brookfield, S. (1995). *Becoming a critically reflective teacher*. San Francisco, CA: Jossey-Bass.

Brookfield, S. (1998). Critically reflective practice. *Journal of Continuing Education in the Health Professions*, *18*, 197–205.

Cook, J., & Rouse, E. (2014). *Leadership and management in the early years*. Albert Park, VIC: Teaching Solutions.

Department of Education, Employment and Workplace Relations. (2009). *Belonging, being, becoming: The early years learning framework for Australia*. Canberra, ACT: Government Printers.

Goleman, D. (2001). Emotional intelligence: Issues in paradigm building. In C. Chernis & D. Goleman (Eds), *How to select for, measure, and improve emotional intelligence in individuals, groups, and organizations* (pp. 13–27). San-Francisco, CA: Jossey-Bass.

Harrison, J.K., Lawson, T., & Wortley, A. (2005). Mentoring the beginning teacher: Developing professional autonomy through critical reflection on practice. *Reflective Practice: International and Multidisciplinary Perspectives*, *6*(3), 419–441.

Killen, R. (2007). *Effective teaching strategies*. South Melbourne, VIC: Thompson Cengage Learning.

Rogoff, B. (1995). Observing sociocultural activity on three planes: Participatory appropriation, guided participation, and apprenticeship. In J.V. Wertsch, P. Del Rio, & A. Alvarez (Eds), *Sociocultural studies of mind* (pp. 139–164). New York, NY: Cambridge University Press.

Rouse, E. (2012). *Reflective practice: A handbook for early childhood educators*. Albert Park, VIC: Teaching Solutions.

Ryan, M., & Bourke, T. (2013). The teacher as reflexive professional: Making visible the excluded discourse in teacher standards. *Discourse: Studies in the Cultural Politics of Education*, *34*(3), 411–423.

Schön, D.A. (1983). *The reflective practitioner: How professionals think in action*. New York, NY: Basic Books.

Schön, D.A. (1987). *Educating the reflective practitioner.* San Francisco, CA: Jossey-Bass.

Warwick, R., & Board, D. (2013). *The social development of leadership and knowledge: A reflexive inquiry into research and practice.* London, UK: Palgrave MacMillan.

Wenger, E., McDermott, R., & Snyder, W. (2002). *Cultivating communities of practice: A guide to managing knowledge.* Boston, MA: Harvard Business School Press.

Wright, G.A. (2008). *How does video analysis impact teacher reflection-for-action?* Unpublished doctoral thesis, Brigham Young University. Retrieved from http://scholarsarchive.byu.edu/etd/1362

Chapter 4
Te Whāriki: A sociocultural framework for mentoring
Viv Shearsby

Introduction

The critical role of socially and culturally mediated learning and reciprocal, responsive relationships is centrally positioned within leadership and mentoring. *Te Whāriki* (Ministry of Education, 1996) states:

> This curriculum emphasises the critical role of socially and culturally mediated learning and of reciprocal and responsive relationships for children with people, places, and things. Children learn through collaboration with adults and peers, through guided participation and observation of others, as well as through individual exploration and reflection. (p. 9)

Over the last 5 years I have been investigating mentoring as part of my own personal and professional learning. I have played an increasing role as a mentor, both in professional supervision with centre managers/leaders and through extensive work mentoring provisionally registered teachers. This has led me to consider the further application of *Te Whāriki* as a tool to support critical thinking in mentoring early childhood teachers. This chapter identifies and unpacks the ways in which the principles and strands of the curriculum can be applied in early childhood teacher mentoring to support successful outcomes for learners and families.

Te Whāriki applied as curriculum

Te Whāriki is presented metaphorically as a woven mat, with the principles of the document likened to the weft and the strands to the warp of the mat. The weaving of these principles and strands enables each valued concept to be considered in relation to the others. Metaphorically speaking, this weaving creates for each child a floor covering or foundation for life. In order to utilise *Te Whāriki* as a mentoring tool, it is crucial to have a fundamental knowledge of its structure and application. When enacted for its original purpose as the early years curriculum, all considerations are grounded in the foundational principles of *relationships, empowerment, family and community*, and *holistic development*.

The principle of *relationships* indicates recognition of learning taking place within, and as being critically shaped by, a wider sociocultural context. This principle guides teachers to strive to provide responsive, reciprocal relationships as a primary avenue for children's learning. The three further principles specifically place value on relationships with families and the wider community, showcase equity through the lens of empowerment, and position a holistic and connected view of children's learning and development. The strands of the curriculum refine the assessment lens, enabling teachers to develop goals and planning specifically and individually in relation to a child's learning.

Each of the principles and strands of *Te Whāriki* can be applied in relation to one another. By overlaying aspects of the curriculum, a teacher can reflect as they assess possible courses of action for the child's learning. This reflective process may include discussions with colleagues, parents and the child/ren, all enabling a holistic perspective of the child in the specific context of the early childhood setting and as part of a wider world. This shared engagement in reflective discussion forms the basis of a community of practice (Curtis, Lebo, Cividanes, & Carter, 2013) and provides a platform for mentor relationships to establish the value of reflection to consolidate in practice.

Mentoring utilising the framework of Te Whāriki

During my journey and experiences as a mentor working with early childhood teachers and leaders, I have sometimes recognised positive intentions thwarted by insufficient pedagogical knowledge. I have also noticed that investigation led to more questions, and I have acknowledged that, as with children, the wider context of life influences learning. I began to recognise three key concepts, which position my approach, attitude and beliefs about mentoring.

For a start, I believe that every teacher has the intention of doing their best for and with children, and that no-one goes to work to do a 'bad job'. As teachers gain experience and insight into learning and development, and come to grips with the complexity of family and community dynamics, they strive to expand their practice. Secondly, maintaining openness to the ideas, approaches and thinking of others is paramount. The journey of learning can take many paths and is not necessarily linear, and providing space for different ways of knowing, being and doing opens the world of diversity. It is not the mentor's job to control everything: it is the mentor's job to help the mentee work their way through complexity (Robertson, 2005).

Finally, I view mentoring as a 'whole life' experience, and I see the mentee in the holistic context of their whole life (Ehrich, Tennent, & Hansford, 2002). My experience has shown me that situations and events outside of the work–life context often influence the mentees' perspectives, attitudes and actions. As a mentor, I encourage mentees to investigate and consider any issues affecting their practice, either professional or personal.

My view is that establishing, consolidating and sustaining a mentor relationship begins with a desire to share experiences and enhance understanding of experiences. Foundations for this relationship must be grounded in mutual trust in the partnership, where both mentor and mentee learn, grow and experience satisfaction (Zachary, 1997). Trust begins with acceptance and is nurtured over time through warm, encouraging and honest conversations (Zachary, 2012). It is vital that both partners share responsibility for the direction, learning and calibre of discussions, and engage wholeheartedly in an authentic and meaningful process. The advantages of a mentor relationship can only come to full fruition when the "mentor provides an enabling relationship that facilitates another's personal growth and development" (Ehrich, Tennent, & Hansford, 2002, p. 5).

With this as a personal foundation to mentoring teachers and education leaders, I began to consider the ways in which I could guide conversations, build confidence and create a trusting relationship without unduly influencing the mentee's thinking. I used typical mentoring practices such as sharing readings, discussing theoretical and pedagogical topics, and exploring mentees' values, philosophies and aspirations for who they want to 'be'. I would pay careful attention to the language, terms and descriptions used by the mentee and guide them to investigate their values and views further, encouraging multiple perspectives and striving for deeper and wider concepts without negating initial points of view (Dahlberg, Moss, & Pence, 1999). I began to think about the potential of the principles and strands of *Te Whāriki* for prompting thinking and encouraging theoretical and pedagogical critique within mentoring relationships.

In order to apply the curriculum framework to mentoring situations, it was necessary to make a slight move in viewing the original curriculum statements and broaden their application to adult learners in the context. I also recognised the importance of professional reflection as the crucial tool for enabling teachers to work their way through complexity and meaningfully engage in learning collaboratively (Curtis et al., 2013), which was my aim in mentor discussions. Tables 2 and 3 show how I came to expand each principle and strand of *Te Whāriki*. The tables identify the curriculum statements, present an alternative mentor statement, then provide examples of applications to mentoring, along with potential reflective questions for mentor and mentee to consider as a starting point.

Table 2: Principles, positions and possibilities

Principles–Ngā kaupapa whakahaere	As a mentor the statement becomes:	What does this mean for the mentor and mentee?	Possible reflective questions
Relationships – ngā hononga Children learn through responsive and reciprocal relationships with people, places and things.	We all learn through responsive and reciprocal relationships with people, places, and things.	A mentor may be seeking to understand the mentee's values and approaches in working through professional differences with others. A mentee can benefit from gaining insight into the effects of their own practices and behaviours on others.	How are relationships affected by the issue? In what ways do you see your practice, perspective or attitude as one that supports relationships?
Empowerment: whakamana The early childhood curriculum empowers the child to learn and grow.	Mentee values, attitudes and practices can empower learning and growth.	A mentor might be inquiring into a mentee's engagement with families, attitudes to diversity or personal judgements that are evident in discussions. The mentor might choose to use this lens when a mentee perceives misuse of power or control in the situation being discussed.	Whose voice is not being heard? How can you find out more from them? What actions could you take to help and participate in finding a shared resolution?
Family and community: whānau tangata The wider world of family and community is an integral part of the early childhood curriculum.	The wider world of family and community is an integral consideration for mentees in their reflection and practice.	A mentor may be interested in extending a mentee's lens from that of teacher, to be more aware of the perspectives of a parent or family. Considering the perspective of families or seeking advice, information and guidance from a family can increase the mentee's insight and confidence.	How are families affected by this issue? How are you sharing information and consulting with families to find solutions?
Holistic development: kotahitanga The early childhood curriculum reflects the holistic way children learn and grow.	Mentee values, attitudes and practices reflect their understanding of the holistic way we all learn and grow.	A mentor can encourage a mentee to look at the bigger picture, consider the direction or path the service is on, and reflect on and align practices with a wider vision and philosophy. This lens also enables the consideration of development and change happening over time in a progressive and formative way.	How does your action support or enhance the vision for the whole centre? In what ways do you see your practice, perspective or attitude as one that supports or enhances the whole service?

Table 3: Strands, positions and possibilities

Te Whāriki strand	As a mentor the statement becomes:	What does this mean for the mentor and mentee?	Possible reflective questions
Wellbeing: mana atua The health and wellbeing of the child are protected and nurtured.	We all engage and perform at higher levels when our health and wellbeing are protected and nurtured.	When struggling with a professional issue, mentees can benefit from reflecting on the wellbeing of those involved in the situation. Mentors prompting consideration of the mentee's own wellbeing can take the discussion directly to the seat of an issue.	How are you taking care of yourself? Where is your personal support coming from? Tell me about how you view your colleagues' personal satisfaction, engagement and joy at work. How could you contribute to this?
Belonging: mana whenua Children and their families feel a sense of belonging.	We all engage and perform at higher levels when we feel a sense of belonging.	A mentor may assist the mentee to identify divisions in a team or levels of engagement. Investigating the sense of belonging mentees have often indicates how successful they feel and can be reflected in their professional practice and learning progress.	Tell me about belonging in this centre/team? What makes you feel at home here? How can you support the engagement and individual responsibility taken within the team?
Communication: mana reo The languages and symbols of their own and other cultures are promoted and protected.	The languages and symbols of our own and other cultures are promoted and protected.	A mentor may be interested to find out more about a mentee's approach with colleagues and/or families. Prompting a mentee to reflect on who they share information with and the way they share information can enable them to recognise features of communication that are either highly successful or unsuccessful.	Who do you think is best to raise this with? How might you enter into a professional discussion about this? How might you move towards a shared resolution?
Contribution: mana tangata Opportunities for learning are equitable, and each child's contribution is valued.	Opportunities for learning are equitable, and each person's contribution is valued.	A mentor may be interested to encourage a mentee to expand their practice, or to support others around them to participate more fully. Inquiring about personal contribution and support for collegial efforts can provide insight into their role and professional practice.	What do you bring to this situation? How might you collaborate with others? How can you utilise your strengths and capabilities to enhance outcomes?
Exploration: mana aotūroa The child learns through active exploration of the environment.	We learn through active exploration of our learning environment.	A mentor may be eager to prompt a mentee to undertake some data gathering, research or professional reading and investigation. Considering active exploration as a tool for learning allows the mentor to prompt the mentee to reflect on the active ways in which they can extend their own knowledge.	I wonder what current research says about this? How can you find out more? What avenues do you see for your own professional growth and development?

Mentoring and the principles of Te Whāriki

Thus began my newly refined approach to mentoring, based on the view that just as *Te Whāriki* principles underpin the considerations of learning for young children, they can also be applied to learning for teachers. Early childhood teachers working with *Te Whāriki* generally have insight into the ways children grow, learn and develop in relation to the curriculum framework, and I quickly found that utilising this well-understood framework in mentoring enabled rapid insight for the mentee into their own practice, challenges and development.

Considering the principle of *empowerment* highlights the fact that culture and deeply held beliefs affect the way we hear, see and value others (Dahlberg, Moss, & Pence, 1999). This leads me to listen attentively in mentee discussions and draw out mentees' own beliefs. I encourage them to consider issues from other perspectives, seek (or explore) wider values, and move from the narrow lens that can only provide narrow solutions (Dahlberg et al., 1999). The children and families we work for and with bring with them multiple ideas, beliefs, expectations, assumptions, desires and aspirations, and the principle of *empowerment* calls on early childhood teachers to seek to understand and respond to these as we work with their children. In order to do this, my role as a mentor is to help teachers build deeper insight into their acceptance of difference, to value and work with the perspectives of others (even when these may challenge their own views), demonstrate respect for equal rights, and develop their cultural intelligence (Van Dyne, Ang, & Livermore, 2010).

The principle of *relationships* reminds me to take into account that mentees work in collaboration with other teachers, which creates a complex context fraught with opportunities for miscommunication. Differences in philosophy and pedagogy, coupled with few opportunities to discuss deeply what they are doing together, can create a focus on problems and complaints, which in turn can strain relationships (Curtis et al., 2013). I have found value in beginning an investigation by unpacking and scrutinising a relationship and/or interaction in accordance with the *Te Whāriki* principle of *relationship*s in order to give insight into this important facet of a teacher's work. Trust sits at the heart of relationships and provides a crucial foundation for successful outcomes (Covey, 2008; Robertson, 2005: Robinson, 2009). Prompting deeper consideration of trust in a relationship can enable identification of barriers and pathways and the enhancement of trust can strongly influence the relationships the mentee shares with their colleagues, families and children.

The third principle of *Te Whāriki* acknowledges and values the place and role of the family/whānau and views them as paramount in the child's life and experience. As a mentor, prompting teachers to view a situation or decision from the lens of the family can often have a profound effect. It provides the teacher with the opportunity to remember the importance of this partnership, consider the child's and family's "funds of knowledge" (González, Moll, & Amanti, 2005, p.133), and reflect on the nature of the families' involvement in the early learning service. This consideration can also support relationship-rich solutions. A critical attitude towards a family regarding the food a child brings for lunch, for example, may alter when reflecting on the family's wider situation. Alleviating the criticism can allow the mentee to consider more supportive ways of working with the family. Reflecting on issues from the perspective of the wider community also allows the mentee to consider how the centre/service might be viewed from an outside perspective.

Considering the holistic nature of the early childhood setting can be particularly valuable for those in management and leadership roles. This can enable a leader to see all the parts of the centre's operations as one—every decision made or action taken has a ripple effect and outcomes for the wider group. Early childhood centre policies and procedures, annual and strategic plans, registration and performance reviews, etc. create the platform for the experiences of children and families. Mentees can limit problem solving or new insight by focusing on an issue in isolation, or by pinpointing at a micro-level without consideration of the wider ramifications. Inviting a mentee to consider a holistic perspective can set the scene for considering many parts of the whole situation and can support shared leadership approaches. It can also highlight the value of having leaders at all levels of the organisation in order to achieve collective progress and development over time (Fullan, 2001).

Mentoring and the strands of Te Whāriki

I have found that of the five strands of *Te Whāriki*, those of Belonging and Wellbeing generally require attention first within mentoring conversations, because they have the biggest impact on involvement in the context mentees work within. When someone experiences a lack of belonging, they are likely to find it hard to fit in, feel a part of the group and participate confidently. This lack of belonging is likely to affect their identity, and in turn their sense of wellbeing because they may feel uncared for, which again affects their participation. Without belonging and a sense of wellbeing, teaching can be a very lonely place (Curtis et al., 2013). Within mentor discussions, relationships regularly sit at the fore, and investigating the principle of relationships, coupled with the strands of wellbeing and belonging, can enable a teacher to move to reflecting on the situation with a deeper consideration of other individuals, rather than remaining entrenched in their own standpoint.

Early childhood teachers notice that when a child has a sense of belonging with the group and their personal wellbeing is attended to, they are better able to share in communication exchanges, contribute more fully within the programme and explore new opportunities in a safe and supported way. My experience has shown that this is also true for those I have mentored. Within mentoring, where challenges in relationships are to the fore, I often question the mentee about the wellbeing of the person they are experiencing challenges with, and also inquire about their own wellbeing. I encourage them to consider the ways they experience belonging within their early childhood context and prompt them to consider the belonging of colleagues, families and children. Drawing attention to these issues often enables a shift—a 'softening' of views—which provides more openness and compassion, which can then lead to more relationship-focused solutions.

The curriculum strands and principles may be blended in many ways to provide alternative perspectives for the mentee's consideration. For example, a mentee may express their values in a way that judges a colleague. As a mentor, I could respond by inquiring about the relationship the mentee and colleague share, their communication and the ways they each contribute to the centre. Supporting mentees to reflect on their assumptions and the validity of their perspectives can enable them to evaluate the quality of their own thinking (Robinson, 2009). As the mentee considers and discusses these perspectives, they will often recognise aspects of communication that hinder their relationship and begin to recognise some of the more positive aspects of their colleague's performance. They may identify ways they can improve their approach to this person and look for strategies to engage in more successful ways.

The strand of Contribution reminds me as a mentor to consider and showcase the mentee's participation in terms of strengths, areas of interest, and the ways the mentee contributes to the holistic progress and success of children and families, and of the centre. Reflecting on Contribution can build self-confidence (by acknowledging aspects of strength), confidence in others (by recognising their strengths) and the confidence of others (by encouraging the mentee to offer more or better of themselves professionally). This lens can enable teachers to critique their own engagement, recognise the engagement and talents of others, and develop personal goals to enhance their performance.

This reflective lens can also highlight areas for exploration, such as untapped passions and areas for professional growth and personal development. Those interested in transformational learning, transformational leadership and developing a shared culture in a community of practice are likely to understand the importance of this journey and recognise the advantage of exploring issues, values and topics over time (Brown & Posner, 2001). Mentees benefit from seeing themselves as active participants in learning and development, with the influence to lead, provoke and encourage new insights (Curtis et al., 2013). In conjunction with the principle of *empowerment*, the strand of Exploration allows mentor and mentee to investigate the level of empowerment the mentee feels, and to highlight any blocks in their engagement, professional development or the level of responsibility they take for their practice. Inviting them to consider how they might explore new practices and take learning opportunities can create solutions to their struggles and pathways for them to move forward.

Conclusion

This chapter has discussed how the principles and strands of *Te Whāriki* can guide mentors and mentees. My experience of applying this framework in mentoring has demonstrated that it can provide a sound pedagogical tool for prompting professional consideration, reflection and critique. It can be used as a useful platform or framework within a community of practice, and as a tool to progress the professional development of an individual or group. Weaving the principles of *empowerment, relationships, family and community* and *holistic development* with the strands of Wellbeing, Belonging, Communication, Contribution and Exploration enables the mentor to maintain alignment with theoretical perspectives, ethical boundaries and shared early-years values in a way that is familiar and meaningful to mentees. These facets of the curriculum draw the mentee's attention to the foundations of practice and pedagogy.

References

Brown, L.M., & Posner, B.Z. (2001). Exploring the relationship between learning and leadership. *Leadership and Organizational Development Journal, 22*(6), 274–280. doi:10.1108/01437720110403204

Covey, M.R. (2008, May). *Trust is a competency.* Retrieved from http://www.coveylink.com/blog/trust-is-a-competency-chief-learning-officer-magazine/

Curtis, D., Lebo, D., Cividanes, W., & Carter, M. (2013). *Reflecting in communities of practice: A workbook for early childhood educators.* St Paul, MN: Redleaf Press.

Dahlberg, G., Moss, P., & Pence, A.R. (1999). *Beyond quality in early childhood education and care: Postmodern perspectives.* London, UK: Falmer Press.

Ehrich, L.C., Tennent, L., & Hansford, B.C. (2002). *QUT ePrints.* Retrieved from http://eprints.qut.edu.au

Fullan, M. (2001). *Leading in a culture of change.* San Francisco, CA: Jossey-Bass.

González, N., Moll, L.C., & Amanti, C. (2005). *Funds of knowledge: Theorizing practice in households, communities, and classrooms.* Mahwah, NJ: L. Erlbaum Associates.

Ministry of Education. (1996). *Te whāriki: He whāriki mātauranga mō ngā mokopuna o Aotearoa: Early childhood curriculum.* Wellington: Learning Media.

Robertson, J. (2005). *Coaching leadership: Building educational leadership capacity through coaching partnerships.* Wellington: NZCER Press.

Robinson, V. (2009). *Open-to-learning conversations / leadership dilemmas / problem solving / home-educational leaders.* Retrieved from http://www.

educationalleaders.govt.nz/Problem-solving/Leadership-dilemmas/Open-to-learning-conversations

Van Dyne, L., Ang, S., & Livermore, D. (2010). Cultural intelligence: A pathway for leading in a rapidly globalizing world. In K. M. Hannum. B. McFeeters, & L. Booysen (Eds), *Leading across differences* (pp. 131–138). San Francisco, CA: Pfeiffer.

Zachary, L.J. (1997, July). *Creating a mentoring Culture.* Retrieved from http://www.centerformentoringexcellence.com/articles[RGP9]

Zachary, L.J. (2012, October). *A little more conversation.* Retrieved from http://www.centerformentoringexcellence.com/articles

Chapter 5
Fostering pedagogical leadership through peer mentoring groups
Raewyn Penman and Kathryn O'Connell Sutherland

Introduction

In 2011 Kidsfirst Kindergartens, an association of 61 kindergartens operating in Canterbury and Westland, New Zealand, introduced a new initiative that evaluated specific indicators for quality performance in all areas of the kindergarten programme. This initiative increased the expectations of the role of the head teacher. As the pedagogical leader, their role is to inspire teachers, provide critical feedback and help the teachers to set and attain robust professional goals, thus improving learning outcomes for children and building capacity within the teaching team (Murray & McDowall Clark, 2013; Notman, 2011). The pedagogical leader is also expected to connect with and engage the parents, whānau and wider community in order to support the children's learning and wellbeing. At Kidsfirst this is a dual role of leading a team of up to eight qualified teachers and teaching children from 2 to 5 years of age for 5½ hours per day.

To support head teachers, our Education Team, the professional support arm of the association, investigated ways to provide effective mentoring with a focus on supporting each participant to fully develop their potential and personal goals in a holistic way. This chapter details a model of mentoring, implemented from 2012, that uses a collaborative approach to support and encourage pedagogical leadership. The impact on personal growth and professional leadership is discussed, and feedback on the benefits and challenges from participating head teachers is included. The content of the peer group meetings is confidential, but the consent of the head teachers was sought to include their voice in this chapter. It is hoped that sharing what has been successful at Kidsfirst Kindergartens will be of benefit to others in the early childhood sector.

Professional supervision

At the end of 2011 the authors attended a course entitled 'The Power of Peer Supervision', facilitated by the New Zealand Coaching & Mentoring Centre (NZCMC). We were introduced to peer supervision and trained in the use of seven structured tools that were developed to facilitate discussion and guide feedback for groups of three or more professionals during regular meetings. The goals of the model are "to enable the development of professional skills and competence" through using "structured processes that tap the resources within the group to enhance their ability to learn from experience" (NZCMC, 2000, p. 1). This model of peer supervision had the potential to offer the head teachers opportunities to develop their leadership practice by participating in contextualised dialogue with peers. It also provided opportunities to meet with others who have similar levels of expertise and interests, to develop a professional learning network and have ownership over this aspect of their professional development. The model had the potential to enable head teachers to develop their capacity as peer mentors.

The NZCMC model includes a range of different processes designed as tools to support specific purposes. Each participant takes turns to determine what they want from the group and then intentionally chooses an appropriate process. The processes support the individual to:

- seek feedback and gain multiple perspectives
- undertake a critical review of their practice
- explore a professional or ethical issue

- practise an upcoming situation
- raise professional challenges
- celebrate practice.

Each process includes guidelines and questions to prompt discussion and ensure effective outcomes for all members in rounds of 8 to 10 minutes.

Historically, professional supervision had its roots in social work and psychology, where authority and expert guidance were used to respond to child and adult welfare practice, especially regarding judgement and critical clinical decision making (Lietz, 2008). Most models for supervision have been a one-on-one professional meeting with a more expert person who has oversight of the supervisee's work (Counselman & Weber, 2004; Newman, Nebbergall, & Salmon, 2013). More recently there has been an emergence of research into the effectiveness of peer supervision groups, both with and without a leader (Counselman, 2013; Goodman, Calderon, & Tate, 2014; NZCMC, 2000; Newman et al., 2013; Turner, 2010).

Peer mentoring

The NZCMC peer supervision model provides a structured approach, with no designated/formal leader. Counselman and Weber (2004) and Newman et al. (2013) found many benefits in groups with no formal leader, including;

- a reduction in professional isolation and burn-out
- increase in safety and trust over time
- access to a range of expertise
- reduction in feelings of shame as participants hear of others' struggles with similar situations
- development of a shared history.

Other benefits were:
- shared leadership
- equal responsibility for ensuring the success of the meetings
- sharing and learning from successes and challenges
- giving and receiving feedback

- learning new strategies from others experiences
- low or no cost.

Counselman (2013) identified a few challenges with leaderless groups, such as:

- maintaining the group
- "task drift"—moving away from professional discussions
- being open to new members while maintaining the processes established
- member drop out due to risks to a person's self-esteem when presenting.

As supervision has expanded to include group and peer models, so, too, has mentoring (Miller & Miller, 1987). In recent years an increasing amount of international research has included reports on peer mentoring groups for teachers in pre-service training (Ambrosetti, Knight, & Dekkers, 2013; Smardon & Charteris, 2014), and for teachers in schools where teachers who work independently are brought together to increase joint advancement of the school's goals and improvements in teaching practice (Langelotz, 2013). These reports show benefits from a peer mentoring approach. Strengthening teacher co-leadership and professional inquiry, improved relationships within a professional learning community, and avoidance of hierarchical issues are some of the benefits reported. All the studies referred to recommended the area of peer mentoring as worthy of further research.

Implementing the peer mentoring model in an early childhood education context

The decision was made to do a staged roll-out of head teacher peer mentoring groups throughout the association using the NZCMC model. It was important that the head teachers be given training so that they were able to use the model successfully and their time effectively. Peer mentoring training was carried out over 3 years, beginning in 2012 with 24 teachers at each 1-day training session. During the training, the head teachers practised the processes in groups of four or five. At the end of the day they were asked to form groups, which would then become their leaderless head teacher peer mentoring group.

Many of these groups were made up of head teachers who had not worked together before, and many—although working for the same association—had little previous contact.

To support the head teachers to begin their meetings, they were given 2 hours' professional release time. Each group then organised their own meeting times and places. With head teachers being geographically spread, some teachers used digital technology, such as Skype, to include all members at meetings. Because head teachers change within the association, the composition of about half of the groups has changed since establishment. The Education Team facilitate new head teachers' inclusion in an already-formed group through discussions with existing group members to ensure they are open to, and able to support, a new member.

The effectiveness of the programme has been evaluated throughout the training and implementation period, and the Education Team have had discussions with head teachers during visits and performance appraisal reviews, at all times respectful of the fact that the content of peer mentoring group discussions remains confidential to the group. The head teachers' voices quoted throughout the next sections come from both focus group meetings and written feedback.

Head teachers' perspectives on the peer mentoring model

As a result of the training day, head teachers recalled learning new strategies and many saw this as an opportunity for increasing professionalism, making connections, and "in a really formal kind of way, limiting time". They took control of forming groups, with some head teachers needing to know members in their group in order to feel a sense of trust right from the start; for others, the prospect of a completely new group of peers was desirable. Some intentionally looked for fresh perspectives, with a thirst to "hear some other things": "I was really purposeful about not sticking with ones I usually have telephone conversations with". One head teacher referred to the Education Team, saying it is important they have "a little bit of a role in making sure that the group suits people".

The head teacher feedback in support of the programme was overwhelming, with head teachers describing it as worthwhile, valuable and an efficient use of time. They talked about prioritising it and described the programme as "precious" and "unique". Here is a selection of the feedback:

> It's a different type of meeting for a different reason, this is more personal.

> It's short and sharp.

> It's a good investment because of the actual rigour, the effect of it is probably much greater than the cost.

Head teachers appreciated the 2 hours' additional professional learning time for their first meeting and are very keen to see the meetings prioritised with further investment in release time. Although more sessions are preferable, most agree that once a term is sufficient and manageable in terms of juggling their myriad teaching and leadership responsibilities.

Benefits of the peer mentoring model

There are a number of benefits of the peer mentoring model, as derived from the head teacher feedback, which we have analysed and grouped into three themes.

1. Collective responsibility and leaderful practice

A key aspect of the peer mentoring programme is the leaderless context and the need for collective responsibility. The groups all operate quite differently, with a natural set of practices that emerge to fit the individual group, and reflect its members and their length of time together. An example is one group met in the morning and felt this was key because they did not feel tired and distracted. This group often went on to have professional release time and talked of being inspired for the day. Head teachers are effective at delineating between the social and formal mentoring aspects of the meeting: "It's structured enough that there's no gossip".

The level of organisational responsibility and regularity has been a crucial indicator of success and sustainability. Groups that function well meet regularly, prioritise the meetings, value the time together, set dates well in advance, and take turns to host their peers. Raelin (2005, cited in Cooper, 2014) describes this collaborative work as "leaderful practice", based on commitment, mutual engagement, responsibility and action.

2. Personal growth: Building relational trust, self-efficacy and agency

The relational qualities fostered through this programme are central to the practice of leadership. Trust is prevalent in the head teacher reflections, as is the notion of vulnerability in learning, and these are desirable components of effective mentoring relationships. Robinson, Hohepa and Lloyd (2009) write about the critical importance of relational trust in group contexts, where the success of one's efforts is reliant on the contribution of others. Most head teachers identified using the framework and sticking to the whole process as necessary to build trust in the early stages. The challenges offered new learning, and the group mentoring has been described as inclusive, safe and fair.

As they have become more adept, developed relationships and grown trust, groups have modified the structure. In one focus group discussion, the depth and growth after 3 years was evident in the head teachers' reflections, the language they used and the way they discussed and explored topics. In newly formed groups, one head teacher commented that it took a while for the process to become natural and the booklet was still a useful guide. Overall, there is both support for and awareness of the value of each process, and, interestingly, many referred back to the model for discussions of ethical dilemmas.

Similar to the findings of a New Zealand study (Thornton, 2010), head teachers talked of feeling isolated and how their peer group helped them feel connected. They valued the opportunity to think aloud and practise their conversations before engaging with their teaching team and seeking feedback. Thornton (2010) refers to this leadership development as "blended action learning", because it involves an active questioning and learning process. The following questions are one example of this: "Did I handle that right?" and "Did I make the right decision?" Many teachers talked about feeling affirmed, empowered and validated in their feelings, frustrations and decisions: "It's great to get with other people who are in exactly the same situation".

These practices of seeking others' perspectives, hearing the successful stories of their peers and practising conversations to support decision making have a positive impact on head teachers' sense of self-efficacy as leaders. In particular, combating feelings of isolation has increased confidence and belief in their own abilities as leaders:

> We talked about being isolated ... but it's also more than that. It's that thing of what it really feels like to be a head teacher and the kind of things you have to cope with, and you really only know what it's like if you're doing it.

The combination of being both vulnerable and affirmed is linked to improvement, and when applied to the context of leadership self-efficacy has a strong influence on pedagogical outcomes. Developing confidence and self-efficacy was a key objective of a New Zealand research project, Developing Pedagogical Leadership in Early Childhood Education (Ord et al., 2013).

The influence of peers in shifting thinking and changing practice

Peer groups have been a vehicle for discussing pedagogical practices, and a rich culture of inquiry has emerged in these learning communities. Some examples of this depth and its potential are as follows:

> It made me think more about how I demonstrate my leadership.

> Feedback has made me reflective of my practice and look at things from a different perspective.

> I have used strategies provided by my peers to support my leadership goals.

Head teachers talked of seeking different perspectives to inform self-review, appraisal goals, teaching practices, programme routines, transitions to school and caregiving routines. These types of discussions resulted in shifts in thinking and changes in practice. Caring for 2-year-olds in kindergartens is still new practice for many teachers, and conversations with peers has been influential. One head teacher sharing her approach to toileting was significant for another. This head teacher reported:

> It was just a tiny spark that changed me suddenly ... it snapped me out of a bit of a negative side. She shared her philosophy and how it works so well that I'm more open to that idea.

Another teacher in the group also recognised this as a shift: "you changed that view of how you look at things".

Head teachers have benefited from time together, contextualised dialogue, the space to make sense of arguments, and actively assist their peers to find meaning through reflection on practice (Benade, Gardner, Teschers, & Gibbons, 2014). Examples of this dialogue are:

We ask questions to explore and get the philosophy behind something.

It doesn't make sense to me.

I was asking quite pointed questions.

We drew you out, you explained well.

One specific example is a head teacher arriving at a meeting prior to the session beginning and discovering a peer using the association's online platform for assessment. "I knew we needed to get into the 21st century, we're a little bit reluctant … I've been feeling the push for getting technology into the programme more." It was the informal and collaborative aspect of the programme that presented the opportunity for this head teacher to see in action, explore and hear a peer positively share the learning and positive outcomes for children, parents and whānau. This resulted in the head teacher embracing a new way of engaging with parents and whānau online. Head teachers described this practice as quite natural, and they felt comfortable to ask questions and clarify thoughts. One head teacher explained this: "You have to be honest and have a vent and do all of that to take things that will change or grow and develop".

Two of the seven processes that head teachers preferred encourage a devil's advocate role "because it's probably the bit we don't do", and the professional issues process, which has been used to explore new ideas, concepts and readings. As a fully qualified group of teachers, one head teacher noted that they very quickly got on to using this process: "Meetings have been a great benefit for my pedagogy". One group talked of the importance of setting their own agenda, the more intimate nature of the gatherings, and having time to "bite into the issue".

Challenges of the peer mentoring model

Head teachers identified some challenges in the peer mentoring model, which have been summarised in this section. One challenge identified arose from not following the processes. This resulted in members of one group feeling that some people talked more than others and some personalities dominated. The discipline of this supervision model and specified tools are designed to combat this complexity of power dynamics. The Education Team continue to promote the idea of using the whole process, which provides unexpected outcomes and enables quiet people to talk. Many head teachers talked about its structure, with statements such as "waiting your turn, that was hard, really, really hard". The discipline of listening and not giving advice was a personal challenge for some.

Other challenges relating to lack of time to meet and the organisation and regularity of the group's meetings were recognised, with a possible solution identified being to develop a group contract. "Part of the issue is we need to get ourselves organised, allocate tasks and take responsibility … even turn taking". For one group the concept of being leaderless was quite foreign initially: "we've kind of floundered a bit because nobody wants to be in control". Trust was identified as important, and for some this was a factor in group composition that affected the time it took to fully engage and participate. Overall, it appears head teachers feel comfortable to contribute, share and discuss a range of topics. The challenge of task drift identified in the literature was not apparent in these groups.

Opportunities and potential

Head teachers have transferred newly developed strategies and the facilitation practices from the model into individual team contexts to guide ethical situations, conflict in the team and difficulties in communication with parents. The programme offers this versatility, and there is a strong correlation between these emerging peer mentoring groups and the nature of professional learning communities, as explored by New Zealand writers in early childhood (Cherrington & Thornton, 2015; Thornton & Wansbrough, 2012). With this platform there is the opportunity to explore new initiatives such as the New Zealand Leadership in Early Childhood Education for '5 out of 5' Children resource (Ministry of Education, 2014). This includes thought-provoking questions designed to stimulate leadership conversation. Head teachers involved in these peer mentoring groups are well positioned to use this material in the manner for which it was designed to co-construct new knowledge.

While respectful of the nature of peer group mentoring and the elements that make it successful, the Education Team are keen to ensure a strong link between the individual learner and peer groups. Lovett, Dempster and Flückiger (2015) recommend greater awareness and accountability of self in leadership programmes and have tailored a self-assessment tool to help leaders identify their current knowledge and future needs. Using this tool alongside the mentoring process could increase head teacher personal agency as they make choices to further their professional knowledge in targeted areas. Future opportunities for collaboration include the formation of new groups and connecting with professional leaders in other early childhood settings to build leaderful communities. This practice is transformational: as one head teacher exclaimed, "We can change the world". There is potential for co-constructed learning opportunities with leaders in cross-sector collaboration.

Progressing pedagogical leadership

Pedagogical leadership is crucial in the context of a fully qualified association of early childhood teachers. These peer mentoring groups have been a catalyst for change, as is evident in the examples of subtle and naturally evolving language and content. Providing this space to be vulnerable as a learner among peers is a powerful mechanism for building pedagogical leadership capability. It requires confidence and efficacy to be the person responsible for establishing and maintaining a culture of ongoing improvement and inquiry within teams. The relational qualities of trust, vulnerability, and personalised and contextualised learning conversations are a great combination to support the critical reflection of head teachers' own pedagogical practices. The structure and discipline were instrumental in helping establish the culture, with the use of purposeful conversation skills to ensure people don't fall into the trap of 'excessive niceness' and 'therapy type' discourse (Langelotz, 2013).

Conclusion

The examples presented in this chapter reveal rich dialogue among leaders about philosophical and curriculum tensions. The two examples—new ways of viewing caregiving routines in kindergarten and embracing digital technology for assessment purposes and whānau engagement—have resulted in shifts in thinking and transformation in practice. Both have had a direct impact on positive outcomes for children, parents and whānau.

There is strong alignment of the NZCMC peer mentoring model to current thinking and constructs of leadership. Writers in education today identify times of significant and rapid change (Benade et al., 2014; Cooper, 2014) characterised by complex views of knowledge and different ways of thinking about learning (Bolstad & Gilbert, 2012). Understanding leadership as a dynamic learning practice of relationships and responsibility (Robertson, 2008) has informed our summation.

Three main benefits that contribute to our understanding of effective leadership development programmes have emerged from this peer mentoring programme: personal growth through relational trust and self-efficacy; an understanding of the significance of collective responsibility; and the benefits of critical inquiry into pedagogy and how this transforms practice through interaction and peer influence. Achieving these outcomes without the presence of the Education Team is a good example of *enablement* and *collective responsibility*, which are two of our Kidsfirst Kindergarten values. Raelin (2005, cited in Cooper, 2014) warns that building leadership capacity does not happen on its own: it needs to be nurtured and grown by intentionally mobilising resources in an organisation and ensuring sustainability. Our approach to the co-ordinated leadership programme has been system-wide (Hargreaves & Fullan, 2013), and the effectiveness of this initiative would not have been possible without a combination of supportive structural and relational conditions (Cherrington & Thornton, 2015).

References

Ambrosetti, A., Knight, B.A., & Dekkers, J. (2013). Perceptions and experiences of peer mentoring in pre-service teacher education. In M.F. Shaughnessy (Ed.), *Mentoring: Practices, potential challenges and benefits* (pp. 125-144). New York, NY: Nova Science Publishers.

Benade, L., Gardner, M., Teschers, C., & Gibbons, A. (2014). 21st century learning in New Zealand: Leadership insights and perspectives. *Journal of Educational Leadership, Policy and Practice, 29*(2), 47-60.

Bolstad, R., & Gilbert, J., with McDowall, S., Bull, A., Boyd, S., & Hopkins, R. (2012). *Supporting future-oriented learning and teaching: A New Zealand perspective*. Report prepared for the Ministry of Education. Wellington: New Zealand Council for Educational Research & Ministry of Education.

Cherrington, S., & Thornton, K. (2015). The nature of professional learning communities in New Zealand early childhood education: An exploratory study. *Professional Development in Education, 41*(2), 310-328.

Cooper, M. (2014). 'Everyday teacher leadership': A reconceptualisation for early childhood education. *Journal of Educational Leadership, Policy and Practice, 29*(2), 84-96.

Counselman, E. (2013). In consultation, peer supervision groups that work: Three steps that make a difference. *Psychotherapy Networker, 37*(3).

Counselman, E.F., & Weber, R.L. (2004). Organizing and maintaining peer supervision groups. *International Journal of Group Psychotherapy, 54*(2), 125-143.

Goodman, R.D., Calderon, A.M., & Tate, K.A. (2014). Liberation-focused community outreach: A qualitative exploration of peer group supervision during disaster response. *Journal of Community Psychology, 42*(2), 228-236.

Hargreaves, A., & Fullan, M. (2013). The power of professional capital. *Journal of Staff Development, 34*(30), 36-39.

Langelotz, L. (2013). Teachers' peer group mentoring: Nine steps to heaven? *Education Inquiry, 4*(2), 375-394.

Lietz, C. (2008). Implementation of group supervision in child welfare: Findings from Arizona's supervision circle project. *Child Welfare, 87*(6), 31-48.

Lovett, S., Dempster, N., & Fluckiger. (2015). Personal agency in leadership using an Australian heuristic. *Professional Development in Education, 41*(1), 127-143.

Miller, R., & Miller, K. (1987). Clinical supervision: History, practice, perspective. *NASSP Bulletin, 71*(503), 18–22.

Ministry of Education. (2014). *Leadership in early childhood education for '5 out of 5' children.* Retrieved from: http://www.education.govt.nz/early-childhood/teaching-and-learning/educational-leadership/5-out-of-5/,

Murray, J., & McDowall Clark, R. (2013). Reframing leadership as a participative pedagogy: The working theories of early years professionals. *Early Years: An International Research Journal, 33*(3), 289–301.

Newman, D.S., Nebbergall, A.J., & Salmon, D. (2013). Structured peer group supervision for novice consultants: Procedures, pitfalls, and potential. *Journal of Educational and Psychological Consultation, 23*(3), 200–216.

Notman, R. (2011). Building leadership success in a New Zealand education context. In R. Notman (Ed.), *Successful educational leadership in New Zealand: Case studies of schools and an early childhood centre* (pp. 135–152). Wellington: NZCER Press.

NZCMC (New Zealand Coaching & Mentoring Centre). (2000). *The power of peer supervision: 7 tools for supervision groups.* Auckland: Author.

Ord, K., Mane, J., Smorti, S., Carroll-Lind, C., Robinson, L., Arvay-Armstrong-Read, et al. (2013). *Te whakapakari kaiārahi aahuatanga ako kōhungahunga: Developing pedagogical leadership in early childhood education.* Wellington: Te Tari Puna Ora o Aotearoa: New Zealand Childcare Association.

Robertson, J.M. (2008). *Coaching educational leadership: Building leadership capacity through partnership.* London, UK: Kogan Page.

Robinson, V., Hohepa, M., & Lloyd, C. (2009). *School leadership and student outcomes: Identifying what works and why: Best evidence synthesis iteration.* Wellington: Ministry of Education.

Smardon, D., & Charteris, J. (2014). Strengthening teacher co-leadership through professional inquiry. *Journal of Educational Leadership, Policy and Practice, 29*(2), 73–83.

Thornton, K. (2010). Developing leadership through blended action learning. *Early Childhood Folio, 14*(1), 7–12.

Thornton, K., & Wansbrough, D. (2012). Professional learning communities in early childhood education. *Journal of Educational Leadership, Policy and Practice, 27*(2), 51–64.

Turner, S. (2010). Developing a non-medical prescribers' peer supervision group. *Nursing Standard, 25*(29), 55–61.

PART 2: MĀORI PERSPECTIVES

Chapter 6
Applying te ao Māori considerations within mentoring relationships
Jenny Ritchie and Carol Smith

Introduction
Central to the mentoring relationship is deep connection and respectful reciprocity, with caring nested within a commitment to social justice (Daloz, 1990). This chapter begins with an overview of previous research conducted at the request of the New Zealand Teachers Council (NZTC) that outlined desirable aspects of processes for supporting new teachers across a range of educational settings (Aitken, Piggot-Irvine, Bruce Ferguson, McGrath, & Ritchie, 2008; Piggot-Irvine, Aitken, Ritchie, Bruce Ferguson, & McGrath, 2009). We then outline key considerations from te ao Māori (the Māori world view) in relation to the support of beginning teachers. Finally, we draw on the extensive experience of Whaea Carol Smith in illuminating the application of these kaupapa Māori values within her mentoring practice across a variety of different early childhood care and education contexts (Smith & Ritchie, 2013).[1]

---

1 Whaea is an honorific term for a respected woman such as an Aunty or other senior female whānau member.

Effective mentoring: A New Zealand study

In 2007 the NZTC commissioned a piece of research[2] aimed at identifying the components of effective mentoring of provisionally registered teachers (PRTs) across early childhood, primary, secondary and Māori-medium settings. Using a 'success case' methodology, which focused on identifying research case study sites that represent effective models of practice, mentors and beginning teachers from 20 different 'success' sites were interviewed.

Consideration of this data, alongside a range of research literature, gave rise to some useful findings and insights (Aitken et al., 2008; Piggot-Irvine et al., 2009). Prominent across all the settings was the finding that the service or schools in which PRTs felt they were being nurtured within a community or family of support were places where managers and teachers had intentionally worked to create a culture of support. After close examination of the case studies it became clear that there were elements of support for PRTs within Māori-medium settings that were common with other sites. These included:

- support for and valuing of the PRTs
- having close physical proximity between the PRT and the mentor teacher
- clarity regarding the setting's learning culture, reinforced in the induction and mentoring process
- the provision of ongoing constructive feedback to the PRTs
- regular checking by mentor teachers of ongoing registration documentation.

In addition to these components, there were a number of elements of successful mentoring processes that were distinctive to Māori-medium settings (i.e. kōhanga reo, kura kaupapa, and whānau rumaki). Most distinctively, in these kaupapa Māori settings the notion of 'mentoring' was not confined to an individualistic, one-on-one, dyadic relationship between experienced and provisionally registered teachers. Instead, the responsibility of including and supporting the PRT was shared by the wider whānau (extended family, collective) of that setting. Effective communications between teachers and staff facilitated

---

2 This project received ethical approval from the Unitec Research Committee.

mutual understanding, respect and co-operation, creating an affirming climate in which the mentoring relationships were nested and nurtured. The following comments are drawn from interviews with a PRT and mentoring teacher from one kōhanga reo:

> We've got a happy whānau here. I think a happy whānau are easier to gain support from than people who've got moans and groans all the time so they must be happy with what we're doing for their kids [and] why they're happy to support us. (Kōhanga reo mentoring teacher)

> Having that support from the whānau, that's really a big thing for us, because I think without that we wouldn't be where we are today. (Kōhanga reo PRT 1)

> Our whānau still have that mana, the whakahaere, the operations of the kōhanga in term of the managerial, the administrative side of things … They really respect and support our feedback to them at our monthly meetings. They support us in terms of our needs for our tamariki … they're happy with the care, the programmes that are running … We take on board what they suggest and always offer feedback. (Kōhanga reo PRT 1)

The staff did, however, raise questions about managing the 'fit' between registration requirements and their kaupapa Māori setting:

> Wondering where kaupapa Māori situations fit within all this. Going to pōwhiri, taking tamariki to tangihanga, even writing my own reports for the kōhanga, but how often do you submit this within your advice and guidance programme? How much do I do? (Kōhanga reo PRT 1)

> How do you demonstrate wairuatanga? How do you write it down on paper? (Kōhanga reo PRT 2)

> How do you document it? Where does it fit under those dimensions?[3] (Kōhanga reo PRT 1)

Both mentors and PRTs grounded their practice in the kaupapa Māori values and philosophy of the kura kaupapa movement's philosophy document, *Te Aho Matua* (Ministry of Education, 2008), and

---

3 At the time of the study, this terminology of 'dimensions' was being used to describe what are now termed 'criteria'.

the early childhood curriculum, *Te Whāriki* (Ministry of Education, 1996):

> I think I have a really good working knowledge of Te Whāriki. I'm not at all too worried about it. I feel that it absorbs my every fibre. I do go back to it for specific wording when it comes down to documentation … Working with children especially, just finding the right question to help them get to where they need to get. (Kōhanga reo PRT 3)

In the following section we consider some of the underpinning values from te ao Māori and explore how they contributed to effective mentoring situations.

Key considerations from te ao Māori

In te ao Māori-focused settings the collectivist, holistic philosophies of wairuatanga (spiritual interconnectedness), manaakitanga (caring, generosity, hospitality), whanaungatanga (interconnected relationships), and aroha ki te tangata (reciprocal obligation to care for others) provided a broader platform of support for both mentor and registering teachers. This meant there was a sense of respectful inclusion, and a lack of traditional hierarchies that might have positioned the registering teacher below the more experienced mentor teacher, thereby contributing to a restricted form of relationship. According to the literature on mentoring, when "novice teachers are treated as an equal in the relationships, inductions are far more fruitful" (Cameron, 2007, p. 33). The induction process is supported within and is consistent with the wider culture of the educational setting; for example, in the conducting of pōwhiri to welcome new teachers, in the provision of regular time allocation for meetings between teachers and mentors, and in the collective celebration of achievement when a teacher is awarded full registration.

Communication channels were similarly holistically integrated, woven into the fabric of the everyday practices in the Māori-medium settings that were part of the study: "flowing communication appears to be constant, ongoing, open, regular, and informally integrated into everyday processes" (Aitken et al., 2008, p. 90). This open communication represented enactment of the expressions of kanohi ki te kanohi (face-to-face), and āheinga kōrero, āheinga whakaaro (free to speak, free to think) (Aitken et al., 2008, p. 93). The value placed on listening was also an enabling strategy identified in the data.

Wairuatanga and whakapapa underpinned all relationships, as explained by a tumuaki of a kura kaupapa:

> From a Māori perspective it's about that taha wairua, and it is saying honour each person's uniqueness and the dignity of each person. Don't trample on the mana of another person, because they carry all the mana of their tupuna—that is part of the beauty of being Māori too. (quoted in Aitken et al., 2008, pp. 91–92)

> The thinking process in Māori is quite different. We always go back to whakapapa, we always go back to atua, whanaungatanga where we are all connected, there is a level that is always operating. (quoted in Aitken et al., 2008, p. 101).

The notion of aroha ki te tangata is evident in the question frequently posed to the PRT by a mentor teacher: "Do you love your children and do they love you?" This is viewed as "indicating the continued reflective practice of child-centred learning required under Te Aho Matua" (Aitken et al., 2008, p. 92). Mentors and PRTs valued the input of kaumātua and links to local marae as supporting the wider collective processes. They also appreciated opportunities for ongoing professional learning, and national networks such as those provided by the teachers' union, the New Zealand Educational Institute, Te Riu Roa, and Te Tari Puna Ora o Aotearoa / the New Zealand Childcare Association[4] (Aitken et al., 2008).

When contacting the teachers who had been part of the NZTC study to obtain permission to use some of the material from one of the original case studies in this chapter, it was heartening to hear that all the PRTs who had been participants in the study had since obtained registration. The response from one of these teachers was illuminating:

> Somewhere around the time of your case study interviews (or not too long after), the registering process changed and clarity surrounding the entire process became vaguely a little more visible. There still wasn't enough support structures for Māori teachers though, and I guess we just fumbled our way through the process without too much

---
4   Te Tari Puna Ora o Aotearoa / The New Zealand Childcare Association has recently been renamed Te Rito Maioha Early Childhood New Zealand.

exterior support. Ultimately collective self-determination got us all over the line. Since then I know all of the PRTs involved have gained full registration. It really did feel like it took an eternity though (four years in one person's case). We all managed to assist the others who followed behind us too. I guess we were able to share our experiences and help guide them through the maze. (Email communication, 2014, used with permission)

This comment points to some highly salient aspects of te ao Māori: the rangatiratanga (self-determination) and kotahitanga (unity), collectivity and solidarity that serve to wrap a korowai (cloak) of support around those who are in need of it. In the final section of this paper, an experienced mentor of provisionally registered early childhood teachers, Whaea Carol Smith, outlines her mentoring process, in which the importance of reciprocity, wairuatanga and whanaungatanga are exemplified.

Mentoring journeys: An experienced mentor teacher shares some insights

I (the second author) have played a mentoring role for 10 years, and although the requirements of the Teachers Council have provided a framework, the kaupapa of my engagement with teachers has always been grounded in the ways of knowing, being, and doing of my Māoritanga (Māoriness). I have mentored teachers who are of Māori, Tokelauan, Samoan, Indian, Turkish and Pākehā descent, both in collectives and as individuals, in a wide range of early childhood settings. In the collective circumstance, this mentoring became whole-centre professional development and in the individual circumstance often the PRT became the kaiwhakahaere (leader) in moving the centre forward with different kaupapa (focuses).

Being Māori, no te uri o Te Rarawa (of Te Rarawa descent), there is a way of knowing, being and doing for me which is normal and natural in all processes of whakawhanaungatanga (relationship building) where I am the kaiwhakahaere (mentor, coach, teacher). I do not seek out this mahi (work), but I am contacted by PRTs by way of others I have mentored, or by PRTs who were students with whom I was previously engaged in my role as a teacher education lecturer. Therefore, already a sense of whanaungatanga (relationship) has been formed, even though I may not have physically met the prospective PRT. The wairua (spiritual interconnectedness) and whanaungatanga built with one person has been passed to another, thus serving as the basis of the new relationship.

A wā hui (meeting time) is made, either to meet outside or within the centre, and at that initial hui (meeting) I present my kawa (process) for mentoring. If the hui is held in the centre, then the management are invited to the hui as well. Information is left with the PRT, who will contact me if they wish to continue. It is important for the PRT and me to determine the wairua (connectedness of being) between us to ensure that we are able to proceed as part of a process that is tika (correct, valid) and pono (honourable, true). This is essential if the whanaungatanga is to become one of engagement. The concept of kanohi ki te kanohi—not only to physically connect but also to spiritually connect—is the hā (essence) of the relationship. This hā is the papa (foundation) of the relationship, for if these components for establishing a respectful relationship are not acknowledged, the mentoring process becomes one of a power relationship rather than an "engaged pedagogy" (hooks, 1994, p. 15). hooks states that "teachers must be actively committed to a process of self-actualization that promotes their own well-being if they are to teach in a manner that empowers their students" (p. 15).

The enactment of concepts of kaupapa Māori, which include acknowledging wairua, whanaungatanga, hā, tika and pono, also bring the PRT into the waka Māori (Māori canoe) for our shared journey. This enables the PRT to have an engaged pedagogy of authenticity when applying and presenting evidence required for the Registered Teacher Criteria (RTC) 3: "demonstrate commitment to bicultural partnership in Aotearoa New Zealand" (NZTC, 2009, p. 1). Our initial hui not only sets the papa for a relationship that is mutually respectful; it also allows for growth within te ao Māori and is one of incorporating the whānau of the centre as well. During the minimum 2-year mentoring period, regular observations are made of the PRT in her engagement with tamariki (children), hoa mahi (colleagues) and whānau, and the expectation is that practices of kaupapa Māori are being implemented.

My role as a mentor is to move PRTs forwards, to take responsibility for their evidence collection and presenting of their practice, and even, within a trusting relationship that allows for both support and challenge, to "make them scratch where they are not itching" so that their practice of incorporating and implementing kaupapa Māori is enhanced. Teachers must have an engaged pedagogy if children are to benefit from being citizens of Aotearoa and the world (Durie, 2001). Tamariki (children) are ultimately ā tātou rangatira mō āpōpō (our leaders of tomorrow).

No reira:
Ko Whangatauatia te maunga
Ko Karirikura te awa
Ko Te Rarawa te iwi
Ko Carol Smith taku ingoa

Conclusion

In early childhood education in Aotearoa we have a paradigm grounded strongly in a commitment to Te Tiriti o Waitangi (the Treaty of Waitangi), as evidenced in *Te Whāriki*. For example, Goal 1 of the Belonging strand asks educators to consider, "In what ways do the environment and programme reflect the values embodied in Te Tiriti o Waitangi, and what impact does this have on adults and children?" (Ministry of Education, 1996, p. 56). *Te Whāriki* and Te Tiriti o Waitangi both imply respectful, responsive relationships between parties, whether they be teacher and child, Māori and Pākehā, or mentor teacher and PRT. We are still working out how to apply this Tiriti-based philosophy within our pedagogical practices. Too often, still, we see a mainstream or 'whitestream' service with only token add-ons of te reo and/or tikanga Māori (Ritchie & Skerrett, 2014).

It behoves us, then, to consider ways in which both our teaching *and* our mentoring practices are inclusive and reflective of te ao Māori values and practices. Wally Penetito has pointed out that a "Māori inclusive system would prioritise a knowledge base but it would also need to take into account Māori 'ways of knowing' (language, organisation), 'ways of thinking' (evaluations, accountability), and 'ways of doing' (pedagogy, reciprocity)" (Penetito, 2005, p. 25).

The model of mentoring described above by Whaea Carol is in keeping with traditional te ao Māori pedagogies, whereby concepts such as wairuatanga, whanaungatanga, hā, tika and pono underpin the mentoring process. It should be noted that this process, which is responsive to and respectful of both individuals and cultures, has been applied effectively by Whaea Carol in mentoring a large number of teachers from a wide range of different cultural backgrounds. In applying her te ao Māori process, Whaea Carol is creating a culture of support which has benefited a large number of different PRTs and their early childhood care and education services. Her process also models the *Tātaiako* competencies of *ako, manaakitanaga, tangata whenuatanga* and *wānanga* (Ministry of Education & NZTC, 2011). It also reflects the relationship-based, collaborative, educative, contextually informed model advocated in the *Guidelines for Induction and Mentoring and Mentor Teachers* (NZTC, 2011).

The examples given in this chapter have pointed to caring, responsive, collaborative, shared journeys between mentors and PRTs, in which the relationships are founded on mutual respect, wairuatanga (spiritual interconnectedness) and aroha ki te tangata (loving concern for others). These qualities sustain a balance of support and challenge, whereby the PRT is gently prodded to extend and enhance their practice. In the description of Whaea Carol's practice and in the case study examples provided earlier, potential imbalances in power dynamics are mediated by the collective ethos generated by shared te ao Māori values. The same engaged pedagogies of attunement, receptivity and listening that are applied in teaching young children are also enacted throughout the journey of these mentoring relationships (Daloz, 1990; hooks, 1994; Rinaldi, 2006).

References

Aitken, H., Piggot-Irvine, E., Bruce Ferguson, P., McGrath, F., & Ritchie, J. (2008). *Learning to teach: Success case studies of teacher induction in Aotearoa New Zealand*. Wellington: NZTC.

Cameron, M. (2007). *Learning to teach: A literature review of induction theory and practice*. Wellington: New Zealand Council for Educational Research.

Daloz, L.A. (1990). *Effective teaching and mentoring*. San Francisco, CA: Jossey-Bass.

Durie, M. (2001, February). *A framework for considering Māori educational advancement*. Paper presented at the Hui Taumata Mātauranga, Turangi/Taupo.

hooks, bell. (1994). *Teaching to transgress: Education as the practice of freedom.* New York, NY: Routledge.

Ministry of Education. (1996). *Te whāriki: He whāriki mātauranga mō ngā mokopuna o Aotearoa: Early childhood curriculum.* Wellington: Learning Media. Retrieved from http://www.educate.ece.govt.nz/~/media/Educate/Files/Reference%20Downloads/whariki.pdf.

Ministry of Education. (2008). Official version of *Te aho matua o ngā kura kaupapa Māori and an explanation in English. Supplement to New Zealand Gazette, Pursuant to Section 155a of the Education Act 1989* (Vol. 32). Wellington: Department of Internal Affairs.

Ministry of Education, & NZTC. (2011). *Tātaiako: Cultural competencies for teachers of Māori learners.* Wellington: Author. Retrieved from http://www.minedu.govt.nz/~/media/MinEdu/.../Tataiako/TataiakoWEB.pdf.

NZTC (2009). *Registered teacher criteria.* Wellington: Author. Retrieved from http://archive.teacherscouncil.govt.nz/rtc/rtcposter-english.pdf.

NZTC. (2011). *Professional learning journeys: Guidelines for induction and mentoring and mentor teachers.* Wellington: Author. Retrieved from http://www.teacherscouncil.govt.nz/content/guidelines-induction-and-mentoring-and-mentor-teachers-2011-englishpdf.

Penetito, W.T. (2005). *A sociology of Māori education: Beyond mediating structures.* Unpublished doctoral thesis, Victoria University of Wellington. Retrieved from http://researcharchive.vuw.ac.nz/handle/10063/485.

Piggot-Irvine, E., Aitken, H., Ritchie, J., Bruce Ferguson, P., & McGrath, F. (2009). Induction of newly qualified teachers in New Zealand. *Asia-Pacific Journal of Teacher Education, 37*(2), 175-198.

Rinaldi, C. (2006). *In dialogue with Reggio Emilia.* London, UK: Routledge.

Ritchie, J., & Skerrett, M. (2014). *Early childhood education in Aotearoa New Zealand: History, pedagogy, and liberation.* New York, NY: Palgrave MacMillan.

Smith, C., & Ritchie, J. (2013). Enacting indigenous wisdom within higher education pedagogies: An example from early childhood teacher education in Aotearoa. In J. Lin, R.L. Oxford, & E.J. Brantmeier (Eds), *Re-envisioning higher education: Embodied pathways to wisdom and social transformation* (pp. 143-160). Charlotte, NC: Information Age Publishing.

Chapter 7
A Māori perspective of mentoring for early childhood settings

Kuni Jenkins, Meremaihi Williams, Emily Sinclair,
Paeakau Harris, Heeni Jenkins and Pearl Waaka

Introduction

The purpose of this chapter is to present a Māori perspective of mentoring in early childhood through the teacher education programme that has been operating at Te Whare Wānanga o Awanuiārangi (TWWoA). TWWoA, as a New Zealand Qualifications Authority-accredited tertiary organisation, has a history of engagement with Māori communities as an early childhood education provider. In the 1970s the imminent death of the Māori language was predicted (Benton, 1979). This announcement shocked the Māori world to the extent that Māori attitudes completely changed towards teaching and learning in the home, on the marae and in early childhood facilities. Early childhood options up to that point had been sadly lacking in Māori communities. Expectations in Māori communities were suddenly elevated to saving the Māori language.

Context of induction and mentoring in Māori educational settings

Historically, the growth of Māori interest in early childhood options outside of the mainstream is traceable back to 1982, with the call from Māori leaders to establish te kōhanga reo (Māori-language nests), which would be the vessel to save the Māori language from the language death that Benton (1979) predicted. Suddenly, the elevated focus on saving the Māori language was no longer about the state policies of advancing Māori achievement through enrichment programmes designed to help Māori children learn English more efficiently; it was now focused on the demand for early childhood options in Māori communities, where young Māori children could have access to quality developmental educational programmes and where they could be taught through the vernacular of Māori language by knowledgeable practitioners.

Kuni Jenkins (with Tania Ka'ai) described the Māori response as being led by "options outside of the State" (Jenkins, 1994, cited in Coxon, Jenkins, Marshall, & Massey, 1994, p. 162). Such options included Māori reporting back in 1985 to the Waitangi Tribunal[1] which found that the state's education system judged on its own criteria was a failure (Waitangi Tribunal, 1986).

The Waitangi Tribunal was recorded as having made the summation of the shortcomings of the educational system and how it had failed Māori (Waitangi Tribunal, 1986). In making such a statement the report challenged the explanation of Māori educational underachievement. Jenkins argued that the state had long seen that underachievement in terms of cultural deprivation theory (Jenkins, 1994, cited in Coxon et al., 1994, pp. 162–163; Ramsay, 1984). Māori groups demanded that te kōhanga reo initiatives should embrace traditional Māori proverbs such as "Ko te reo te mauri o te mana Māori" (The language is the very principle of Māori mana) and "Me kōrero Māori i ngā wā katoa i ngā wāhi katoa" (Speak Māori at all times and in all places).

---

1 The Waitangi Tribunal (Māori: Te Rōpū Whakamana i te Tiriti) is a New Zealand permanent commission of inquiry established under the Treaty of Waitangi Act 1975. It is charged with investigating and making recommendations on claims brought by Māori relating to actions or omissions of the Crown, in the period largely since 1840, that breach the promises made in the Treaty of Waitangi (https://en.wikipedia.org/wiki/Waitangi_Tribunal).

Underpinning these imperatives was the determination of Māori leaders never again to accept dominant educational theoretical policies and practices that did not fit within the frameworks of their cultural heritage. Rather, they wanted a pedagogy based on tino rangatiratanga (absolute sovereign right), where te kōhanga reo espoused Māori ideals and practices as the norm. They could then expect that their children would be educated in the frameworks and practices that were acceptable to Māori communities (Jenkins, 1994, cited in Coxon et al., 1994, p. 163).

A key intervention strategy developed by the TWWoA team in the period 2007 to 2009 was Te Hāpai Ō, the name our team gave to our part in the induction and mentoring pilot, a programme that was established from and funded as a professional development project by the Ministry of Education. Te Hāpai Ō became our team's descriptor for contextualising mentoring practice within Māori settings. The mechanism became significant for our team in the production of Māori mentors, whom we chose to call pou tautoko, and beginning teachers, to be called pia. The early childhood induction and mentoring pilot project set up by the NZTC created a platform for our research team at TWWoA to co-ordinate a network of early childhood centres and kura kaupapa Māori in the Mataatua rohe in the Bay of Plenty region. It included some early childhood centres and maintream schools that had arisen to deliver parts of their curriculum in Māori language. These are often referred to as Māori-medium schools.

Te Hāpai Ō: A programme for mentor teachers in early childhood and primary school levels to assist with the development of a Māori perspective

Te Hāpai Ō (NZTC, 2012) describes how mentoring had always taken place during the registration process of teachers, but it had not been the formal and recognised process that is now a key part of the NZTC protocols. What is exciting from a Māori perspective is the role of the pou tautoko (mentors) in the new process. When we decided to apply for the initial research in 2007, we did so because we thought this was an opportunity to come up with practical solutions for our kōhanga and other early childhood centres to devise strategies where we could be part of the renewed registration process for Māori beginning teachers.

A Māori perspective to induction and mentoring

Induction and mentoring is a pedagogical process that TWWoA focused on as one of the NZTC Induction and Mentoring Pilot projects during 2008 to 2010. The whakataukī that inspired the thinking of TWWoA's application was "Te amorangi ki mua, te hāpai ō ki muri". The whakataukī is divided into two sections:

- model and organisation (te amorangi ki mua)
- practice and implementation (te hāpai ō ki muri).

The Māori perspective in teacher education approaches by wānanga sectors to early childhood settings

TWWoA saw the need to train their kaiako for the early childhood context. There was a gap in the teacher education sector in the provision of a cultural teaching programme for the early childhood sector that offered a holistic delivery approach: ā wairua, ā tinana, ā hinengaro (mind, body and spirit). Professor Tāmati Reedy and his wife Tilly Reedy were presenters at the World Indigenous Peoples Conference in Education held at Waikato University in 2009. They spoke about their contribution as co-writers, with others, in *Te Whāriki: He Whāriki Mātauranga mō ngā Mokopuna o Aotearoa: Early Childhood Curriculum* (Ministry of Education, 1996). As a curriculum statement, the document is historic within Māori education in Aotearoa because it assisted with guidelines for teachers and students in the first bilingual classes that were to be found in schools operating under the Tomorrow's Schools reforms (Ministry of Education, 2010).

Te Iti Rearea pedagogy

The philosophy and purpose of TWWoA's Te Iti Rearea[2] pedagogy and the curriculum provision of its bachelor degree were specifically designed to address the threatened indigenous heritage language of Aotearoa New Zealand through the cultural contexts found in te kōhanga reo and kura Māori. The children who participate in this language reclamation process are often referred to as ngā manu, the birds of the forest. Their instruction was to be provided for in the 'early years' programme, within a tino rangatiratanga model for te kōhanga reo and Māori-medium early childhood centres.

---

2   A metaphor used to describe early childhood as tiny birds.

The tino rangatiratanga model came about as a means of developing Māori self-definition and determination, as advocated by a number of theorists (Bauer, 1997; Durie, 2001; Fishman, 2001). By 2011 the implications of its language planning, pre-service and in-service training, professional development, pedagogy and praxis in te kōhanga reo and kura kaupapa Māori had been furthered through its research output on the induction and mentoring of beginning teachers in its Ministry of Education publication *Te Hāpai Ō* (NZTC, 2011).

TWWoA provides a mentoring programme for the teacher and learner, named after a 1985 Ruātoki waiata (song) that Manawa wera, the Ruātoki kapa haka group, performed in the 1980s. The imagery in that waiata stems from the proverb about the achievements of a tiny bird, a korimako, which darts around the tallest trees of the forest. Such achievements for a tiny bird in reaching the tallest heights in the forest inspired TWWoA to use this metaphor to name their early childhood Bachelor of Education degree, Te Tohu Paetahi Ako: Te Iti Rearea.

Te Amorangi ki Mua and Te Hāpai Ō

Te Amorangi ki Mua is the model and organisational plan the research team used for the professional educative development of mentors (pou tautoko), and the professional development of beginning teachers (pia) towards full registration. It is the achievement of the taonga (treasure) of full teacher registration that is revered and aspired to. Such aspiration is articulated in the imagery of 'Te amorangi ki mua te hāpai ō ki muri'. This approach promotes mātauranga Māori (Māori knowledge and values) and te ao Māori (Māori perspectives / world views). Tikanga Māori (Māori cultural values and practices) guide induction and mentoring. Whakataukī Māori (Māori metaphor and symbolism), stated as proverbs and sayings, is used to relate Māori philosophy in terms of belief and practice. Māori proverbs are language tools and strategies that articulate cultural belief and practice, and in doing so reveal the necessity to understand the importance of language to explain culture. The whakataukī is used to put a cultural framework alongside the registered teacher criteria.

Te Hāpai Ō, as we said earlier, was a name we used to contextualise the mentoring practices within the Māori settings of the research. In our attempts to define the way these cultural practices or ideas might work in the NZTC induction and mentoring programme, the ideas did become complex. The team attributed the essence of the idea to an indigenous (Māori) cultural practice whose conceptual framework emanates from a Māori world view. Te Hāpai Ō is an integral part of the fuller model of Te Amorangi ki Mua. From this combination of the two parts we believed, as a team, that we had a formula that could help us validate a Māori practice (tikanga) for induction and mentoring.

Figure 1: Te Amorangi ki Mua model

Note: Pia are positioned and supported by pou tautoko and Te Hāpai ō ki Muri. Pou tautoko = mentor(s); Te Hāpai Ō = professional development and resources; ako = a cultural practice that exists as a facilitative relationship in forums of knowledge communication, such as whānau, wānanga, kura, and within the practice of Te Hāpai Ō.

Ako is the pedagogy of induction and mentoring. This iterative and pragmatic process is symbolised by the pā harakeke, the flax bush, and draws on the strengths of the group for the wellbeing of the relationship and its maintenance. Ako is dynamic in that āhuatanga Māori (Māori practices) emanate and integrate. The model Te Amorangi ki Mua utilises these practices to explain its organisational structures as follows:

- whanaungatanga—to gather in collaborative, supportive and effective relationships
- manaakitanga—to develop a spirit of caring and sharing, where the idea of reciprocity becomes a firmly rooted practice
- kaitiakitanga—to use culturally responsive strategies to embrace and protect what are respected as taonga
- rangatiratanga—to recognise the leadership attributes of a person
- wairuatanga—to place an ethical responsibility on a person in the way they engage with others
- kōtahitanga—to focus on the unity of purpose to achieve
- mātauranga—to ensure the acquisition of knowledge and intellectualisation.

These practices inform the rituals of engagement, such as professional conversations. Within early education and care communities, educational communities, professional communities and learning communities, iterative opportunities are highlighted where pou tautoko and pia can deliberate, reflect, ask questions, learn from each other and others, and share. There is a collaborative approach to what professional learning is and how this is achieved, and a whole-school approach to mentoring and induction. Networking provides capacity and capability. It does not operate in isolation (Pihama, Lee, Taki, & Smith, 2004), but, as Te Hāpai Ō articulates, mentoring and induction are pedagogies that are holistic and contextual. Professional learning and development is not just an event for 'kura': its outreach is to its local and national communities, focused as it is on quality teaching and learning.

The aim of the research publication *Te Hāpai Ō* is to incorporate the Te Amorangi ki Mua model with the teaching criteria in the guidelines set by the NZTC as the Registered Teacher Criteria in 2011 (p. 8). *Te Hāpai Ō* works within those guidelines to develop a Māori perspective that is comprehensive, educative and evaluative in order to assist the pou tautoko and provide guidelines following a set of āhuatanga (cultural practices) for the pia.

In their mentoring practice, the pou tautoko brings the Māori perspectives together through their experiential knowing, professional passion and shared vision of what makes for good teaching practice. The pia works in collaboration with the pou tautoko to engage in a programme of professional learning that focuses on how to be an effective teacher for diverse ākonga in Aotearoa New Zealand (NZTC, 2012, p. 12). Effective teachers are committed to ongoing inquiry (NZTC, 2012, p. 12) of their professionalism, practice and relevance to the Aotearoa New Zealand social, cultural and educational context.

A retrospective view of past mentoring experience and practice of mentors in Māori-medium settings was their limited emphasis on preparing the mentee for life in a classroom filled with Māori children. Jenkins argues that the common sense ideas that persisted among people of the 1960s–80s who mentored or worked out solutions for improving their teaching strategies to overcome the failure rates of Māori children, centred on 'enrichment programmes' (Jenkins 1994, cited in Coxon et al, 1994 p. 151). These programmes simply meant increasing the 'dosage' of English and Western culture for Māori pupils as the solution to improving Māori performance rates at school; that is, there was no sense of the need to 'be a Māori teacher' and to understand or believe that cultural norms had a place in the classroom.

Instead, it seemed that mentors had the task of making professional learning and development monocultural, where good practice was equated with 'we are one people'—the theoretical underpinning of the assimilation model. The idea of Māori language revival did not fit into such a mentoring approach, where the possibility of deviating from what had become a standard norm in the mentoring of teachers to a more cultural, social and educational view of providing professional development was based on the needs of the pia.

Te Hāpai Ō as an induction and mentoring initiative within Māori perspectives for schooling

After the introduction of kōhanga reo and kura kaupapa Māori, an opportunity to use Te Hāpai Ō arose within the NZTC 2007 to 2010 research pilot on mentoring and induction. In this way, Te Hāpai Ō could be made available to educational agencies with Māori programmes to broaden their teacher education initiatives on induction and mentoring provision for their beginning teachers. Te Hāpai Ō is based on a relationship whereby both the pou tautoko and the pia have the dual profile of being learners as well as teachers, acknowledging the reciprocal nature of educative mentoring and facilitative relationships. The forward vision for TWWoA is to be committed to a culturally responsive strategy that guides and facilitates the pedagogy of mentoring for the pia by the pou tautoko. *Te Hāpai Ō* (NZTC, 2011) is consistent with *Te Whāriki* (Ministry of Education, 1996) and the values of early child education and care.

Te Hāpai Ō (NZTC, 2012) has a comfortable fit within the early childhood education (ECE) objectives and practices as required in the curriculum of *Te Whariki*. As a curriculum *Te Whāriki* is designed to be the document for all ECE environments whether Māori or Pākehā, so that whole child is catered for, for a child who grow up to be socialised within a bi-cultural society, which New Zealand claims to be. Te Amorangi ki Mua (NZTC, 2012, p. 4, 12)—the high status leaders—that the ECE children will become, is embedded in the futuristic designs of the mentoring and induction (NZTC, 2012, p. 6) process right from the outset of the children's educational journey under an umbrella of Te Amorangi ki Mua, Te Hāpai Ō ki Muri.

Implicit in the methodology of Te Hapai Ō is whanaungatanga and āhuatanga as they link to the raising of tamariki. In the āhuatanga, each member of the whānau has a responsibility to facilitate learning and development. Similarly, the pia, as the kaiako (beginning teacher), should expect the same approach. Te Hapai Ō was designed to embrace inclusive mentoring, and so this aspect in our pilot dictated the direction of the mentoring programme.

The pilot we are describing here was about how the settings included other cultures using the Māori perspective. Concern with 'inclusivity', where the practices of learning are group oriented, was a feature of whānau learning units. Hemara (2000) has written extensively on the realm of Māori pedagogies in his review of eponymous ancestral influences. Hemara recounts the nature of intergenerational learning—just like the whānau learning units. Smith (2007) also reflects Hemara's ideas and affirms that learning is based on assistance from elders and occurs in the wider community (p. 70).

Berghan (2007), Hemara (2000) and Smith (2007) open up the idea of collective learning as an indicator of the way in which learning circles fit within the whanaungatanga model, where the nature of reciprocal relationships is established and has become taken for granted in terms of the ways of teaching and learning. Based on their model, early childhood programmes should benefit from the implementation of those descriptions of shared and collective learning.

Durie (2001) proposes a framework for considering Māori educational advancement in terms of the outcome of the aspirations of our tīpuna (ancestors), mai rā nō (handed down from generation to generation). The first principle of those aspirations is 'to live as Māori', which means:

- being able to have access to a Māori world
- being able to have access to Māori language and culture/tikanga, the marae, whānau, land and kai.

Outcomes from a Māori perspective of early childhood education practice

Durie (2001) argues that being Māori is something that educational establishments should ensure is a reality for whānau. Such a notion fits with TWWoA's philosophical curriculum plan, whereby to live as Māori—the right of every Māori child—is an indigenous right. May (2001) refers to Convention 169 of the International Labour Organisation (Article 1.1), which provides a view of how indigenous peoples might be regarded:

> [Indigenous peoples are] peoples in independent countries who are regarded as indigenous on account of their descent from the populations which inhabited the country, or a geographical region to which the country belongs, at the time of conquest or colonisation or the establishment of present state boundaries and who, irrespective of their legal status, retain some of their own social, economic, cultural and political institutions. (p. 275)

Articles 14 and 15 of the Draft Declaration of the Rights of Indigenous Peoples (2003) state:

> Indigenous peoples have the right to revitalise, use, develop and transmit to future generations their histories, languages, oral traditions, philosophies, writing systems and literatures, and to designate and retain their own names for communities, places and persons. ... Indigenous children have the right to all levels and forms

of education of the State. All indigenous peoples also have this right and the right to establish and control their educational systems and institutions providing education in their own languages, in a manner appropriate to their cultural methods of teaching and learning.

The importance of citing the Draft Declaration of the Rights of Indigenous Peoples in their programme document was to emphasise the conscious effort in the wānanga to establish a degree that was based on the cultural revitalisation of their oral traditiona as a political and cultural right. They said of the education programme of Iti Rearea that it was for:

> … Māori-medium early childhood practitioners it is about supporting the children to make links between situations in their bilingual, bi-literate, bi-cognitive and bicultural development, and supporting their movement between those situations competently and confidently (Iti Rearea *Tohu Paetahi Ako… Early Years* pp. 31 and 32).

Conclusion

In recent conversations with kaiako in early childhood education and care, there is respect for and recognition that pou tautoko are essential for maintaining the integrity of the profession and the assurance of quality teaching and learning. Te Amorangi ki Mua, in terms of ongoing professional learning and development, is a priority for pia, but even more so for pou tautoko, so that their voices can appraise and review their practices, professionalism and profession.

The group workshops revealed many interesting activities going on at each kura that aligned easily to the Registered Teacher Criteria, the āhuatanga and the whakataukī. The pia and the pou tautoko present included a kaiako who had recently received her full registration. Her feedback was invaluable in terms of the way she had collected evidence for each criterion. In addition, the Resource Teacher of Māori in that region shared her experiences as a pou tautoko, reinforcing the notion that this Māori model offers many opportunities already practised within kura. The TWWoA team is confident that the creation of a new framework (Te Amorangi ki Mua and Te Hāpai Ō) within New Zealand's educational standards of registration works across all sectors—early childhood education, primary and secondary schools.

References

Bauer, W. (1997). *The Reed reference grammar of Māori.* Auckland, New Zealand: Reed

Benton, R. A. (1979). *Legal status of the Maori language: Current reality and future prospects: A special report.* Wellington: Maori Research Unit, New Zealand Council for Educational Research.

Coxon, E., Jenkins, K., Marshall, J., & Massey, L. (Eds). (1994). *The politics of learning and teaching in Aotearoa / New Zealand.* Palmerston North: Dunmore Press.

Durie, M. (2001, March). *A framework for considering Māori educational advancement.* Opening address at Hui Taumata Mātauranga, Taupo, New Zealand.

Fishman, J. (2001). Why is it so hard to save a threatened language? In J. Fishman (Ed.), *Can threatened languages be saved?* (pp.1–22). Clevedon, NY: Multilingual Matters.

Hemara, W. (2000). *Māori pedagogies: A view from the literature.* Wellington: New Zealand Council for Educational Research.

May, S. (2001). *Language and minority rights: Ethnicity, nationalism and the politics of language.* UK: Pearson Education.

Ministry of Education. (1996). *Te whāriki: He whāriki mātauranga mō ngā mokopuna o Aotearoa: Early childhood curriculum.* Wellington: Learning Media.

NZTC. (2011). *Professional learning journeys: Guidelines for induction and mentoring and mentoring teachers.* Wellington: Author.

NZTC. (2012). *Professional learning journeys: Te Hāpai Ō: Induction and mentoring in Māori-medium settings.* Wellington: Author.

Pihama, L., Lee, J., Taki, M., & Smith, K. (2004). *A literature review on kaupapa Maori and Maori education pedagogy.* Auckland: The International Research Institute for Maori and Indigenous Education.

Smith, C. (2007). Cultures of Collecting. In M. Bargh (Ed.), *Resistance: An Indigenous Response to Neoliberalism,* (PP. 65–74). Wellington: Huia Publishers.

Waitangi Tribunal (1986). *Report of The Waitangi Tribunal on The Te Reo Maori Claim.* Wellington: Author.

Chapter 8
Kia tiaho Tamanuiterā: A metaphor for mentoring

Jacqui Brouwer, Gail Pierce, Julie Treweek and Tristan Wallace

Anei te moemoeā, mō ngā ririki tokomaha
Whaia te kahurangi, rewa ki Tāwhiti.
Kia tīaho Tama nui te rā
Kia tīaho tamariki ma.
E tipu kia rite e, ki te ika mangō ururoa.
Ana Rangiatea, te toi o ngā rangi.

Here are our dreams for the
future leaders of this nation.
Pursue your most treasured desires
beckoning to you from afar.
Tamariki are named in the image of Tamanuiterā,
your light shines strong in this world.
Draw your strength from the prowess
of a hammerhead shark.
There lie your origins,
descended from the pinnacle of the heavens above.

Introduction

This chapter tells the story of a team of professional leaders within an early childhood context engaging with the notion of mentoring. Our methodology was developed by unpacking multiple narratives to create ways of knowing and being—threads to weave into a conceptual framework for mentees and mentors. The authors drew on their funds of knowledge to identify inclusion, social justice, culture and distance mentoring as key elements of mentoring.

Kia tiaho Tamanuiterā is the metaphor we have chosen to represent mentoring in this chapter, because it symbolises the connection between the sun (our organisation's logo), the above whakatauakī, and our organisation. This whakatauakī affirms our organisation's underlying belief that children's place in the world should be awarded the highest status. The word 'tamariki' (children) derives from Tamanuiterā (Sun), as a constant reminder that children are the divine representation of ongoing life. Mangō ururoa (hammerhead shark) is a metaphorical reminder that with the dawning of each day we have to stand with courage to ensure that children shine like the sun.

This chapter will share the honest, humble and at times critical journey of a team of professional leaders as they strove towards creating a mentoring programme that would allow all ākonga (teachers and learners) to shine like the sun. Special emphasis will be given to reflective learning and the value of understanding 'he taonga te he'—that mistakes are a gift presented to us to seek new learning and move towards clarity. The authors draw on their experiences by discussing the value and application of reciprocal, responsive, authentic relationships when developing a mentoring programme.

Our story

Our story takes place in a kindergarten trust with a diverse employee base that stands firmly on Te Ika a Maui (the North Island of Aotearoa New Zealand) and is responsible for 56 care and education centres spread over a large geographical area. The Trust has a mission to ensure that educational programmes reflect Te Tiriti o Waitangi (the Treaty of Waitangi) and the dual heritage of Aotearoa. We, the authors, are leaders in this organisation and had undertaken a self-review of the teacher registration programme within the service. One of the findings of the review was that while mentoring was present within the organisation, there was a need for a more robust mentoring programme to support both mentors and mentees.

Back in 2009 two of the authors, Treweek and Wallace, were returning from an early childhood hui (meeting) in Christchurch, abuzz with new learning, ideas and possibilities. From our respective 'thinking seats' (solitary places of reflection) we came together to form a shared mentoring vision for our organisation. We were excited about the mentoring programme and could visualise the future—one that we believed would challenge and support teachers to reach their true potential. With a passion fuelled by professional development, we felt sure we would project rays of light to guide our followers. Research suggests that leaders who are committed to their own learning and that of the teams they work with have a greater chance of causing 'followership' (Avolio & Gardner, 2005; Walumbwa, Wang, Wang, Schaubroeck, & Avolio, 2010). In our imaginations we had, like the legendary figure Maui (indigenous eponymous ancestor) ensnared Te Rā (the sun).

Robertson claims that the success of a mentoring framework "lies in the power of reciprocity within a relationship of trust, self-awareness, commitment to the learning journey, and co-creation of new knowledge and understanding" (2011, p. 5). This is supported by Boreen and Niday (2000), Pavia, Nissen, Hawkins, Monroe and Filimon-Demyen (2003) and Rodd (2006), who suggest that the mentoring relationship benefits both the mentee and the mentor. Robertson (2011) alludes to the reciprocal significance within the teacher and learner relationship and relates this to the Māori value of ako. *Tātaiako* (Ministry of Education, 2011) describes ako as a dialogic, interactive relationship

Our intuition was telling us that quality mentoring needs to be intentional, meaningful, planned and well executed, in line with many writers in the field (Clutterbuck, 2008; Colky & Young, 2006; Hawkins, 2010; Pavia et al., 2003; Rodd, 2006). Rodd (2006) suggests that mentoring is an opportunity to engage in a reflective relationship and has its foundation in open dialogue that supports feelings of confidence, along with an appreciation of and aspiration for lifelong learning. The effectiveness of mentoring is arguably dependent on the quality of the relationship (Robertson, 2005; Rodd, 2006). Mentoring is a proven form of leadership development and building capacity in others (Philippart & Gluesing, 2012; Robertson, 2004, 2005; Thornton, Wansbrough, Clarkin-Phillips, Aitken, & Tamati, 2009). Hence we strode forward with our new, self-proclaimed vision, fuelled by determination and, in hindsight, a certain amount of arrogance.

Our vision was to implement our espoused theory of creating an authentic, meaningful relationship-based mentoring programme within a heterarchical leadership model. A 'heterarchy' of leadership allows for greater collaboration and consultation between all members of an organisation (Gronn, 2008). We had discovered there was a tension between management and leadership. Humphries and Senden (2000), as cited in Thornton et al. (2009), suggest that leaders focus on the development of others, whereas managers control and direct the effective organisation of the service. A mentoring mind set requires a focus on empowering, helping, developing, supporting, and removing obstacles for the mentee (Ellinger, Beattie, & Hamlin, 2010).

To realise the potential of all ākonga, we aspired to develop a mentoring programme that would upskill mentors who could build teachers' capacity as critical thinkers. As leaders we had received training in active listening, but not in the skills needed to directly mentor a mentee. Some participants in our teacher registration self-review claimed that they had had unsuccessful guidance from their mentors. Muijs and Harris (2006) argue that student outcomes improve when the educational environment is "a professional community, where learning and leadership is shared" (p. 961). This indicated to us that mentoring was a relatively misunderstood practice. Making connections, modelling and ongoing dialogue are essential components of successful mentoring and building capacity in the people we work with (Avolio & Gardner, 2005; Robertson, 2005; Walumbwa et al., 2010).

Implementation of our vision evolved into a frustrating, but at the same time profound, learning opportunity. Mists had shrouded Te Rā and our visibility was restricted. We became distracted by other aspects of our job and the urgency and excitement faded. Te Rā was escaping from our net. Every now and then Te Rā would taunt us, as, unlike Maui, we were unable to control him. Mentoring is complex, and, as we discovered on our journey, the path is not cleared for us but instead needs to be discovered and revealed. As Blackmore (2010) and Zembylas

(2010) point out, emotional effort goes into the journey of discovery.

In 2013 four members of our team attended an NZTC conference on mentoring. This resulted in us identifying the holes in our net that needed urgent attention or Te Rā would escape completely. The absence of connection between our espoused theory and our practice had become evident. We had not considered the potential contributions of others within the organisation towards the development of an effective mentoring programme. We needed the courage to delve into a deeper understanding of how we actually value, respond to and acknowledge what we supposedly believe as a collective (Kanter, 2007). We were a perfect example of walk theory and talk theory existing in separate houses: we could talk the talk of our beliefs and understanding of effective mentoring being grounded in reciprocal relationships, but our walk (way of working) was not consistent with that theory.

We decided that it was essential to slow down and take time to involve others in the development of the mentoring programme. Freire (1970) emphasises that "thinking critically about practice, today or yesterday, makes possible the improvement of tomorrow's practice" (cited in Eagan, 2010, p. 429). Bishop and Glynn (1999, cited in Keown, Parker, & Tiakiwai, 2005) argue that when people experience having something done *to* them rather than *with* them, they will feel left out of the learning interactions and conversations with others.

To align our newly espoused theory of inclusiveness, we restructured our mentoring journey to include self-review practices that would provide a forum for ākonga to contribute their knowledge. The Education Review Office report on self-review (2009, p. 16) states:

> in services where self-review was well understood and implemented common themes about what was working well included, having
>
> the whole team working together on self-review
>
> a sense of ownership of the process and outcomes of self-review.

With the elements of inclusion and social justice resonating, we sent an open invitation to all ākonga within our organisation to join our mentoring self-review. At the inaugural meeting our expanded group shaped the review question: we formulated indicators of the characteristics of an effective mentor. Finally, we felt we were on the right path, but, paradoxically, we were still not making progress. We asked ourselves, "What is the problem?" Answer: we went for the 'quick fix'. We realised that we had created indicators about a mentoring process without a shared understanding of what the characteristics of a successful mentor should be. There seemed to be confusion between the terms 'coaching' and 'mentoring', which were being used interchangeably.

Our next phase was to clarify these differences and create a definition of mentoring for our organisation. An eventual unpacking of the gathered data from teachers' voices led to the indicators of a successful mentor, which we refer to as "ways of knowing" and "ways of being", as outlined in Table 4.

Table 4: Indicators of a successful mentor

Ways of knowing	Ways of being
Reciprocity	· Learning from each other—ako · Belief in mentees · Offering and receiving feedback · Establish agreed ways of working together · Sharing ideas · Encouraging ongoing dialogue · Co-creator of new knowledge and understanding
Proactivity	· People coming up with their own ideas through reflective questioning · Building a learning community · Seeking to understand
Self-efficacy	· Understanding self · Being reflective
Trustworthiness	· Reliability · Authenticity
Inspirational	· Exemplary practitioner · Affirming · Motivating · Encouraging others to challenge themselves · Challenging · Modelling
Ethical	· Observing what is seen without judgement · Value diversity · Professional · Confidential
Engaged listener	· Being present · Positive growth mind set · Being open minded · Listening more than talking · Listening for the message
Mentee centred	· Encouraging risk taking in learning · Developing critical thinking · Committing to the learning journey
Respectful	· Encouraging uniqueness · Non-judgemental

To facilitate sharing of information and foster pedagogical discussion within the review team, we created a blog to allow ideas to be shared in a communal forum. It appeared light had been shone onto our path, and from here we moved forwards, empowered by the belief that we were moving together in the right direction this time. We analysed current practice and developed plans for improvement. Our group was reduced in number to those who were available to formulate and implement concrete plans. Unfortunately, we stalled once again, as the outcomes seemed bureaucratic and unwieldy and lacked heart or soul. Is this what we had envisioned all those years ago as we travelled from Christchurch? Forms to fill in and procedures to follow? Wisely, we didn't panic or become disheartened. As the sun set on this day, a time of reflection and contemplation ensued while the world turned.

The new day dawned to the realisation that our mentoring programme required a philosophical underpinning that would arise only when we investigated key elements of inclusion, social justice, culture and distance mentoring. Sitting at the heart of these key elements are trust, shared leadership, transparency, capacity building, tradition, enacting espoused theory, learning relationships, and relevance for teachers in today's contexts.

Key elements of a successful mentoring programme

Individually the authors considered the characteristics of mentoring and combined these to form a consensus of what they believed to be the key elements of a successful mentoring programme in the context of an early childhood setting. These are discussed in turn below.

Inclusion

In early childhood, inclusion focuses on the rights of all ākonga to be equal partners in their own learning, and to have their opinions listened to and their learning styles catered for. The *New Zealand Code of Ethics for Registered Teachers* requires us, as registered teachers, to "cater for the varied learning needs of diverse learners" (NZTC, 2004). Relationships that encourage participation as equal partners are created within an atmosphere of trust. Burbules and Berk (1999, cited in Grey, 2011, p. 25) state that, "improvements or changes to practice are achieved through striving for greater understanding, inclusion of alternative viewpoints and by encouraging participation". Leaders within an organisation have a responsibility to create an atmosphere of trust, where teachers feel empowered to contribute to improvements on an equal footing. Empowerment motivates teachers to be active participants in the development and delivery of programmes.

McCaleb and Mikaere-Wallis (2005, p. 4) theorise that "people learn how to be people largely through their *early* involvement with other people". This theory could be transferred into the workplace. To promote participation, those in positions of power in an organisation need to act in a way that allows for all viewpoints to be freely expressed without fear of ridicule. Formal leaders promote a climate of shared leadership by using strategies such as 'open-to-learning conversations' (Robinson, Hohepa, & Lloyd, 2009), where the views of participants are given equal weight and where outcomes are win-win (Covey, 1989). Positional leaders have a responsibility to provide openings for collaborative, transparent decision making, but this takes time and multiple opportunities in a variety of mediums (Sinek, 2009).

Social justice
Mentoring is a social affair, which relies heavily on a culture of commitment to building a trusting, reciprocal relationship (Bosu, Dare, Dach, & Fertig, 2011; Robertson, 2005; Rodd, 2006). In any relationship there is a power differential, and to believe that in the realm of mentoring, mentors and mentees are able to have an equal share of this power may be naïve, especially when we consider the social norms that abound in an organisation (Bosu et al., 2009).

We invited teachers to participate in significant decision-making opportunities for the organisation, which exposed the fact that it may be risky to explore contentious values and beliefs in the presence of those who have positional power (Thornton, 2013). This highlights the role of the relationship between the leaders and employees, and how it can make a profound difference to the success of the self-review's outcome. The pivotal role of trust is explained by Kouzes and Posner (2010), such that trust encourages risk taking, and that to inspire a new future there must be options for people other than the leaders to take risks. Our goal is to structure an environment in which diversity is seen as positive in the move towards a shared vision, and those in a supposed position of lesser power have the confidence to have their voices heard.

Culture

Deep at the heart of our thinking in the development of this mentor programme was our desire to be genuine in our inclusion of a Māori world view. The lead review team spent hours searching for common threads and interconnectedness, based on the belief that there are links to all people, and that common ground is a sacred place of significant potential. The medium of storytelling was the forum where common ground could be signposted and linked interculturally. Maenette and Nee (2008) refer to the value of storytelling, and believe that a "healthy and engaging learning environment requires that we live 'in', that we walk 'in', leadership that is rooted in our stories and traditions, our homeland (place), and our mother tongue language" (p. 53).

Metaphor was considered as a significant learning pedagogy, but, interestingly, our team could not see the metaphor of our own whakatauakī, which was circling around us. In keeping with early childhood origins, we considered the metaphors of pā harakeke (flax bush), of a whāriki (a specially woven mat), and of a korowai (a woven cloak), but the synergy of these images was not in keeping with our journey thus far. Eventually 'kia tiaho Tamanuiterā' became our metaphor for mentoring. Our whakatauakī states that our primary goal is that children will shine bright like Tamanuiterā (Sun). The basis of this thinking is that life is complex; therefore, as the world turns each night, a new learning heralds each new day. In essence, the Māori world view that resides in this chapter arose from seeking mirror images of experience across cultures, weaving the threads of metaphor, and then allowing the multiple versions of each participant's truth to unfold.

Distance mentoring

Operating within a large, geographically dispersed organisation provides unique challenges for mentoring relationships. Our vision included the creation of a mentoring programme that would provide a range of mentoring options for ākonga. For mentors, who work alongside mentees, opportunities to be relational and work through challenges can happen on a daily basis, but for those who are mentoring from a distance, building relationships needs to be deliberate and planned. Our aim was to provide choice for mentees so that they could connect with mentors they related to and who were able to acknowledge their varied aspirations and unique ways of being, doing and knowing. One way of being resourceful is by utilising a range of mentors throughout the organisation for different objectives. Research by Kram and Higgins (2001) in the United States highlights the importance of a range or "constellation of learning relationships for people working in organisations" (cited in Hunt, 2005, p. 9).

Being available and being aware of the limitations of successful mentoring through space and time is an ongoing challenge. By providing choice for mentees, issues of presence, process and technology can be addressed (Ocker, Huang, Benbunan-Fich, & Hiltz, 2009). There is a need for mentors to prioritise regular time with mentees to build trusting relationships, which ideally would mean the provision of specifically trained mentors across the whole organisation. With this in place, mentees could connect with mentors locally, allowing face-to-face contact. However, given the distance constraints, contact could potentially occur through a mix of face-to-face and telepresence interactions.

Although the use of technology and virtual communication may work for some, it is clear that there is no one method that meets the needs of everyone, but more likely a variety of methods that can be tailored to meet the differing ways of working for individuals. Mentors need to continue to motivate others in their learning by using a range of tools and resources to keep the learner feeling valued, encouraged and motivated to continue with their learning (Clarkin-Phillips, 2007).

Conclusion

Our journey started with our determination to provide an effective mentoring programme for our Kindergarten Trust. Like the legendary Maui, we tried to tame Te Rā by capturing him and forcing him into submission. This experience taught us that despite the best intentions, careful consideration must be given to the sanctity of trust and all aspects of relationship building. This is not an element that can be born from hierarchical arrogance, but rather from heterarchical models of mentoring and self-review. In returning to our origins we reflected on our whakatauakī, and were reminded of the strength, resilience and courage of the mangō ururoa (hammerhead shark), and were reminded of the strength, resilience and courage of te ika mangō ururoa, which has the unique ability to see the world with an expansive view. As the sun sets on this chapter of our story, we will courageously remove the net from Tamanuiterā and allow the unfolding of inclusion, social justice, culture and distance mentoring to light our path. What the dawn will bring is a whole new story.

References

Avolio, B., & Gardner, W. (2005). Authentic leadership development: Getting to the root of positive forms of leadership. *The Leadership Quarterly, 16,* 315–338.

Blackmore, J. (2010). Preparing leaders to work with emotions in culturally diverse educational communities. *Journal of Educational Administration, 48*(5), 642–658.

Boreen, L & Niday, D. (2000). Breaking through the isolation: Mentoring beginning teachers. *Journal of Adolescent and Adult Literacy, 44*(2), 152–164.

Bosu, R., Dare, A., Dach, H., & Fertig, M. (2011). School leadership and social justice evidence from Ghana and Tanzania. *International Journal of Educational Development, 31*(1), 66–77.

Clarkin-Phillips, J. (2007) *Distributing the leadership: A case study of professional development.* Unpublished master's thesis, University of Waikato. Retrieved from http://hdl.handle.net/10289/2449

Clutterbuck, D. (2008). What's happening in coaching and mentoring? And what is the difference between them? *Development and Learning in Organisations, 22*(4), 8–10.

Colky, D., & Young, W. (2006). Mentoring in the virtual organisation: Keys to building successful schools and businesses. *Mentoring & Tutoring: Partnership in Learning, 14*(4), 433–447.

Covey, S.R. (1989). *The seven habits of highly effective people.* London, UK: Simon & Schuster.

Eagan, J. (1968). Paulo Freire's pedagogy of the oppressed. *Administrative Theory & Praxis, 32*(3), 429–430.

Education Review Office. (2009). *Implementing self-review in early childhood services.* Retrieved from http://www.ero.govt.nz/National-Reports/Implementing-Self-Review-in-Early-Childhood-Services-January-2009

Ellinger, A., Beattie, R., & Hamlin, R. (2010). The manager as coach. In E. Cox, T. Bachkirova, & D. Clutterbuck (Eds), *The complete handbook of coaching.* London, UK: Sage.

Grey, A. (2011). Professional dialogue as professional learning. *New Zealand Journal of Teachers' Work*, *8*(1), 21-32.

Gronn, P. (2008). The future of distributed leadership. *Journal of Educational Administration*, *46*(2), 141-158.

Hawkins, P. (2010). Coaching supervision. In E. Cox, T. Bachkirova, & D. Clutterbuck (Eds), *The complete handbook of coaching* (pp. 381-393). London, UK: Sage.

Hunt, K. (2005). E-mentoring: Solving the issue of mentoring across distances. *Development and Learning in Organisations*, *19*(5), 7-10.

Kanter, R. (2007). Organizational Change. The enduring skills of change leaders. *NHRD Journal, Special issue, 1,* 53-60.

Keown, P., Parker, L., & Tiakiwai, S. (2005). *Values in the New Zealand curriculum: A literature review on values in the curriculum.* Report for the Ministry of Education, New Zealand, by the Wilf Malcom Institute of Educational Research, School of Education, University of Waikato.

Kouzes, J.M., & Posner, B.Z. (2010). *The truth about leadership: The no-fads, heart of the matter facts you need to know.* San Francisco, CA: Jossey-Bass.

Maenette, K.P., & Ah Nee, B. (2008). Living leadership: Indigenous educational models for contemporary practice. *In Our Mother's Voice, 11,* 53-57.

McCaleb, M., & Mikaere-Wallis, N. (2005). The first years: Ngā tau tauatahi. *New Zealand Journal of Infant and Toddler Education*, *7*(2), 1-10.

Ministry of Education. (2011). *Tātaiako: Cultural competencies for teachers of Māori learners.* Wellington: Author.

Muijs, D., & Harris, A. (2006). Teacher led school improvement: Teacher leadership in the UK. *Teaching and Teacher Education*, *22,* 961-972.

NZTC. (2004*). Code of ethics for registered teachers and those granted a limited authority to teach.* Retrieved from http://www.teacherscouncil.govt.nz

Ocker, R., Huang, H., Benbunan-Fich, R., & Hiltz, S. (2009). Leadership dynamics in partially distributed teams: An exploratory study of the effects of configuration and distance. *Springer Science and Business Media*, *20*, 274-292.

Pavia, L., Nissen, H., Hawkins, C., Monroe, M., & Filimon-Demyen, D. (2003). Mentoring early childhood professionals. *Journal of Research in Childhood Education*, *17*(2) 250-260.

Philippart, N., & Gluesing, J., (2012, March). *Global e-mentoring: Overcoming virtual distance for an effective partnership.* Paper presented at ICIC '12. Proceedings of the 4th International Conference on Intercultural Collaboration, Bengaluru, India.

Robertson, J. (2004, January). *Coaching leaders: The path to improvement.* Paper presented at the Biennial Conference of the New Zealand Educational Administration and Leadership Society, Dunedin, New Zealand.

Robertson, J. (2005). *Coaching leadership: Building educational leadership capacity through coaching partnerships.* Wellington: NZCER Press.

Robertson, J. (2011). *Coaching and mentoring through partnership* [course handout]. Waiheke Island, New Zealand.

Robinson, V.M.J., Hohepa, M., & Lloyd, C. (2009). *School leadership and student outcomes: Identifying what works and why: Iterative best evidence synthesis programme.* Wellington: Ministry of Education.

Rodd, J. (2006). *Leadership in early childhood* (3rd ed.). Maidenhead, UK: Open University Press.

Sinek, S. (2009). *Start with why: How great leaders inspire everyone to take action.* New York, NY: Penguin.

Thornton, K., Wansbrough, D., Clarkin-Phillips, J., Aitken, H., & Tamati, A. (2009). *Conceptualising leadership in early childhood education in Aotearoa New Zealand.* Occasional paper published by the NZTC. Retrieved from http://www.teacherscouncil.govt.nz

Thornton, K. (2013). *The educational leadership role of mentors.* Visiting scholar presentation to the New Zealand Educational Leadership and Administration Society. Retrieved from http://www.nzeals.org.nz/magellan/pages/ezines.aspx11

Walumbwa, F., Wang, P., Wang, H., Schaubroeck, J., & Avolio, B. (2010). Pyschological processes linking authentic leadership to follower behaviors. *The Leadership Quarterly, 21,* 901-914.

Zembylas, M. (2010). The emotional aspects of leadership for social justice: Implications for leadership programs. *Journal of Educational Administration, 48*(5), 611-625.

PART 3: MENTORING STUDENT TEACHERS

Chapter 9
Dual roles: Mentoring and assessment in the early childhood practicum

Karyn Aspden

Introduction

Practicum is a core feature of initial teacher education (ITE) in Aotearoa New Zealand. It is a key site of induction and mentoring, intended to support student teachers in their move from neophyte to graduating teacher. Student teachers consistently report that their experiences while on practicum are the most significant and influential moments in shaping their professional growth and identity as a teacher (Cameron & Baker, 2004). However, it cannot be assumed that simply placing student teachers in a teaching setting with the support of an associate teacher and teacher educator will ensure the desired outcomes (Hickson, Fishburne, Berg, & Saby, 2005; Hill, 1999). Quality mentoring and support lie at the heart of the practicum experience, but practicum is also a key point of assessment in initial teacher education programmes. Those responsible for supporting and mentoring student teachers are also tasked with providing assessment feedback and determining assessment outcomes that have high-stakes implications for student teachers.

This chapter explores the role of mentoring within the early childhood practicum, with particular attention paid to the challenge of maintaining the dual (and potentially duelling) roles of assessor and mentor in the practicum context. The following discussion will consider the way in which associate teachers and teacher educators conceptualise their role as mentors during practicum and identify the hopes and expectations of student teachers being mentored. In identifying the potential for tension between the mentoring role and the assessment responsibilities of associate teachers and teacher educators, the need for skilful, prepared mentors who can navigate the different tasks of mentor and assessor is highlighted.

The research study

Between 2009 and 2014 I conducted a doctoral study entitled *Illuminating the Assessment of Practicum in Early Childhood Initial Teacher Education* (Aspden, 2014). The aim of the study was to examine the way in which practicum assessment was experienced and enacted by student teachers, associate teachers and teacher educators in early childhood initial teacher education programmes, and to understand the cultural and institutional contexts within which the assessment of practicum takes place. The findings of the study revealed that mentoring and guiding students was viewed by associate teachers and teacher educators as the primary task of their role, with assessment responsibilities taking a secondary, albeit important, place.

The study was a large, multi-phase project involving four New Zealand ITE institutions that were providing 3-year early childhood ITE programmes. Data were gathered through three phases. The first was an interview with key informants at each participating institution. The second phase of the study was an online survey, which was distributed to all student teachers, associate teachers and teacher educators associated with the early childhood programme at the four institutions. In total, 120 responses to the survey were received, comprising 74 student teachers, 26 associate teachers and 20 teacher educators. The final phase of the research involved four case studies, comprising a practicum triad from each institution. The student teacher, associate teacher and teacher educator agreed that I could be present for the final practicum visit and then interview them afterwards about their experiences of the practicum and its assessment.

Ethical approval was given by the Massey University Human Ethics Committee, as well as the relevant ethics committee at each of the four institutions. Preserving the anonymity of the participating institutions, as well as that of the individual participants, was the key ethical responsibility of this project, given that the population of early childhood teacher education providers in New Zealand is relatively small.

Mentoring in the practicum triad: Thoughts from student teachers, associate teachers and teacher educators

The 'practicum triad' is a term used to refer to the relationship between the student teacher, associate teacher and teacher educator. The triad model has been a constant in New Zealand teacher education for many years (Grudnoff & Williams, 2010; Kane, 2005), whereby a student teacher is placed in a variety of educational settings for a specified time, allocated an associate teacher, and then observed and assessed by a staff member of the ITE institution. The move to a triadic assessment model emerged from greater recognition of the mentoring role of the associate teacher, as well as a desire to increase the fairness of assessment and empower the individual participants in their different but complementary roles (Haigh & Ell, 2014). A key task of the associate teacher and, to some degree, the teacher educator is to mentor the student teacher, induct them into the profession, and support and guide their professional and personal growth during the practicum. Findings reveal this to be a rewarding yet complex task, and one that participants may not be well prepared for.

Student teacher perspectives

The focus of the triadic practicum is the student teacher, as the associate teacher and teacher educator support their journey into the teaching profession. The practicum is a critical time in the initial formation and ongoing development of the student teacher's identity as a professional teacher (Cattley, 2007), and the associate teacher and teacher educator play a key mentoring role in supporting this journey. Students' beliefs about themselves, both personally and professionally, are intensively illuminated during this time, shaped by the feedback, affirmation and guidance provided by the associate teacher and teacher educator. Student teachers enter the teacher education programme with an already established set of beliefs about teaching and learning, derived from their own schooling and other educational experiences (Pajares, 1992). Part of the role of the mentor is to encourage a process of transformation, during which existing beliefs are challenged in relation to theory and practice (Goodfellow & Sumsion, 2000). However, this process is complex, and transformation is not guaranteed (Clift & Brady, 2005).

In my study, when asked to describe a positive experience of practicum, students gave a strong message that the relationship with the associate teacher was the most significant factor in determining the quality of the practicum. Student teachers desired positive relationships with those who mentored and assessed them and felt that conflict, or broken relationships at times, led to unfair assessment feedback, and increased vulnerability to subjective assessment decision making, as also reported by Moody (2009) and Gulikers, Bastiaens, Kirschner and Kester (2008). Positive relationships were seen to provide a safe space within which the students were able to receive feedback. As one student commented: "You can't really take information from someone else unless you've got that relationship and they know where you are from."

The feedback received from associate teachers and teacher educators was identified by student-teacher participants as the most critical feature of a positive practicum assessment. Students highly valued mentoring relationships that allowed for honest feedback that identified their strengths and gave advice and support in areas of weakness. Students identified a strong sense of affirmation, empowerment and encouragement when someone in a position of influence, such as an associate teacher or teacher educator, could see strengths in their practice, as reflected in the following comment, "After an observation I was told of good teaching practices I had shown: this led to me feeling more empowered and confident about my practice."

Relational issues were clearly evident in the description of difficult practicum experiences provided by student teachers. Student teachers had expectations of the support, guidance and positive interactions to be given by the associate teacher and teacher educator, and felt concerned when these expectations were not met, as also reported by McGee,

Ferrier-Kerr and Miller (2001). As one student teacher commented:

> I thought my AT [associate teacher] wasn't as involved or as interested as she should have been if she accepted the AT role. I would have liked more interaction and feedback from her. This would have built my confidence a lot more.

Student teachers revealed that their experiences of the mentoring relationship were highly variable. Some triad relationships had a strong connection, and sometimes relationships endured past the end of the practicum, even leading to subsequent employment. For others, there was a breakdown of relationships, with open conflict, limited interactions and little support. Students found such situations to be distressing and highly stressful, although comments indicate that concerns may be mitigated if other relational support is in place, such as teacher educator support for a student when their relationship with the associate teacher was problematic.

Associate teacher perspectives

The associate teacher is the qualified, experienced teacher within the practicum setting who has responsibility for mentoring and guiding the student teacher, as well as contributing to the assessment process, most typically in formative ways throughout the practicum (Mitchell, Clarke, & Nuttall, 2007), although also by contributing to varying degrees to final summative outcomes. Associate teachers typically report that their role is both rewarding and challenging (Beck & Kosnik, 2000), with the opportunity to mentor a new member of the profession frequently cited as a key motivation for taking on the mentoring role, along with the opportunity to keep up to date with current research and practice.

When asked to identify what they considered to be their primary role in the assessment of practicum, the majority of associate teachers in my study (74 percent, $n = 17$) indicated that it was to mentor and support student teachers: "to assess the student teacher's achievement of goals to provide individual feedback, support and guidance for professional growth". Only 26 percent ($n = 6$) believed that their primary role was "to assess the student against the institution's required standards to determine if they are meeting expectations". The descriptions of a successful practicum offered by associate teachers portrayed a desire for the practicum to be a rich, effective and positive experience that fosters growth in the student teachers' professional practice. In considering the role of mentoring as a tool in this process, associate teachers highlighted the need for assessment to occur within an environment of positive relationships, respect and trust, and to identify and support the student's strengths as well as their areas of weakness.

When asked to identify the challenges that may arise in mentoring and assessing student teachers, relationship concerns were again highlighted. Associate teachers reported that they were seeking positive working relationships with student teachers, but that this did not always happen for a variety of reasons. Sometimes the only reason that could be cited was a clash of personality between the student and mentor that could not be resolved. Associate teachers reported difficulty in cases where they felt the student teacher was not open to feedback, did not seek advice or meet the expectations of the associate teacher or the setting.

The challenge of building effective relationships within the short time frame of some practicum experiences was also acknowledged, as associate teachers tried to manage their existing workload while also making time for the student teacher. The associate teachers reported that the short time frames of practicum, as well as the assessment process, affected the development of an open and trusting relationship between associate and student that allowed for open discussion, critical feedback and risk taking. Limited preparation and support for the responsibilities of mentoring and assessing student teachers was also a frequently cited concern, one that was acknowledged at an institutional level as the ITE providers sought to find meaningful and practical ways to enhance induction and ongoing professional development for associate teachers.

Teacher educator perspectives

The final member of the triad is the teacher educator, the representative of the institution in which the student teacher is completing their programme of study. Their role is both to support and to assess the practice of student teachers while on practicum (Haigh, 2001). The teacher educator serves as the intermediary between the student, the early childhood centre and the ITE institution, and typically holds responsibility for the summative component of assessment.

When asked to identify how they conceptualised their primary role in the assessment of practicum, 72 percent of the teacher educators identified this as "assessing the student teacher to provide feedback, support and guidance for professional growth", reflecting an emphasis on mentoring and support. Only 28 percent of teacher educators placed greater emphasis on assessment for summative purposes, i.e. ensuring a student teacher had met the required standards in order to pass the practicum, or to graduate. This emphasis on mentoring supports the findings of Ortlipp (2009) and Ciuffetelli-Parker and Volante (2009), who suggest that teacher educators are committed to supporting the professional development of student teachers and that summative assessment is necessary, but secondary in importance. As one teacher educator commented:

> it doesn't matter who the student is, the job is to support them and find out where they are, and what's happening for them, and give them opportunities I guess to make sense of what it is they're doing and why they're doing it, really.

This finding is of particular interest in that teacher educators define their role more strongly in relation to a mentoring focus, whereas student teachers and associate teachers more often identify the teacher educator as 'the assessor'. The findings of this study suggest that teacher educators define their role in multiple and complex ways (Haigh, 2001), and in ways that may not align with the preconceptions and expectations that other participants have of them.

Both associate teachers and teacher educators in the study indicated that they had received little induction or training for their role, and commented that more professional development in this area was desired. The teacher educators expressed a deep personal and philosophical commitment to positive mentoring-oriented practicum relationships, but were challenged by the institutional constraints, particularly relating to time and finances, which limited the length of time they could spend in a practicum setting.

In acknowledging the constraints of limited time spent with a student teacher on practicum, teacher educators highly valued the mentoring role of the associate teacher, which complemented their own.

However, teacher educators also shared concerns when the associate teacher was not present regularly throughout the practicum, and where they did not provide the regular feedback, guidance and support necessary to facilitate professional growth, as reflected in the following quote from a teacher educator:

> One of the most common situations I have seen … is when the associate teacher has not spent a great deal of time with the student teacher and therefore has not been in a position to give accurate feedback to and about the student … Sometimes the student has been completely unsupported by the staff and has not had the opportunity to grow and develop as a result of this.

Mentoring and assessment responsibilities

One of the challenges for both associate teachers and teacher educators is the tension that can arise between assessment *for* learning, with a focus on learner support, and the need for assessment *of* learning, within a political and institutional climate that requires accountability and gatekeeping (Bates, 2004; McDonald, 2005). International literature indicates that the requirement for accountability in teacher education is increasing (Autry, Lee, & Fox, 2009). There is a growing call for teacher education providers not only to demonstrate the quality of their programmes, but also to provide evidence of the effects of the programme on the student teacher and, potentially, the children they subsequently teach (Barrie, 1999; Cochran-Smith, 2005, 2006).

While there is often theoretical agreement about the importance of equal and reciprocal relationships in the practicum (Roberts & Graham, 2008), achieving this outcome in practice can be very difficult. Lomas (1999) goes so far as to suggest that it is almost impossible due to the "evaluation bind" that is "created by assessment requirements on the supervisor and supervisee which acts against the establishment of a climate of openness and trust necessary for an effective professional development focus" (p. 24). Tillema, Smith and Lesham (2011) question whether those who are responsible for mentoring and supporting a student on practicum can also take a role in summative assessment without jeopardising the open relationship required for mentoring.

There are indications, in both the literature and the current study, that the assessment requirements of practicum can influence the relationships the student teacher develops with both their associate and the teacher educator, and that their concerns over assessment outcomes have an impact on the authenticity, openness and critical discussion they engage in. Beck and Kosnik (2000, p. 217), for example, found that

> the Associate Teachers repeatedly said they did not think their evaluative role affected their relationship with the student teachers, but this was not how the students saw it: again and again they expressed fears to the faculty about their evaluations.

Students reported feeling at risk if they openly discussed areas of weakness or lack of knowledge, and actively sought to present themselves in the best light, actions that can militate against potential growth and transformation. Student teachers saw themselves as vulnerable to the opinions of the assessors, and suggested that good relationships were equated with positive assessment outcomes, and poor relationships with negative assessment experiences. However, this is a somewhat simplistic proposition, which minimises the role of professionalism and professional judgement in assessment practices (Joughin, 2009), and suggests that students may need reassurance as to the dual role of mentor and assessor, and greater transparency in the way assessment decisions are reached.

The focus on assessment outcomes and trying to please the assessor has implications not only for the teaching practice demonstrated, but also for the student's ability to fully engage in mentoring relationships. Research suggests that student teachers may be afraid to share openly because they are concerned about the effect this may have on their relationships and their subsequent assessment (Beck & Kosnik, 2000; Haigh, 2001), with the theme of needing to 'please' the mentor/assessor common in student reflections (Turnbull, 1999). A number of authors have raised concerns about this 'need to please', arguing that it manifests itself in the guise of conformity (e.g., Goodnough, Osmond, Dibbon, Glassman, & Stevens, 2009), whereby student teachers do exactly what their associate teacher does, whether or not this reflects best practice or is supported by the theoretical teaching of their teacher education programme (Kersh, 1995). Tension may then arise when the teacher educator comes into the educational setting to assess the student teacher, particularly if practices modelled by the associate teacher differ from those espoused by the training institution (Brown & Danaher, 2008). Does the student teacher continue to model the actions of the associate teacher, or do they amend their practice to demonstrate competence in qualities desired by their training programme? Who should students aim to please in this situation?

Roberts and Graham (2008) indicate that student teachers often use 'tactical compliance' in order to ensure that relationships are maintained and assessment outcomes protected. Certainly the students in my study reported that they shaped their actions to fit the expectations of the mentor and the institution, juggling to maintain relationships while meeting assessment requirements. Cattley (2007) further argues that:

> preservice teachers who take risks in their pedagogies are particularly vulnerable if by doing so, their mentor teachers identify them as being out of tune with their own way of thinking ... If the chosen pedagogy is substantially different to that of the mentor teacher and this in turn leads to criticism of the pre-service teacher, the latter's growing sense of professional identity could well be shaken. (p. 338)

The challenge of dual mentoring and assessment roles was evident in the triadic meetings that typically serve as the formal assessment point of the practicum, providing an opportunity for discussion of a student's progress. In the four case studies in my study, it was evident that the triadic meeting served three key purposes: to build relationships; to yield assessment information about the practicum; and to share feedback for the purpose of supporting the student's ongoing development. Each triadic meeting navigated the mentoring and assessment elements in different ways, with associate teachers and teacher educators indicating that the balance between functions was influenced by how successful the student was in meeting practicum expectations, as well as the stage of study that they were at. When students were clearly meeting expectations, the emphasis tended towards feedback that was affirmative and future oriented, such as advice about future practica or the student's entry to the profession. However, when there were concerns about a student's practice, the emphasis was more likely to be placed on adherence to assessment criteria and desired outcomes. Likewise, more scope for mentoring and future growth was given to students earlier in the ITE programme, with students close to graduation held to higher standards, as associate teachers and teacher educators felt they needed to serve as gatekeepers to the profession.

Conclusion

This chapter has explored the challenge and complexity of mentoring in the early childhood practicum. There can be no denying that the relationships between the student teacher and their associate teacher and teacher educator have the greatest significance in shaping the practicum experience and the professional learning of the student teacher during practicum. The challenge of mentoring in the practicum is made even greater by the short-term nature of many practicum experiences, as well as by the many intra-personal, interpersonal and institutional variables that interact to shape each individual practicum experience, in particular, the demand for summative assessment.

Such complexity means that it is impossible to apply a recipe or formula to mentoring in the practicum, and implies that each practicum will have a story of its own. Given the concerns raised by associate teachers and teacher educators in relation to induction and ongoing support for the mentoring role, it appears to be important to place greater emphasis on training and support in this area, along with ongoing conversation about ways to address tension between mentoring and assessment roles in the practicum.

References

Aspden, K.M. (2014). *Illuminating the assessment of practicum in early childhood initial teacher education*. Unpublished doctoral thesis, Massey University.

Autry, M.M., Lee, J., & Fox, J. (2009). Developing a data-driven assessment for early childhood candidates. *Journal of Early Childhood Teacher Education, 30*, 138–149.

Barrie, S. (1999, November/December). *Assessment: Defining the worth of professional practice.* Paper presented at the Annual Conference of the Australian Association for Research in Education (AARE), Melbourne, Australia.

Bates, R. (2004). Regulation and autonomy in teacher education: Government, community or democracy? *Journal of Education for Teaching: International Research and Pedagogy, 30*(2), 117–130.

Beck, C., & Kosnik, C. (2000). Associate teachers in pre-service education: Clarifying and enhancing their role. *Journal of Education for Teaching, 26*(3), 207-224.

Brown, A., & Danaher, P. (2008). Towards collaborative professional learning in the first year early childhood teacher education practicum: Issues in negotiating the multiple interests of stakeholder feedback. *Asia-Pacific Journal of Teacher Education, 36*, 147-161.

Cameron, M., & Baker, R. (2004). *Research on initial teacher education 1993-2004: Literature review and annotated bibliography.* Wellington: Ministry of Education.

Cattley, G. (2007). Emergence of professional identity for the pre-service teacher. *International Education Journal, 8*(2), 337-347.

Ciuffetelli-Parker, D., & Volante, L. (2009). Responding to the challenges posed by summative teacher candidate evaluation: A collaborative self-study of practicum supervision by faculty. *Studying Teacher Education: Journal of Self-Study of Teacher Education Practices, 5*(1), 33-44. doi: 10.1080/17425960902830385

Clift, R.T., & Brady, P. (2005). Research on methods courses and field experiences. In M. Cochran-Smith & K. Zeichner (Eds), *Studying teacher education* (pp. 309-424). Mahwah, NJ: Lawrence Erlbaum Associates.

Cochran-Smith, M. (2005). Teacher education and the outcomes trap. *Journal of Teacher Education, 56*(5), 411-417.

Cochran-Smith, M. (2006). Evidence, efficacy and effectiveness. *Journal of Teacher Education, 57*(1), 3-6.

Goodfellow, J., & Sumsion, J. (2000). Transformative pathways: Field-based teacher educators' perceptions. *Journal of Education for Teaching: International Research and Pedagogy, 26*(3), 245- 257.

Goodnough, K., Osmond, P., Dibbon, D., Glassman, M., & Stevens, K. (2009). Exploring a triad model of student teaching: Pre-service teacher and cooperating teacher perceptions. *Teaching and Teacher Education, 25*(2), 285-296.

Grudnoff, L., & Williams, R. (2010). Pushing boundaries: Reworking university-school practicum relationships. *New Zealand Journal of Educational Studies, 45*(2), 33-45.

Gulikers, J.T.M., Bastiaens, T.J., Kirschner, P.A., & Kester, L. (2008). Authenticity is in the eye of the beholder: Student and teacher perceptions of assessment authenticity. *Journal of Vocational Education & Training, 60*(4), 401-412.

Haigh, M. (2001, December). *Coherence and congruence of perceived roles within practicum partnerships: A case study*. Paper presented at the Annual Conference of the New Zealand Association of Research in Education, Christchurch, New Zealand.

Haigh, M., & Ell, F. (2014). Consensus and dissensus in mentor teachers' judgments of readiness to teach. *Teaching and Teacher Education*, 10–21. doi: 10.1016/j.tate.2014.01.001

Hickson, C., Fishburne, G.J., Berg, S., & Saby, C. (2005, July). *Preservice and practicum experiences: Are they complementary?* Paper presented at the Annual Conference of the Australian Association of Research in Education, Cairns, Australia.

Hill, L. (1999, November/December). *"Just tell us what to teach": Preservice teachers thinking about teaching*. Paper presented at the Annual Conference of the Australian Association for Research in Education (AARE), Melbourne, Australia.

Joughin, G. (2009). Assessment, learning and judgement in higher education: A critical review. In G. Joughin (Ed.), *Assessment, learning and judgement in higher education* (pp. 13–28). Dordrecht, The Netherlands: Springer.

Kane, R. (2005). *Initial teacher education policy and practice: Final report*. Wellington: Ministry of Education.

Kersh, M.E. (1995). Coordinating theory with practice. In G.A. Slick (Ed.), *The field experience: Creating successful programs for new teachers* (pp. 99–109). Thousand Oaks, CA: Corwin Press.

Lomas, G. (1999). Supervision of classroom practice. *ACE Papers*, *4*, 18–25.

McDonald, L. (2005). Teacher education, training and experience: Knowing what, how, when, why and with. *New Zealand Annual Review of Education*, *14*, 131–151.

McGee, J., Ferrier-Kerr, J., & Miller, T. (2001, December). *Student teachers' initial perceptions about the role and the professional and personal qualities of associate teachers*. Paper presented at the Annual Conference of the New Zealand Association of Research in Education, Christchurch, New Zealand.

Mitchell, J., Clarke, A., & Nuttall, J. (2007). Cooperating teachers' perspectives under scrutiny: A comparative analysis of Australia and Canada. *Asia-Pacific Journal of Teacher Education*, *35*(1), 5–25.

Moody, J. (2009). Key elements in a positive practicum: Insights from Australian post-primary pre-service teachers. *Irish Educational Studies*, *28*(2), 155–175.

Ortlipp, M. (2009). Shaping conduct and bridling passions: Governing practicum supervisors' practice of assessment. *Contemporary Issues in Early Childhood, 10*(2), 156-167.

Pajares, M.F. (1992). Teachers' beliefs and educational research: Cleaning up a messy construct. *Review of Educational Research, 62*(3), 307-332.

Roberts, J., & Graham, S. (2008). Agency and conformity in school-based teacher training. *Teaching and Teacher Education, 24*(6), 1401-1412.

Tillema, H.H., Smith, K., & Leshem, S. (2011). Dual roles—conflicting purposes: A comparative study of perceptions on assessment in mentoring relations during practicum. *European Journal of Teacher Education, 34*(2), 139-159. doi: 10.1080/02619768.2010.543672

Turnbull, M. (1999). Assessment in the early childhood practicum: A triadic process. *ACE Papers, 4*, 26-39.

Chapter 10
Contextual factors that affect the mentor–mentee relationship
Cheryl McConnell

Introduction
This chapter has as its focus the mentoring experience of student teachers while on weekly field-based placement. I refer to this placement as the 'field-based practicum'. The student teachers work in a paid, voluntary or relieving position in an early childhood centre for 12 hours per week as part of a 3-year field-based teacher education (FBTE) programme.

In this chapter I examine the views and experiences of four graduate teachers reflecting on their time as student teachers, and of 26 mentors and six teacher educators in the context of students' continuous weekly placement. Nolan, Morrissey and Dumenden (2012) suggest that the voice of mentees is under-reported in early childhood teacher education. Therefore I pay specific attention to the student teachers' experience of the mentoring relationship, alongside the mentors' perceptions of the employed or volunteer status of student teachers. I report on what the participants in my master's research (McConnell, 2010) believed made a difference to the mentor–mentee relationship, and consequently to student teachers' professional learning.

The research procedures, ethical guidelines and protocols of Deakin University, Melbourne, Australia, and the Eastern Institute of Technology, Napier, New Zealand, directed and informed this research. A qualitative methodology within an interpretative paradigm was used in this study (Charmaz, 2006).

Context

In this FBTE programme the student teachers are mentored by a qualified teacher at their early childhood centre, who provides collegial support and meets in a triadic discussion with the visiting lecturer three times a year. The teacher educators' expectations are that the student teachers will experience increasing levels of responsibility in their role as teachers and authentic engagement in the life of the learning community. The student teachers also undertake one block practicum (per year) at another early childhood centre, where an associate teacher provides guidance, supervision and a summative assessment. In this chapter, the block practicum (called teaching practice in this programme) is not under investigation. However, the lessons learned from mentors and mentees in the 12-hours-per-week field-based practicum are applicable to other practicum contexts.

In this discussion there is no intention to simplify the multi-faceted and complex nature of all the relationships involved in the weekly FBTE setting, including those with the teacher educators. Each setting is unique and each participant is unique. However, specific lived experiences and the perceptions of individuals lend insight into the mentor-mentee relationship. Three themes emerged from the data regarding the expectations of the student teachers of their mentors and the teaching team: the importance of belonging, reciprocity, and authentic participation. The data also reveal how the expectations and attitudes of mentors and mentees may either constrain or create opportunities for student teachers' professional learning.

Participants

Of the four graduate teachers who volunteered to be interviewed, three completed their FBTE practicum in education and care settings and one in a kindergarten. Two were employed for the 3 years, and two did a combination of employed and voluntary hours in different years.

Their ages ranged from 18 to 43. Pseudonyms, selected by them, are used: Millie, Kate, Jane and Amber. Henceforth they will be referred to as student teachers, because they are reflecting on their time as student teachers.

Of the 26 mentors who answered the questionnaire, 17 gained their teaching qualification from providers other than the Eastern Institute of Technology (EIT). Eighteen had more than 10 years of teaching experience and 13 had been a mentor for between 5 and 10 years with EIT's programme. Mentors are offered two professional development and support meetings per year by the Institute. Six teacher educators, including myself, who were employed full time contributed reflective journals.

The importance of belonging

The key to establishing an effective mentoring relationship with the student teacher is, firstly, to establish a sense of belonging. *Te Whāriki*, the New Zealand Early Childhood Curriculum (Ministry of Education, 1996), emphasises the importance of belonging for children and families, and it is just as critical for student teachers. In the initial establishment of the mentor–mentee relationship, the power of feeling welcome must not be underestimated. Initially it is the mentor who sets the climate for establishing a constructive relationship (Zachary, 2012).

The student teachers clearly articulated how belonging and respect, or the lack of it, affected their learning. All four mentioned that respect from the mentor included acknowledgement of them as people with a history, and sometimes considerable experience. When they did not feel respected or did not gain a sense of belonging, they moved to another setting for the field-based practicum: two after their first year. Millie, as an employed mature student, became frustrated when she was not encouraged by the mentor to share her learning or contribute to children's learning and development in her first year. She felt that her considerable experience was also ignored. She made the financial sacrifice to be voluntary in her second year, preferring a mentor who would maximise her learning and who made her feel respected and valued.

Some student teachers gain this sense of belonging quickly, while others grow into it slowly. Regardless, the mentor needs to be proactive in supporting the student's sense of belonging rather than assuming it will occur automatically. One mentor teacher summarised it like this:

> [When] students experience a sense of belonging, they know they have a place and that their contribution to the centre with current theory and practices is valued. This partnership is beneficial to both parties in affirming practice and extending learning for all children.

This mentor articulated the reciprocal nature of the relationship and the possibilities of professional development for herself and the teaching team. Both mentors and teacher educators suggested that, as this sense of belonging develops, students benefit. Margaret, a teacher educator, reflected:

> This [ongoing relationship] supports the student's professional knowledge by offering constructive feedback that can be acted on immediately ... goals can be worked on in an environment where the student is part of a team and where they are valued and known by staff and children alike.

Thus a sense of belonging and the ongoing positive mentor relationship contributes to students' professional development when they are able to debate practice, receive feedback, set goals and enact content and curriculum knowledge. Howie and Hagan (2011, 2012) also found that once student teachers gained a sense of belonging and were treated as team members by their peers, participation and engagement increased. Developing a sense of belonging is a reciprocal process and depends on both mentor and mentees actively building the relationship.

Student teachers thrive and gain a sense of belonging when mentors are supportive and encourage participation by creating inclusive opportunities. The student teachers in this study desired inclusion, regardless of their voluntary or employed status. However, sometimes the beliefs of the mentors made a difference to the degree of involvement. For example, 12 of the mentors considered that employment expedited inclusion because the mentors' expectations were different. One explained that employed students could be "given more responsibility" because they have set roles and duties and are therefore "included in team discussions," and another stated: "I believe I can have more expectations and she has a sense of belonging."

This contrasted with the expectations of the volunteer student teachers in my study, who expected to be included, and contradicted the teacher educator's expectations that students, regardless of their status, take on increased responsibility and become more involved in each year of their programme. Disturbingly, for those student teachers who were voluntary, some mentors appeared to lower their expectations of participation. One considered that if you expect student teachers to fully participate then they should be employed, and one even believed that the "voluntary student is not able to be given responsibility." These responses suggested that the beliefs of the mentor about the employed or voluntary status of the student teacher influence the degree of inclusion, and consequently their sense of belonging. When expectations are lowered, the student teacher is more likely to be an observer rather than a participant in the learning community, and the full potential of the field-based practicum is unrealised. Critically, the reciprocity essential in the mentor–mentee relationship will be undermined.

Reciprocity and respect

When reciprocity underpins the mentor–mentee relationship, mutual respect is an outcome. Reciprocity may be defined as a mutual or co-operative exchange.[1] In relation to education, this may include the exchange of knowledge, values, ideas and experiences. I found that student teachers' professional learning was enhanced when their mentor and the teaching team exhibited respect by actively encouraging the student's voice and valuing their ideas. Millie described the respect she experienced from both the mentor and the teaching team when she changed settings: "I guess they valued it [knowledge she brought from class], they listened and they encouraged you to try things out."

The mentor in this setting actively encouraged Millie to have a voice in decision making, valuing her perspective as well as expecting her to actively co-operate in the provision of children's learning and development. Here the mutual exchange of ideas and knowledge is practised. As Loizou concludes, "a healthy professional relationship allows for parallel contributions" (2011, p. 373). A mentor who welcomes parallel contributions places value on the knowledge and ideas of the student teacher. The students in my research emphasised their

---

1 *Merriam-Webster Dictionary*. Retrieved from http://www.merriam-webster.com/dictionary/reciprocity

desire to be treated with respect, and to be viewed as a valuable team member who could contribute. When this occurred, it increased their confidence and enthusiasm, and enhanced their professional learning. Respectful mentors did not make the student teachers feel different or inferior because of their voluntary status. This suggests that a more democratic and inclusive approach to the mentor–mentee relationship supports student teachers' learning (Loizou, 2011; Zeichner, 2010).

For all of the students, reciprocity enabled legitimate participation in the life of the centre. Amber shifted to an employed position in her second year and described the experience as follows: "to become part of a team, like teachers, and to be involved in the staff meetings and have my own say and my own opinions heard and valued." Amber compared this with her 1st-year experience as a volunteer and occasional reliever, where she had not felt valued. Consequently, as a 1st-year student she doubted her career choice and considered leaving the programme. A lack of reciprocity by the mentor and/or the teaching team has the potential to undermine student teachers' confidence. In this case, Amber changed settings and found herself in a respectful learning community with a supportive mentor, and she began to thrive.

Authentic participation

Professional learning in the field-based practicum is contingent on student teachers' authentic participation in effective learning communities. In effective communities, student teachers are able to engage with the complexity of practice in the early childhood setting and can fully engage with the routines, practices and work of teachers (Howie & Hagan, 2011; Lave & Wenger, 1991; Renshaw, 2003). As a result, the mentee and mentor are better able to engage in mentoring dialogue about the complexity of teachers' work.

The following stories illustrate how student teachers experienced authentic participation when they genuinely contributed to improving outcomes for children. Katie, in her second year, shared how she encouraged the team to think about the use of high chairs with very young infants and persuaded the centre to undertake a trial without the highchairs. She initiated this based on course work that was not part of any assessment. The team's initial reluctance developed into eagerness, and leading the change empowered Katie and a fellow student teacher.

She remembered enthusiastically:

> We kind of just had to let it go for a while [the idea met with resistance], even though we had the philosophy and research [behind the idea] and then we brought it up at a staff meeting and sort of just kept pushing it and she [the supervisor] finally relented and we tried it for a week and by the end of the week they [the infants] were great, sitting at the table, and that was really cool for us and it was something we could go back to [class] and say, look what we did.

When authentic participation occurs, the mentee and mentor are better able to engage in mentoring conversations that question and critically review practice (Pollard, 2008). In this process, the student teacher receives feedback and evaluates the contribution made to improved outcomes for children. As Pollard claims, the mentor is able to offer constructive support, and new learning can be created.

As illustrated above, enthusiasm from the mentor and teaching team for the student teacher's learning is important. Furthermore, a willingness to engage with them in professional conversations underpins reciprocity and supports student teachers' authentic participation. Katie's experience also demonstrated the collaborative nature of the mentor's and team's relationships with the student teacher—a critical element of effective learning relationships (Zachary, 2012).

Another example of collaborative mentor relationships is demonstrated by Anna's (the teacher educator's) recall of a Year 2 class. The class content and assessment focused on planning and organising an excursion into the local community. As part of this class, the students examined their FBTE centre's policy and the Ministry of Education regulatory requirements. Anna wrote:

> This week after we had this class one of the students shared that she had been invited to share the content of our discussion and how she felt the centre's policy had measured up at the staff meeting. She stated how nervous she had felt offering her critique but how openly her comments had been received. The policy had been reviewed by the team and she had led the discussions. She commented that this had truly made her feel part of the team and that her contribution was valued.

Both stories reveal how student teachers can be emerging leaders in the field-based setting when they engage authentically and where the mentor and team are open to new possibilities. I believe it also illustrates a high degree of trust and a learning community where teachers are willing to critically engage with evidence to reflect on and refine their practice (NZTC, 2007). Such a high degree of trust is possible when the student teacher is in the setting on a weekly basis and the mentor relationship is developed over time.

These examples demonstrate how authentic participation enables student teachers to lead, with the support of their mentor. These potentially self-empowering roles enable student teachers to "develop into agents of their own learning" (Loizou, 2011, p. 383). As the student teachers built their confidence and knowledge, they felt able to make a difference to practice, in spite of some of the constraints they experienced. For example, Jane felt that her learning was not prioritised by the mentor, but she maintained her own agency and responsibility for shaping her teacher identity. Jane described her contribution enthusiastically:

> I wrote lots of learning stories [assessment in early childhood], and we [the children and Jane] did lots of exciting things, anything new would go straight back into the centre and be used. I did a lot of research within the centre, made a lot of changes.

Ten of the mentors surveyed felt that participation depends on the individual commitment of the student teacher. One noted that one student often rejected opportunities with "I'm only a student", but that this altered once this particular student became employed. Another reported that "students often have firm ideas about what they can and can't do as volunteers". There were definitely conflicting views, with one mentor stating, "I have seen those in voluntary positions working harder and more diligently than those given a permanent employment contract." The mentors' contrasting views indicated that contribution and participation were partially dependent on the individual student teacher's sense of agency and commitment to their own learning. At times, it appeared there was a delicate balance between opportunities for participation and the potential exploitation of voluntary student teachers. Regardless of the status of the student teacher, a mentor needs to find that delicate balance of fostering a caring, respectful relationship while encouraging challenge and participation (Certo, 2005; Goodfellow & Sumison, 2000). In this respect, the mentor–mentee relationship is in a constant state of negotiation and must be nurtured.

Expectations and attitudes

As discussed earlier, the relationship between mentor and student teacher is affected by the expectations and attitudes of the mentor and teaching team. In some situations it appeared there was a mismatch between centre priorities and those of the student teachers. This created tension for the mentor–mentee relationship. Both Millie (employed) and Amber (voluntary) in their first years of study came under pressure to work more than the programme requirement of 12 hours per week. The student teachers wanted to prioritise their study. Jane felt her mentor considered the paid 'work' to be more important than her study.

It is critical for the mentor–mentee relationship that genuine interest is demonstrated by the mentor, and that active engagement in professional conversations occurs regularly. Professional conversations between mentor and mentee send a clear message to the student teacher that they are important and mitigate the potential for mismatched expectations. Competing goals and expectations have been reported elsewhere as being common in the practicum experience (see Valencia, Martin, Place, & Grossman, 2009). I think communication between mentors, student teachers and the teacher educators is critical in minimising the negative impacts of differing expectations.

Communication with and the accessibility of the mentor have been identified in other studies as critical aspects of a healthy mentoring relationship (Graves 2010; Murphy & Butcher, 2011; Strader, 2009). As discussed earlier, a sense of belonging is developed as the mentor and teaching team build an ongoing respectful, reciprocal relationship with the student teacher. This facilitates the student teacher entering fully into the life of the learning community. However, I believe the mentor–mentee relationship needs to be actively facilitated; for example, through regular meetings, recording outcomes and setting goals collaboratively, mutually planning to support children's learning, inviting the student teacher to meetings, offering professional development opportunities, and extending invitations to social events. These practices are particularly important when the student is a volunteer. Such systematic contact also enhances the opportunities for clarification of expectations and facilitates mutual understanding of the student teacher's context. This context is often one of juggling many responsibilities, including family and community obligations (Bell, 2004).

Interestingly, some mentors believed it was an advantage to be voluntary because the student teachers are in addition to the legally required child/teacher ratio. Seven mentors expressed the view that volunteers have less pressure and can therefore focus on their practice and the assessment requirements of their teacher education programme. However, the assessments often involve the work of teachers, including observations of children and planning for children's learning. Rather than viewing these as the 'work' of teachers, some mentors (as in Jane's experience) appeared to perceive assessment tasks as interfering with the daily work of teachers, rather than an opportunity to engage in reflective dialogue about teaching and children's learning.

The mentors who had lower expectations and the student teachers who positioned themselves as 'only a student' indicated a need for the education provider to clearly communicate their expectations for both mentors and student teachers. An employed position for the student teachers should not be a default setting for authentic participation in the experiences of the community. Critically, this participation should not be left to chance (Howie & Hagan, 2011, 2012; Valencia et al., 2009). As Howie and Hagan (2011, p. 96) emphasise, mentors (and, I would suggest, the teaching team) must actively promote the "inclusion of student teachers in the full life of the home centre [field-based setting]". Mentors must also systematically increase the expectations of student engagement in each year of the programme. This requires the mentor to establish a culture of inquiry through regular conversations. Pollard (2008, p. 476) claims that this "relationship between mentoring and reflection is fundamentally important to the professional well-being of individual teachers." Again, this needs to occur regardless of the voluntary or employed status of the student teacher.

The decision to be voluntary, as opposed to being employed, may have implications for student teacher learning. There was some indication from the mentors that there were greater expectations of the student teachers in employment, and that this enhanced their sense of belonging and acceptance of them as a team member. In contrast to the mentors, the student teachers did not focus on their status as a volunteer or employed student teacher. Instead, they focused on the nature of the relationships with their mentor and teaching team and the attitudes and expectations towards them. Student teachers' sense of belonging was enhanced when they felt their study was valued and they were given opportunities to express this learning and contribute to children's learning. As student teachers they wanted to belong to learning communities where mutual respect and trust were developed with their mentor and the team. This would involve a genuine commitment to engage in reflective conversations based on the student teacher's learning and practice.

Conclusion

Respectful relationships based on reciprocity are fundamental to a strong and successful mentor–mentee relationship—one that enables parallel contributions. Student teachers need authentic inclusion and participation that supports them to gain a sense of belonging and to contribute to children's learning. In this chapter, we have seen that the expectations and attitudes of the mentor and/or the teaching team affected students' sense of feeling respected. These expectations and attitudes either constrained or created opportunities for student teachers' learning.

While it is important that all parties facilitate inclusion of the student teacher into the work of teachers, the role of the mentor is critical in supporting student teachers' professional growth and development. Also, the individual student teacher must commit to their own learning and maximise the potential opportunities available. When reciprocity and respect are present between the mentor and mentee, the full potential of student teachers' professional learning in the 12-hour field-based practicum is realised, regardless of their voluntary or paid status.

References

Bell, N. (2004). *Field-based teacher education at multiple sites: A story of possitibities and tensions.* Research Policy Series, No. 2. Wellington: Institute for Early Childhood Studies, Victoria University.

Certo, J. (2005). Support and challenge in mentoring: A case study of beginning elementary teachers and their mentors. *Journal of Early Childhood Teacher Education, 26*(4), 395–421. doi: 10.1080/10901020500413106

Charmaz, K. (2006). *Constructing grounded theory: A practical guide through qualitative analysis.* London, UK: Sage Publications.

Goodfellow, J., & Sumison, J. (2000). Transformative pathways: Field-based teacher educators' perceptions. *Journal of Education for Teaching, 26*(3), 245–258.

Graves, S. (2010). Mentoring pre-service teachers: A case study. *Australasian Journal of Early Childhood, 35*(4), 14–20.

Howie, L., & Hagan, B. (2011). *Practice makes perfect—does it?: Adding value to practicum experience through field-based teacher education.* Retrieved from http://akoaotearoa.ac.nz/ako-hub/ako-aotearoa-northern-hub/resources/pages/teaching

Howie, L., & Hagan, B. (2012). Adding value to practicum experience through field-based teacher education: A self-review process. In J. Hansen, B. Hagan, & L. Howie (Eds), *Fresh provocations: Rethinking practices in early childhood education* (pp. 85–100). Manukau: Manukau Institute of Technology.

Lave, J., & Wenger, E. (1991). *Situated learning: Legitimate peripheral participation.* New York, NY: Cambridge University Press.

Loizou, E. (2011). The diverse facets of power in early childhood mentor–student teacher relationships. *European Journal of Teacher Education, 34*(4), 373–386. doi: 10.1080/02619768.2011.587112

McConnell, C. (2010). *Field-based teacher education: An analysis of a continuous practicum.* Unpublished master's thesis, University of Deakin, Melbourne, Australia.

Ministry of Education. (1996). *Te whāriki: He whāriki mātauranga mō ngā mokopuna o Aotearoa: Early childhood curriculum.* Wellington: Learning Media.

Murphy, C., & Butcher, J. (2011). The intricacies of mentoring and teaching assessment in field-based early childhood teacher education. *New Zealand Research in Early Childhood Education, 14,* 53–66.

Nolan, A., Morrissey, A.-M., & Dumenden, I. (2012). *Mentoring for early childhood teachers: Research report 2012*. Retrieved from http://www.education.vic.gov.au/Documents/childhood/professionals/profdev/mentoringearlychildhoodreport.pdf

NZTC. (2007). *New Zealand graduating teachers standards*. Wellington: Author.

Pollard, C., with Anderson, J., Maddock, M., Swaffield, S., Warin, J., Warwick, P. (2008). *Reflective teaching: Evidence-informed professional practice* (3rd ed.). London, UK: Continuum.

Renshaw, P. (2003). Community and learning: Contradictions, dilemmas and prospects. *Discourse Studies in the Cultural Politics of Education*, *24*(3), 355–370.

Strader, W.H. (2009). The mentor–student relationship: From observer to teacher. *Young Children*, *64*(1), 54–57.

Valencia, S., Martin, S., Place, N., & Grossman, P. (2009). Complex interactions in student teaching. *Journal of Teacher Education*, *60*(3), 304–322.

Zachary, L.J. (2012). *The mentor's guide: Facilitating effective learning relationships* (2nd ed.). San Francisco, CA: Jossey-Bass.

Zeichner, K. (2010). Rethinking the connections between campus courses and field experiences in college and university-based teacher education. *Journal of Teacher Education*, *61*(1–2), 89–99.

Chapter 11
21st century mentoring for 21st century students
Nicole Downie

Introduction

Twenty years ago, when I first started studying early childhood education (ECE), my mentor was the person who helped me to connect what I was learning in class with what I was experiencing in the ECE service. My mentor was the one who told me not to turn my back to the playground, the person who showed me the importance of getting down to the child's level, and the person who helped me to find my own confidence as a teacher.

Today, for students in the Bachelor of Teaching (ECE) programme, the mentor is the person who motivates, supports, clarifies, challenges practice, role models, engages in dialogue, draws on experiential learning, is inspirational, calm, assertive, confident and empathetic (Garvey, Stokes & Megginson, 2014). This is not to say that my mentor did not do any of these things. In fact, as a qualified teacher working alongside me in the ECE service my mentor was an influential navigator in my learning journey, mapping out a path that has inspired me to be in this sector for many years. However, the difference between 20 years ago and today is that today technology is part of the mentor, student and lecturer equation.

This chapter tells the story of the introduction and implementation of e-portfolios into a field-based teacher education practicum model. The mentoring landscape has changed as a result of technology, and this chapter shares the experiences of mentors, students and lecturers when using a technological approach. The challenges, the highlights and the ways in which mentoring through technology has changed the student learning experience will be explored.

The relationship

Once upon a time mentoring was commonly thought of as a relationship between a mentor and a mentee. When the mentee is a student within a teacher education programme, one perspective has been that the mentoring role has been about transferring knowledge from the mentor to the mentee (Lane, Lacefield-Parachinni, & Isken, 2003), where the relationship is based on one learner and one teacher. In an era where learning and teaching are interchangeable, we find ourselves in a time when knowledge is a journey rather than a destination. In my experience, the mentor–mentee relationship has evolved and taken on a co-constructivist sociocultural approach (John-Steiner & Mahn, 1996), where there is not one clear learner and one clear teacher.

Throughout this chapter I talk about the place of technology in the mentor–mentee equation. My hope is that you read this chapter and understand that mentoring through technology has seen a positive and marked progression from the mentoring role of days gone by. I didn't grow up with technological devices. Having a computer in the home was rare when I was a child. Telephones were still wired to shared telephone exchanges, and being connected meant actually writing a letter and posting it through the New Zealand postal service. Therefore, the introduction of technology as a teaching and mentoring tool has come with some resistance from me. However, as a lecturer in a Bachelor of Teaching (ECE) programme, and through my role as professional practice co-ordinator at a tertiary education provider, I now welcome technology for the huge range of possibilities it can offer, and the connectivity between student, mentor and lecturer. It is this connectivity that has proven its worth over the past 3 years.

The context

In this field-based initial teacher education programme, practicum (home centre) means the student is required to complete at least 12 hours per week in a licensed ECE setting (Ministry of Education, 2008). The student works alongside a mentor who is a qualified (minimum Diploma of Teaching [ECE]) and fully registered teacher. The qualified and registered teacher is called the mentor. In this model of teacher education, the mentor and the mentee (student) work closely together. The mentor is available to provide feedback, role model, offer suggestions and give advice. The student is able to learn what it means to be a teacher, practise teaching approaches and become part of the ECE setting's community of practice (Wenger, 2010). Praxis is the underpinning fundamental dimension of such an approach to teacher education, whereby theory and practice interconnect. As well as 12 hours of practicum per week, students in this programme attend one evening class of 3 hours and one day class of approximately 7 hours (including lunch breaks), where they are taught on campus by a lecturer. Students are able to apply what they learn in class to what they are doing in their work with children. Likewise, what they learn in practice can be linked to the theory they are exploring in class (Coombes & Downie, 2014). The sustained relationship of the mentor and mentee allows an immediacy of applying teacher education learning to hands-on work in the ECE setting, and vice versa.

This model of teaching and learning is not new, but the use of e-portfolios for documenting learning has increased. In a report written for the Ministry of Education, Fox, Britain and Hall (2009) discuss the definition of an e-portfolio. They argue that an e-portfolio needs to have a purpose (p. 7), and to be a three-dimensional tool (using technology) "which allows existing learning of all media types to be pulled together into one convenient location with ease of accessibility" (p. 8). This chapter discusses how one tertiary education provider is using e-portfolios to showcase and measure student competence and growth in their teaching practice. The students undertaking practicum are using one form of technology as a vehicle to record, journal and display their examples of practice. The students share these pages with their mentors and visiting lecturers, and what begins is a three-way conversation that not only strengthens and increases the success of the student but also provides the mentor and visiting lecturer with professional learning opportunities.

Increasing the connections

The year 2012 saw the introduction of an e-portfolio system in one field-based teacher education programme. This pedagogical shift came in response to a need for more lecturer connection to students and mentors in the practicum setting. It had become clear through student and mentor evaluations that students needed more ongoing and sustained support to complete their practicum work. The need to strengthen the relationship between the student, the mentor and the visiting lecturer by encouraging deeper dialogue and discourse opportunities became a driver for the change to e-portfolios. Abbey (2012) suggests that what is required in responding to today's changing technological landscape is the implementation of new pedagogies using new technologies. It was timely to move towards a technological platform as a way to connect students, mentors and visiting lecturers and to stay in tune with what was happening with the student in the practicum setting. By using an e-portfolio system, mentors and visiting lecturers are able to gain an insight into the evolving practices, reflection and philosophy of the student, thereby facilitating new insights, knowledge and understanding of this triadic relationship (Abbey, 2012). This pedagogical shift has seen the focus move from lecturer-led instruction methods, to a student-centred approach based on collaboration (Tapscott, 2009). No longer are students documenting their practicum in isolation or on their own. The e-portfolio has encouraged collaboration between the student, mentor and visiting lecturer that builds on learning.

Before the introduction of this e-portfolio system, students had a folder where all documentation of practicum work was collated. The mentor was able to see this folder when the student offered it to them or when they asked for it. The visiting lecturer generally only saw this folder during three visits per year to the student in the practicum ECE setting. Now students are taught in year one how to set up the e-portfolio. They give access to their visiting lecturer and mentor so that the e-portfolio can be seen and commented on in real time. This means that as the student uploads their work, the visiting lecturer and the mentor can go online and make suggestions, give advice, ask the student questions, upload photos or videos and give praise and encouragement. Gone are the days of waiting for a visit from the visiting lecturer before gaining some insight into the student's progress. The days of going to visit the student (as the visiting lecturer) only to find they have forgotten their folder have disappeared. The days when the mentor has to ask to see the student's work are no longer. The e-portfolio system has initiated a stronger and more robust triadic relationship between the student, mentor and visiting lecturer.

The practicum module structure includes the set-up of the e-portfolio, face-to-face meetings between the student and the visiting lecturer, and at least three 'in centre' visits per year (each of 2 hours). Before a visit, the visiting lecturer (who remains the same person for the student throughout the progression of practicum), the student and the mentor will have been conversing via the e-portfolio. When the visiting lecturer visits the student, they use a tablet or iPad (mobile device) to view and contribute to the student's e-portfolio. The visiting lecturer makes comments about the student's practice and how the student is meeting the requirements of practicum. The visiting lecturer and the student then discuss the visiting lecturer's observations and the student experiences of practicum. Soon after, the mentor is included in this discussion. The iPad or tablet can be used as a tool to document the feedback during this triadic meeting, which is then uploaded to the e-portfolio. The number of visits per year to each student has not increased in the move to e-portfolios. However, the connections, the discussions, the depth of these discussions and the amount of contact between the student, the mentor and the visiting lecturer have increased dramatically.

Assessment continues to play a defining role in the student's success of practicum. The e-portfolio is formatively assessed (pass or fail) based on the student's written and practical work, the mentor's feedback and the visiting lecturer's professional judgement. Aspects of the written work within the e-portfolio are summatively assessed (graded out of 100) by the visiting lecturer. In all aspects of the assessment process, the mentor's professional insight, comments, opinions and views about the student inform the result of the practicum for the student.

The challenges

For some ECE settings, this shift to e-portfolios has generated some concern. Understandably some centre managers and mentors have voiced concerns about the safety of online documentation: safety for the students' work, but, more importantly, safety of the images and information about children that may be documented on the e-portfolio. In response to this concern, measures were tested and proven to ensure the safety of children and families. The e-portfolio platform security checks showed that information is safe. Password and multi-level security gates were enforced so that users and industry could feel safe that information and images of children could not be stolen. Students were asked to sign declarations, and a system administrator was given overall site access so that the requirements of the declaration are enforced. This means that one designated staff member has the right of access to check each student's e-portfolio and delete any images if the student has not already done so. If the documentation uploaded by the student has photos, videos or references to the children, families or staff of one setting, these must be removed before a change in practicum setting can happen. Usually students stay in one practicum setting for the length of the Bachelor of Teaching (ECE), but in some cases students do move settings. Any multimedia images must be removed to ensure the privacy of the children, families and staff of the previous setting.

Some concerns were also raised about the cost of the data required to access an e-portfolio in an ECE setting. The visiting lecturers carry mobile data devices, which enable access to the student's e-portfolio through a mobile internet connection, thereby placing the cost on the tertiary provider rather than the ECE setting. Although most students have access to the Internet at home, the tertiary provider offers free Internet connection on campus. For the mentor, some challenges have arisen in relation to having the non-contact opportunity to go online and access the e-portfolio. Not all ECE settings have Internet, due to choice, location or cost. Not all ECE settings allow non-contact time to be used for mentoring of practicum students, or allow the centre data allocation to be used for online mentoring, but these are in the minority.

The important thing is the triadic student–mentor–visiting lecturer relationship rather than the technology or complications in accessing the technology. Therefore, for mentors in this position, handwritten feedback is encouraged and the students can themselves take a photo or scanned copy of this written feedback and upload it to the e-portfolio. In these cases, the student, mentor and visiting lecturer can develop ways to work together and maintain connections based on the needs of the setting.

Understanding the technology

Training in how to use the e-portfolio has been offered (and continues to be offered) to mentors. This can occur in the ECE setting or during evening sessions at the tertiary provider. Although many of us were not born into this technological era, and therefore often resist new technology for fear of 'breaking the system', this particular e-portfolio system is much like other e-portfolios that we are beginning to know and use, such as Educa or Storypark. Jones (2010) refers to the "digital immigrant" (p. 365). This term refers to people like me who were born in a time of very limited digital possibilities.

Although the majority age group of the student cohort in this programme falls between 20 and 30 years of, it is important to realise that age does not translate to digital literacy (Jones, 2010). It cannot be taken for granted that people who are "digital natives"—those born into a technological environment (Jones, 2010)—know how to use an e-portfolio for academic purposes. Regardless of the level of digital literacy, the responsibility falls on the teacher education provider to ensure that students, mentors and visiting lecturers receive and are equipped with the skills needed to engage with the e-portfolio. Many mentors have said that at first it was scary to embark on mentoring a student through an online tool, but the positive outcomes for the student and the mentor far exceed the fear and challenges.

The feedback

Through the use of questionnaires and interviews, 30 mentors were randomly selected as part of the 2014 review of this style of practicum delivery. The results from these data show that mentors feel they have a stronger presence, influence and role in shaping not only the student in their work but the overall programme the tertiary education provider offers. Because mentors can see the work of the student and read the comments made by the visiting lecturer, the expectations, the requirements of the programme and the direction of learning become clearer, thereby giving the mentor an opportunity to be part of this discourse in an immediate and responsive way. What evolves is a conversational, supportive, ongoing dialogue of reflection, action, improvement, learning and teaching. The shift between the learner and the teacher is forever moving and transforming the roles of the student, mentor and visiting lecturer as information is shared and discussed by all three parties. One mentor shared their perspective thus:

> The e-portfolio has given another avenue for discussing practice. The student teaches me things through the e-portfolio as she uploads readings from class and we talk about them on the floor. I think I can help her make more connections between theory and practice because I know what she is studying at the time.

The mentoring of students is not always a success story. Looking back at my own history of academic study, I know all too well the realities and multiple identities of a student (Gibbs, 2006). With these multiple identities come commitments, confidence testers and life-challenging moments, and for some, studying to become a teacher is not an easy road. For some students the road is already filled with pot holes and loose gravel. For the mentor, working with students who are not getting their work completed on time (or not at all) can be frustrating and heart breaking. Through the use of e-portfolios, mentors of these students become more aware of them falling behind and are better able to offer support. Visiting lecturers can also see a lack of presence on the e-portfolio so are alerted to this fact and can contact the student to discuss the individual learning needs of that student. As a result, student failure rates have decreased as the support offered by mentors and visiting lecturers is timely and support structures can be put in place.

Sinclair (2003) suggests that technology cannot replace the "affective nature of education" (p. 92). Face-to-face discussions, experiences and hands-on practical application of teaching strategies and techniques cannot be replaced with technology. We are working in a profession where relationships are key to our ways of being and knowing (Gibbs, 2006), and the way we interact with people, places and things (Ministry of Education, 1996) provides inspiration for our learners—both child and adult. Therefore the use of e-portfolios cannot take away or replace the need for the mentor to be having discussions about practice, and engaging in dialogue where connections between learning and theory can be made, challenges shared and successes celebrated. As one mentor said:

> I still have on the floor discussions all the time with [student]. These happen all the time. But now I can see in her e-portfolio how what she does with on the floor translates into a learning outcome. I can tell [student] exactly a time when she is demonstrating something with children and the most rewarding thing is seeing that light bulb go on—just like a teachable moment with a child. If the e-portfolio system was not there, I would still give feedback but I would not know how it links to her class work as much as I do now. I can see exactly how her actions link to her study and I can help her to see those links as well.

Mentors speak of how being able to access the e-portfolio helps to engage on a deeper level with the student. The e-portfolio gives another dimension to the mentoring role, thereby creating another way to connect the student to their learning. What was once often a discussion alongside children now may start as a discussion within the centre, then turn into an online discussion with input from the visiting lecturer. Photos that link to that discussion being demonstrated on the floor can be uploaded. The student, mentor or visiting lecturer might read something about the topic and upload that to the e-portfolio. The student can link their reflections to those discussions, and so the deepening of learning continues. It is this self-review process that widens and deepens an aspect of learning into something so much greater than what would have happened without this technology.

This is not to say that any one of the students, mentors or visiting lecturers is tied to the computer. Although the immediacy of response can be an asset, it does not mean an immediate reply is required. What is meant by this term 'immediacy' is often and regularly. It would be unrealistic to expect a mentor (which is an unpaid role) to be on call to the e-portfolio. This is not the intention of the system. The idea is that students will weekly upload their work, discussions and documentation, and then the mentor and visiting lecturer will respond. The scope of the e-portfolio is such that if the excitement of a topic transforms into a project-type approach, the mentor and visiting lecturer can enter and exit the project on a time frame that is manageable to them. It has been shown that through this e-portfolio system each party becomes part of the process and wants to add their thoughts, opinions, ideas and suggestions. This often happens outside of their working hours due to their own motivation and passion for the topic of conversation.

Looking forward

As with any new adventure, in the beginning issues caused frustration in this student, mentoring, visiting lecturer e-portfolio system. Over the 3-year journey there have been moderation and change processes. Part of the visiting lecturer's story is of challenges in moving from a paper-based module to an e-portfolio module. Part of the student's story is of Internet connection issues and difficulties uploading videos or photos that exceeded the limitations of the e-portfolio system. Behind all of these frustrations, the need to ensure user training is embedded into the teacher education programme was highlighted. However, these challenges can be expected, and with modifications and change come new and improved opportunities.

The story now is quite different from that of 2012. The story now has a strong mentor narrative that has brought the mentor role to the main stage of this practicum experience. Students talk of the support given by their mentor and often tell a story of admiration of and respect for their mentor. The students speak of being supported not only through their academic work but also in a holistic way. Mentors and visiting lecturers have shared personal experiences whereby they have been able to offer a stronger partnership with the student—a partnership of teaching and learning rather than student, mentor and visiting lecturer separation. It is the daily or weekly dialogue and the connections made in an ongoing way through the e-portfolio that make this practicum model one of success.

Conclusion

This chapter has highlighted the journey of mentors, students and lecturers in the move to an e-portfolio model of practicum. Through the use of technology, the triadic relationship has developed new and exciting ways in which students, mentors and lecturers co-construct knowledge, share ideas and engage in professional dialogue. Through technology, new relationships have evolved. These relationships are not only the triadic relationships of mentors, students and lecturers, but also the relationship with ECE and tertiary educational settings, industry and student cohorts.

I therefore urge you to ponder your own relationship with mentoring. How could you—as a teacher, mentor, student or professional leader—build your own capability and confidence in using technology to build relationships? How could you inspire new ways of connecting with people? How could you build your professional network to include opportunities for sharing ideas, giving feedback and engaging in professional discussion? Do you have a community of practice, which could be strengthened through technological connectivity?

Technology is forever changing, thereby creating endless possibilities for ECE professionals to engage with each other, build communities of practice and inspire new learning. I encourage you to embrace all that these possibilities offer. The teaching and learning destination you have in mind might be just the beginning.

References

Abbey, N. (2012). *Developing 21st century teaching and learning: Dialogic literacy.* Retrieved from http://education.jhu.edu/PD/newhorizons/strategies/topics/literacy/articles/developing-21st-century-teaching

Coombes, C., & Downie, N., with Aitken, H., Burgess, J., Gould, K., Howie, L., et al. (2014). Early childhood field-based initial teacher education in New Zealand: A valid choice? *New Zealand Journal of Teachers Work, 11(*1), 17–29.

Fox, I., Britain, S., & Hall, V. (2009). *E-portfolios: Celebrating learning.* Retrieved from http://www.foxedu.co.nz/2009/07/celebrating-learning

Garvey, B., Stokes, P., Megginson, D. (2014). *Coaching and mentoring: Theory and practices.* London, UK: Sage Publications.

Gibbs, C. (2006). *To be a teacher: Journeys towards authenticity.* Auckland: Pearson Education New Zealand.

John-Steiner, V., & Mahn, H. (1996). Sociocultural approaches to learning and development: A Vygotsky framework. *Educational Psychology, 31*(3–4), 191–206.

Jones, C. (2010). A new generation of learners?: The net generation and digital natives. (Editorial to special edition). *Learning Media and Technology, 35*(4), 365–368.

Lane, S., Lacefield-Parachinni, N., & Isken, J. (2003). Developing novice teachers as change agents: Student teacher placements against the grain. *Teacher Education Quarterly, 30*(3), 77–88.

Ministry of Education. (1996). *Te whāriki: He whāriki mātauranga mō ngā mokopuna o Aotearoa: Early childhood curriculum.* Wellington: Learning Media.

Ministry of Education. (2008). *Licensing criteria for early childhood education centres 2008.* Retrieved from http://www.lead.ece.govt.nz/ServiceTypes/CentreBasedECEServices.aspx

Sinclair, C. (2003). Mentoring online about mentoring: Possibilities and practice. *Mentoring & tutoring: Partnership in learning. 11*(1), 77–94.

Tapscott, D. (2009). *Grown up digital: How the net generation is changing your world.* New York, NY: McGraw-Hill.

Wenger, E. (2010). Communities of practice and social learning systems: The career of a concept. In C. Blackmore (Ed.), *Social learning systems and communities of practice* (pp. 179–198). London, UK: Open University.

Chapter 12

Ka puta ki te ao mārama: Te huarahi o ngā kaiārahi piri—Into the world of light: Mentoring teachers' journeys

Margaret Kempton, Rosemilly Piasi Teaheniu, Arapera Witehira, Susana Smith, Margarette Cantwell and Winnie Korina

Introduction

This chapter draws on recent work our team has done mentoring teacher education students in our research courses at Te Rito Maioha Early Childhood New Zealand (formerly Te Tari Puna Ora o Aotearoa / New Zealand Childcare Association) at our Manukau teaching base. The chapter explores the challenges our team experienced as mentors of a diverse group of students, in particular as the students engaged in teacher education, and how we learned about becoming teacher–researchers. The experience of sharing the students' understanding, knowledge and challenges forms the basis for our critical reflections on effective and respectful ways to mentor. The chapter discusses reflections on journeys as early childhood teacher–researchers into the world of light, te ao mārama.

We highlight that though becoming a teacher–researcher can be complex and potentially marginalising, there is potential for it to become emancipatory and transformative. The implications for those mentoring beginning teacher–researchers from diverse cultural and linguistic backgrounds, particularly, Māori and Pasifika students, are a central focus of our discussion. We give practical examples of how cultural understanding and lived experiences (if they are shared and/or legitimated by those mentoring) can be a way into engaging powerfully with the world of academic research.

While not suggesting that our work is without tensions, some of the promising mentoring practices we have initiated have involved making links between cultural ways of researching within a Pasifika framework, and the parallel processes of undertaking research into teaching practice are just one aspect of the 'bringing into the light' the chapter discusses. Our role as mentors of our students has also caused us to reflect critically on the ways we can and do support and mentor each other within a team context.

Guiding concepts

In terms of effective and respectful ways to mentor, we have reflected on the Māori concept of kaiārahi piri (literally, to closely guide). We consider this concept in terms of our own learning and in terms of how we mentor and set up learning environments for students, and how we mentor and support each other as a teaching team. We also explore how effective and respectful ways to mentor are expressed within Pasifika world views. The concept that has helped us critically reflect across the contexts we mentor and are mentored in is that of 'teu le va'—meaning to value, cherish, nurture and take care of the *va*, the relationship (Amituanai-Toloa, 2005; Anae, 2010; Mara, 2013).

The metaphor of te ao māramatanga, the world of light, is relevant to our work. To us this metaphor refers to moving into the light from relative darkness, or developing a deeper understanding or knowledge after a time of uncertainty. By working as a diverse team of teacher-educators, we draw on our strengths and connections with students while respecting and coming to understand our different world views and experiences. In this sense we are mentoring each other. This happens in practical ways, as those with research experience support those with less, and those with expertise in working and supporting their communities can help those who might not have the cultural understanding necessary to easily experience a "meeting of minds" (McNaughton, 2002, p.1).

Who are we?
We draw on the knowledge and experience of the staff at the Manukau teaching base, who are diverse in age, life experiences, educational qualifications and cultural ethnicities. Our staff have a combined six decades of teaching and research experience in early childhood, primary and tertiary contexts. We come from Pākehā, Māori and Pasifika backgrounds, from Niue, Kiribati and the Solomon Islands.

What is mentoring?
The research literature traditionally describes a mentor as a figure who guides and supports a younger person, often playing an important "role in teaching, inducting and developing the skills and talents of others" (Hansford, Ehrich, & Tennent, 2004, p. 4). Different authors have highlighted various aspects of this role. For example, Anderson and Shannon (1988) identified four aspects of mentoring, arguing that it is: intentional, nurturing, insightful, and supportive and protective.

In the teacher education literature a concern has been expressed at a 'lack of conceptual frameworks', leading Anderson and Shannon (1988) to propose a concept based on essential attributes (nurturing, role modelling, professional development, caring relationship), including "five basic functions (teaching, sponsoring, encouraging, counselling and befriending)" (p. 40). These writers also draw on Katz and Raths's (1985) definitions of essential dispositions for mentors as: being open to mentees observing them, leading over time, and expressing care and concern. Adding to these ideas, Johansson-Fua, Ruru, Sanga, Walker and Ralph (2012) identify essential "positive interpersonal relationships" (p. 243), which satisfy "needs for acceptance, affiliation and belonging" (p. 243) in both mentor and mentee.

Timperley (2001) specifically looks at the mentoring of student teachers and suggests that effective mentoring is based on co-inquiry, where both parties explore and learn from each other, with respect for each other and open sharing. Similarly, relationships are seen as central to Pasifika ways of communicating and understanding, such that the va between people is cared for to enable such open dialogue to occur between mentor and mentee safely. Hook, Waaka and Raumati (2007) also emphasise the importance of relationships, and suggest that within a Māori perspective mentoring is based on āwhina (to "assist, benefit, befriend") (Williams, 2002, cited in Hook, Waaka, & Raumati , 2007, p. 13). They also note that "values of relationality, collectivity, reciprocity and connectivity to prior generations" (Hook, 2007, cited in Hook, Waaka, & Raumati, 2007, p. 13), along with whānau and whanaungatanga, are important in guiding interactions.

In the next three sections we present a selection of effective ways of mentoring that have come together in our diverse teaching team. These are exploratory and are informed in an ongoing way by professional and collegial work and discussions. While three specific aspects/voices are highlighted in these three anecdotes, the chapter is the work of the wider team, who have fed into and refined our thinking in these areas. Firstly, Arapera describes her philosophical approach, focusing on lived experiences. Then Margaret describes working with students to unlock the unfamiliar world of research, and finally we focus on the understanding that Rosemilly has brought to light in relation to working alongside and making sense for students by linking to cultural understanding.

Ways to mentor: 1. Connect with life experiences

In this first section Arapera describes a holistic approach which informs the way she has learned to be a kaiārahi piri (mentor). As pouako (one who ensures the foundation and structure are safe and strong to enable all to participate in learning) for the Manukau base, she leads our team in te reo Māori and tikanga (Māori practices). She discusses the tikanga practices followed on the marae and how these are implemented in the same way within the classroom environment.

Arapera

How have simple everyday chores on the marae, such as helping wash the many dishes in the kaūta/kitchen or playing the game bullrush, impacted on my teaching today? How has listening to aunties call visitors on to the marae, and even being growled at for jumping on mattresses and sitting on tables, shaped me into a kaiārahi piri today?

The way I work is underpinned by the experiences I had while growing up on our family marae. Durie (2001) argues that the ability to hold strong to the values and principles that consolidate a Māori world view occurs through the marae. On reflection, my life was a learning journey, and alongside me in this journey were many kaiārahi piri. In time I would come to reciprocate this learning as a pouako and a kaiārahi piri for student teachers in our teacher education programme.

As children there was a strong reverence when we entered our whare tūpuna. I learned to respect our aunties as I watched in awe while they called to the many visitors of our whare. That same karanga would begin to shape me, too. I would be heard with humility and respect by all my visitors/students, and I, in turn would respect my students. The work of my kaiārahi piri flowed on into the kitchen, where food, drink and nourishment for our visitors was prepared and presented with honour.

Our nurturing, which translated into our mentoring of student teachers, is of another kind. In this context students hungered for knowledge of te ao Māori. I could provide that and present it in an appealing way so that students would come back for more. These are experiences and encounters where they can think, feel and behave as Māori. Not sitting on tables, not jumping on mattresses, not running in the whare, no walking in front of the kaikōrero became my rules in and out of the marae. These have become tikanga in our teaching environment as well. Learning to respect each other by implementing these tikanga ensures everyone will experience a sense of wellbeing, a sense of belonging and a sense of worth, which is the basis of a fruitful relationship between student and kaiārahi piri.

These tikanga come from the accumulated knowledge of generations of Māori and are part of the intellectual property of Māori (Mead, 2003). This intellectual property includes concepts such as tapu (the state of being set apart), mana (prestige), noa (neutrality), manaakitanga (hospitality), take (cause), utu (reciprocation) and ea (satisfaction), which are modified and built upon as people use them (Mead, 2003). In our teacher education context, the depth and real-life application of this learning flows into our mentoring work. In order to mentor students, it is crucial that that they feel the same aroha that I felt on the marae from my kuia, kaumātua and aunties, aroha that, in part, is demonstrated through respectful relationships.

Our role as a kaiārahi piri is more than being a 'mentor'. Our role is one where we ensure these tikanga are understood in their fullest sense. It is not enough to know not to sit on tables, or jump on mattresses: we must also know why these tikanga are adhered to and how they relate to the concepts described above. In the same way, it is not enough just to know one cultural view: it is important to have understanding and acceptance of other cultural views.

Ways to mentor: 2. Unlocking the unfamiliar using the familiar

In this second section, Margaret critically reflects on her challenges as mentor. Her work teaching the teacher-as-researcher components of our final-year courses has meant drawing on ideas from sociocultural approaches to teaching and learning to mentor early childhood teachers into the role of teacher–researchers.

Margaret

My experience trying to mentor our students has highlighted for me that while research can be confusing and marginalising, it can also be emancipatory and transformative. One aspect of my thinking on this has been to try to unlock the unfamiliar using the familiar, so that a "meeting of minds" can happen (McNaughton, 2002, p. 1). Some attempts to mentor in this way have been more successful than others, and have led to more collaborative work (see next section). We have examples of very practical ways that students' cultural understanding and lived experiences (if they are shared and/or legitimated by those mentoring them) can be a way into engaging powerfully with the world of academic research. This is one aspect of 'bringing into the light' the world of research.

One way to bring research into the light has been to seek to privilege the work of researchers who share cultural backgrounds with the students we are working alongside. Māori and Pasifika educational research are burgeoning fields (Amituanai-Toloa, 2009). We have access to research findings in master's and PhD theses, which are mostly written in English but in which researchers have had to make sense of mainstream concepts and have translated and transformed these so that they align with their world views (or are discarded if not useful) and are respectful of the ways of working in their communities.

One way of demystifying I have used has been to utilise indigenous researchers' work that fits with the class content. For example, in a class on data analysis I used a page from a Tongan researcher's PhD thesis (Kalavite, 2010), in which she explained in clear terms her approach to interrogating her data. The topic she looked at is of interest to my Tongan students (while in higher education rather than early childhood education), and she highlights her making sense of Tongan experiences through research. This is one attempt to incorporate some aspects of culturally familiar content and pedagogy into my teaching (McNaughton, 2002)

Sometimes I am made acutely aware (and sometimes I am completely oblivious) of the way my dialogue with students is affected by power dynamics and cultural understanding. Working within a diverse team helps me to develop an empathetic understanding of what is happening when I have trouble reaching my students. My hope is that my passion for research, along with our bringing into the light the world of both the Western research tradition and the critique of this as we mentor the students on their journeys, provides powerful tools for the ongoing work of my students as early childhood teacher–researchers.

For me, this links to ideas expressed by Linda Tuhiwai Smith (2005), involving tentatively recognising that a context that has been historically marginalising can, under the right conditions, become inclusive and transformative. Research, like schooling—once the tool of colonisation and oppression—is very gradually coming to be seen as a potential means to reclaim languages, histories and knowledge, to find solutions to the negative impacts of colonisation, and to give voice to an alternative way of knowing and of being (Smith, 2005, p. 91)

Ways to mentor: 3. Storytelling

In this third section we reflect further on mentoring students participating in our research papers. We have come to recognise that working collaboratively as lecturers from diverse backgrounds and with diverse expertise can make us much more effective in our mentoring. In this section, Rosemilly discusses how working alongside Margaret has become a process of raramana pa ororu ghighila—which is a Ndugore (from Kolombangara Island, in the Solomon Islands) concept of bringing light to intellect, which aligns with te ao māramatanga. She argues that understanding Pasifika students' experiences and working on how these can be incorporated (McNaughton, 2002) into the understanding of research concepts is a fundamental step to mentoring all students, particularly our Pasifika student teachers.

Rosemilly

Our strategy was for me to sit in as Margaret taught the research paper. We had worked out that sometimes during explanations of research concepts students would verbally acknowledge that they had understood, leading the lecturer to move along to other ideas. In sitting in with them I could pick up that their non-verbal language did not demonstrate understanding: in fact it showed confusion, which they were reluctant to express to the lecturer.

We bring to our work an understanding that ways of acting and knowing are culturally organised, with language, gestures and gaze influenced by our voices, by our bodies, and by what and how we see (Duranti, 1992, cited in Amituanai-Toloa, 2005). As colleagues we had discussed this dynamic, and our teaching strategy was to work together at complementing diverse ways of knowing and understanding research.

One example uses *vivinei soloso bangara*, which literally means children's stories in Ndugore. 'Vivinei' means to tell a story, or talanoa. Most Pasifika nations have similar important oral experiences in their cultures (Farrelly & Nabobo-Baba, 2014; Suaalii-Sauni & Fulu-Aiolupotea, 2014). 'Soloso' means within the midst of the jungle, and 'bangara' means god. This shared experience and ways of structuring knowledge within a narrative meant I could create a story around an important concept (and often do this in my teaching and collegial discussions), and explain research concepts using this context with Pasifika students.

In one class the example of a prearranged marriage was used to help students reflect on the research process within their academic course. While this concept of arranged marriages is not shared or understood by all Pasifika students, in this instance it was used successfully to help make links to the process of academic research. Arranged marriages are related to sensitive purposes and obligations for both the young people's families, such as protecting ownership of the tribal land and continuity of kinship within families. I described my own knowledge and asked them to reflect on their understanding of the 'research' a family might conduct in this situation—the planning, the specific methods for collecting information, the analysis and the formalised ways of presenting back of information. We likened this to an oral-based research investigation.

This process links with the understanding in Pasifika communities (Penetito & Sanga, 2003, p. 25) of research as a purposive activity undertaken for the benefit of communities, "rather than merely a good, interesting thing to do". Being able to tell this story (of my own experiences in the Solomon Islands) triggered students to think about important oral processes in their own cultures. It also gave a meaningful purpose for the research, and placed it within their experience; as one student reflected, "I realise I have been doing research practically, in what I do as a teacher, but to write up is the hard bit". We were able to mentor through this close guidance, kaiārahi piri, through vivinei/storytelling/talanoa, which includes empathetic understanding (Farrelly & Nabobo-Baba, 2014). Our mentoring also includes an awareness of looking after our relationships—the *va*, or spaces between us (Anae, 2010).

A further aspect of this work, which can only be briefly described here, is our need to challenge our ways of working at a philosophical as well as a practical level. Is our teaching truly providing spaces for different epistemologies or world views, or are we narrowly channelling our students into required understanding? Are we actually supporting the unpacking of competing stories about knowledge and research, are we creating spaces for the important work of decolonising, listening to silenced voices and developing dialogue across our differences (Smith, 2005)?

Mentoring the team and each other: Recognising our strengths and needs

As we work with mentor students in our teacher education courses, we also try to engage in respectful ways of working together as a teaching team. There is strength in our diversity, but diversity also presents challenges for us. We briefly highlight here some ways we see that our support and mentoring of each other as colleagues has the potential to enhance our work.

Our ways of mentoring each other could be seen as shifting tuakana–teina relationships, respectful reciprocal relationships that are based on the complementary sharing of knowledge (Mead, 2003). For example, those with research experience support those with less experience, and those with expertise in working and supporting their communities help those who might not have the cultural understanding necessary to easily experience a "meeting of minds". We are also trying to take underlying concepts and be respectful of these in joint interactions. Linda Tuhiwai Smith has used the concept of "negotiated space" (2008, cited in Mila-Schaaf & Hudson, 2009, p. 5). This idea keeps relationships central, and our work together has highlighted that respectful relationships are key to effective mentoring. These are not straightforward, and we need to constantly keep in mind that any dialogue is imbued with power dynamics and cultural understanding. This space, Durie (2002) writes, can provide "not only physical territory but also the psychological space to rehearse identity and to confirm the relationship between self and others" (p. 20).

We are involved daily in the work of bringing together incongruent knowledge systems (Mila-Schaaf & Hudson, 2009), and the inequitable histories we represent of dominance and conflict can contribute to the problematic nature of this work (Penetito & Sanga, 2003). We also need to provide our students with ways to critically engage with teaching and researching, and to do this we are often forging new negotiated spaces. It has been suggested that the problem is that "Western thinking tends to provide complete paradigms with little opportunity for indigenous peoples to engage critically with these ways of framing the world" (Mila-Schaaf & Hudson, 2008, p. 68). Some points of contention include the way the construction of knowledge is often individualised within academic research. This is a particular source of tension for Pasifika people, who see knowledge as rightly held by the collective (Du Plessis & Fairbairn-Dunlop, 2009). There is also concern about the way we consider the impact of the historical in terms of the continuing energy of colonisation.

Smith (2014, a co-author of this chapter) has reviewed the work of other Pasifika writers and notes that they draw attention to dire implications for the wellbeing of individuals and groups when relationships are left unattended. Her analysis is that the concept of teu le va can be used as a guide to establishing and sustaining relationships, and has the potential to promote creativity and innovative practice because respectful relationships lead to an environment where everyone is "on board". Smith notes that from a Pasifika perspective, success involves maintaining harmony and balance in our interactions. This has implications for our expectations of each other, our individual behaviours, and, specifically, in our communications (both verbal and non-verbal) (Du Plessis & Fairbairn-Dunlop, 2009, cited in Smith, 2014).

Conclusion

This chapter has given three specific examples of how being mindful of cultural understanding and lived experiences can be a way into successfully mentoring our students. These promising mentoring practices have caused us to reflect critically on the ways we can and do support and mentor each other within a team context. We struggle every day to support our students and each other. We take heart in the idea that it is the struggle and discomfort of these encounters that will create space for new and useful ideas to develop. Like Jones (2012), we hope that "ideas and critiques developed in the spirit of whanaungatanga—that is, ethically, with care and respect for others (along with a consciousness of how power works in everyday interactions)—are surely to be welcomed and debated" (p. 109).

We also take heart in the commitment by our team to take heed of the Samoan concept and practice of teu le va—to value, cherish, nurture and take care of the va. As Smith (2014) highlights, we need to value, nurture and, if necessary, 'tidy up' the physical, spiritual, cultural, social, psychological and tapu 'spaces' of our relationships. The work to develop, let alone maintain, respectful relationships is ongoing, and at a basic level it requires empathic understanding and taking another's perspective (Farrelly & Nabobo-Baba, 2014). To act ethically as mentors of each other and our students requires space for deliberation about what counts as knowledge, resisting homogenisation, and working in positive ways to develop specific local applications of our treasured knowledge and teachings.

References

Amituanai-Toloa, M. (2005). *Ua malie toa: Ua malie tau: Students with silver tongues whip the tail: Enhanced teaching and learning of reading comprehension in Samoan bilingual classes.* Unpublished doctoral thesis, University of Auckland.

Amituanai-Toloa, M. (2009) What is a Pasifika research methodology?: The 'tupua' in the winds of change. *Pacific-Asian Education: A Journal about Education in Pacific Circle Countries, 21*(2), 45-54.

Anae, M. (2010). Research for better Pacific schooling in New Zealand: Teu le va—a Samoan perspective. *MAI Review, 1*, 1-25. Retrieved from http://www.mai.ac.nz/index.php/MR/article/viewfile/298/395.

Anderson, E. M. & Shannon, A. L. (1988.) Towards a conceptualization of mentoring. *Journal of Teacher Education, 34*, 38-42.

Du Plessis, R., & Fairbairn-Dunlop, P. (2009). The ethics of knowledge productions: Pacific challenges. *International Social Science Journal, 60*(195), 109-114. Retrieved from http://hdl.handle.net/10092/5552

Durie, M. (2002). Is there a distinctive Maori psychology?" In L. Nikora, M. Levy, B. Masters, M. Waitoki, N. Te Awekotuku & R. Etheredge (Eds.), *The Proceedings of the National Maori Graduates of Psychology Symposium.* Hamilton: University of Waikato. pp. 19-25.

Farrelly, T., Nabobo-Baba, U. (2014). Talanoa as empathic apprenticeship. *Asia Pacific Viewpoint, 55*(3), 319–330.

Hansford, B.C., Ehrich, L.C., & Tennent, L. (2004). Formal mentoring programs in education and other professions: A review of the literature. *Educational Administration Quarterly, 40*(4), 518-540. Retrieved from http://eprints.qut.edu.au

Johansson-Fua, S., Ruru, D., Sanga, K., Walker, K., & Ralph, E. (2012). Creating mentorship metaphors: Pacific Island perspectives. *Learning Landscapes, 6*(1), 241–259.

Jones, A. (2012). Dangerous liaisons: Pākehā, kaupapa Māori, and educational research. *New Zealand Journal of Educational Studies, 47*(2), 100–112.

Kalavite, T. (2010). *Fononga 'a fakahalafononga: Tongan students' journey to academic achievement in New Zealand tertiary education.* Unpublished doctoral thesis, University of Waikato. Retrieved from http://researchcommons.waikato.ac.nz/handle/10289/4159

Katz, L.G., & Raths, J.D. (1985). Dispositions as goals for teacher education. *Teaching and Teacher Education, 1*(4), 301-307.

McNaughton, S. (2002) *Meeting of minds*. Wellington: Learning Media.

Mead, H.M. (2003). *Tikanga Māori: Living by Māori values*: Wellington: Huia Publishers.

Mila-Schaaf, K., & Hudson, M. (2009). *Negotiating space for indigenous theorising in Pacific mental health and addictions.* Retrieved from http://www.leva.co.nz/file/PDFs/090204-le-va-neg-spaceocc-paper-low-res.pdf

Penetito, W., & Sanga, K. (2003). A conversation on the philosophy and practice of teaching research in Māori and Pacific education. *New Zealand Annual Review of Education, 12*, 21–37.

Smith, L.T. (2005). On tricky ground: Researching the native in an age of uncertainty. In N. Denzin & Y. Lincoln (Eds), *The Sage handbook of qualitative research* (3rd ed., pp. 85–107). Thousand Oaks, CA: Sage Publications.

Smith, S.F. (2014). *Pasifika early childhood educators' understandings and beliefs about Pasifika visual languages and cultures in the ECE curriculum: Implications for teaching and learning.* Unpublished master's thesis, University of Auckland.

Timperley, H. (2001). Mentoring conversations designed to promote student teacher learning. *Asia-Pacific Journal of Teacher Education, 29*(2), 111–123.

Suaalii-Sauni, T., & Fulu-Aiolupotea, S.M. (2014). Decolonising Pacific research, building Pacific research communities and developing Pacific research tools: The case of the 'talanoa' and the 'faafaletui' in Samoa. *Asia Pacific Viewpoint, 55*(3), 331–344.

PART 4: MENTORING THROUGH APPRAISAL AND REGISTRATION

Chapter 13
Mentoring with integrity: A story of teacher registration
Diti Hill and Mele Vete

Introduction
This is the story of a qualified and registered early childhood centre owner's quest to renew her teacher registration and of the relationship with her mentor. The Aotearoa New Zealand teacher registration process offers a strong underpinning message about quality teaching and teacher professionalism. The criteria and indicators for professional relationships, professional values and professional knowledge in practice are clearly presented through a range of media (NZTC, 2015; Watson 2014). However, the very sense of integrity the teacher registration process expects of teachers has the potential to be lost if it is understood as a set of compliances and 'boxes to tick'. This story looks at the context of one teacher's journey and the types of professional dialogue that characterise a meaningful mentoring relationship, a relationship that is easily and seductively compromised by technical 'form filling' and a perfunctory checklist of criteria and indicators.

As the NZTC makes clear on its website, with reference to the Registered Teacher Criteria, "teaching is a highly complex activity" and "(t)he criteria and indicators should be viewed as interdependent and overlapping" (NZTC, 2015). For Mele, the teacher registration process has been experienced as a constant struggle to convey the complexity of her teaching practice, as owner of and lead teacher in a small early childhood education and care centre. As well as conveying the complexity of her everyday practice, Mele wished to do this with integrity and honesty. She was keen to share those aspects of her practice that were complex and not easily resolved.

We (Mele and Diti) have had a longstanding relationship since Mele was a student in Diti's classes in 2007 while completing a Graduate Diploma of Teaching (ECE). Mele would email Diti whenever she had a question or a challenging situation. An email discussion would ensue, where the issue was discussed, debated and resolved 'for now'. Sometimes we would talk on the phone or meet in person over a cup of coffee. This open-ended dialogue, which took place between us over a number of years—always with satisfying yet tentative outcomes—characterised what was already a strong mentoring relationship when Mele began the process of renewing her full teacher registration.

Mele's story

I came to New Zealand from Tonga on a student visa after gaining University Entrance in Form Six. I was sponsored by one of my teachers at Tupou High School. I attended the Seventh Form at Epsom Girls Grammar School before I enrolled at the University of Auckland. After graduating with an MA (Hons), I relieved at Penrose High School and Wesley College. I completed a teaching qualification from the Auckland College of Education and then taught at Seddon High School, which is now Western Springs College. With a falling roll, I was the last one employed and so I was the first to go.

I decided to work for the government, and over 14 years I was employed in two government departments. Then the section I worked in closed as part of restructuring the department. At this point I thought long and hard about what was important to me and decided it was still education. A good friend who owned an early childhood centre suggested I look into early childhood education. I received a Graduate Diploma in Teaching (ECE) in 2007 from the University of Auckland. Shortly after graduating, my husband and I bought an early childhood centre.

Because I was new to the early childhood sector I kept my relationship with Diti Hill, who was one of my lecturers in the Graduate Diploma programme. I had told Diti during the Graduate Diploma year that I was looking to buy a centre, and she mentioned her willingness to be a support person as it would be a stressful pathway. Whenever I experienced challenges and had questions, I emailed Diti. Her responses always lifted me and added a new dimension to the particular question or issue I was uncertain about. It was always refreshing to exchange ideas with her, and the dialogue always opened my eyes to more than I knew.

One of my earliest communications with Diti was when I was considering a name for my early childhood centre. Her thoughtful comments were valued as part of the decision making. My relationship with Diti has continued up to the present. Although I never really considered a label for this relationship, I realise now that it has been a mentoring relationship, set in a context of friendship and collegiality.

The past renewals of my teacher registration have been relatively straightforward. The latest renewal proved to be more challenging. I had heard that the New Zealand Teachers Council was being particularly rigorous when owner–managers of early childhood centres renewed their teacher registration. With a strong commitment to quality teaching, I saw the renewal as a do-able challenge.

Diti has continued to mentor me for my re-registration, and this mentor relationship is now in its 7th year. I continue to send Diti emails when I am 'up against the wall'. Diti's responses have always been timely, current and relevant to what was consuming me at any particular time. At no stage did I wish to hold regular planned meetings. Diti and I have only met in person a few times during the year. The emails, however, have always gone to and fro whenever I needed assistance.

The mentoring relationship that was sparked from the connection I built with Diti as a student was characterised by the depth and breadth of our reflective conversations. I have difficulty explaining this connection, but it is definitely an intellectual connection that I can only explain as a meeting of the minds. There are situations and ways of thinking and being that are not clear to me until someone patiently explains them, providing meaning and relevance. Diti is one of those few people. I believe that I take time to learn, and I believe that the following quote from Guy Claxton (2002) defines me well:

> Good learners do not learn fast. The ability to hang out in the fog, to tolerate the confusion, to dare to wait in a state of incomprehension while the glimmering of an idea takes its time to form is another aspect of resilience and thus of learning power. (p. 25)

It has sometimes seemed to me that mentoring supports compliance with the teacher registration process in the first instance. However, from my mentoring relationship with Diti I realise that my integrity, my honesty and my ability to articulate the uniqueness of my educational setting to others are the key to best practice, and therefore also the key to compliance. I was determined to avoid 'ticking the boxes', to avoid seeing the renewal of my teacher registration as a technical exercise, as 'done'. From my course readings I recall Slattery (2006) stating that when we see curriculum in the present, as small, continuous and responsive moments that form the fabric of children's experience and being, we begin to see that it is our own willingness to address the complexity of the contexts within our practice that gives rise to meaningful experience over time.

For me it is the small, continuous, responsive moments that form the fabric of my teaching experience and of my being as a teacher, owner–manager and leader. Sometimes these moments are about something that appears minor, yet is crucial for holding everything together. Sometimes it is a phase of group development where forming and reforming the group necessitates the repeating of certain understanding. Sometimes it is just an expression of my opinion about something or someone. At other times it is a question in formation, where I do not know exactly what I need to ask. It could also just be a diary entry that is for my eyes only, but, upon re-reading the diary entry the central idea develops to a point where I find myself seeking a response and then grasping for an answer. Once I get 'lost' and do not know where I am, I tend to think that everything I look at is not quite right and disconnected. Then I talk to Diti, and she affirms that we (the teaching team) are on the right track and the dialogue opens my eyes to new connections and new opportunities to extend my current work.

I remember an occasion when I felt that I was adding too much text and meaning to a child's learning story. Although I considered this to be a minor issue at the time, I was sufficiently concerned to email Diti, and she responded in a way that made sense of my concern:

It is interesting that you see the story you have written as 'too long'. To me the length is a necessary part of the way the story has evolved over several weeks. When a story 'grows' like this the focus should be to capture the FLOW of the story over time ... Also, really important, is leaving room for the readers/viewers to interpret the story for themselves.

For me, this online exchange exemplifies our continuous and responsive mentoring relationship.

Discrete criteria and the 'tangle of spaghetti'

From Mele's mentoring story, as told above, we have identified several significant ideas underpinning our mentoring relationship, ideas that we believe can be generalised and shared with others. As we met, online and in person, to talk over the teacher registration process, we would puzzle over how to capture the small but significant shifts in thinking that defied being classified as any one of the Registered Teacher Criteria. We recognised that the criteria are "interdependent and overlapping" (NZTC, 2015), and every discussion would commence as a passionate, holistic and connected dialogue about such things as recent teaching incidents and vignettes, the wonder of children's learning, the frustration of finding the right response to a child's questions, and the challenges of working as a team in an early childhood setting. Every discussion would culminate in both mentor and mentee expressing delight in and satisfaction with our new learning. Some questions were resolved, but new problems and issues also emerged.

We came to the realisation that education and the gaining of knowledge are truly a "tangle of spaghetti" (Loris Malaguzzi's metaphor, as described in Dahlberg & Moss, 2005, p. 117), and yet we still felt compelled, by the power of the process itself, to isolate our thinking and Mele's practice into discrete criteria for the purpose of teacher registration renewal. Through our mentoring relationship we had to find ways of staying true to our mentoring journey (and the integrity of Mele's practice) while also recognising the limitations of presenting the journey to outside scrutiny. We began to look more deeply at the polarisation that exists as part of the human condition and that is found in almost every aspect of our lives as teachers.

Form and function

Education is particularly rife with abstract concepts that pull our thinking apart and manifest themselves in our practice as dilemmas and as contradictory practices. For example, the simple polarisation of the two concepts 'adult' and 'child', together with the related concepts of 'teacher' and 'learner', can lead to a confusion about who adults and children and teachers and learners really are as protagonists in the educative process. By continuing to polarise these abstract concepts, we find that it becomes difficult to acknowledge both adults and children as competent people who have a lot to teach one another as well as learn from each other. The view of ourselves (adults and children) as competent and contributing members of society—as teachers and learners—fits well with Mele's philosophy and is evident in her pedagogy and practice. As part of our mentoring relationship we had to find ways of articulating this dialectic view of polarised concepts so that the theory (the underpinning ideas and concepts) reflected a more holistic practice. 'Dialectic', as the term is used here, means creating a point of view that acknowledges and values both polarised concepts.

In much the same way, we talked about the teacher registration process as potentially polarised into 'form' and 'function', terms that come from the discipline of art but are equally applicable to education (Greenough,1947). The *form* can be seen as the identified framework for teacher registration and the completion of the required paperwork, while the *function* is the values-based, philosophical rationale for the *form*. As part of our mentoring discussion, we agreed that *form* feels restrictive and is like 'putting a square peg into a round hole'; we preferred to talk open-endedly about Mele's values and practice as a flow of ideas, understanding, doubts, questions, responses and decisions.

Yet we also recognised that *form* helps *function* to be readily available to others and to be compared and contrasted for the purposes of accountability and, in this case, teacher registration. The question arose: how could we ensure that the *function* of Mele's philosophy, pedagogy and practice would inform and be visible, with integrity, in the *form*? What would such a *form* look like? Would Mele feel that her connected thinking and holistic, continuous, uncertain everyday practice were adequately represented in the *form*?

Technical practice and critically reflective practice

The focus on form and function led to a mentoring discussion and shared awareness about the notion of critically reflective practice in contrast to the notion of technical practice. Critical reflection is understood to mean a consideration of practice that is ethical and political, where teaching decisions are the political outcome of ongoing ethical and professional discussion. Dahlberg and Moss (2005) talk about "technology as first practice" and urge teachers to "turn to diversity and uncertainty" (p. 34), thus opening up a space "for ethical and political practice itself, so reversing a process which has seen ethical and political practice replaced by technical practice" (p. 63).

To us, as mentor and mentee, this meant scrutinising any of Mele's practices that might be expedient (serving adults) and not enacted in the best interests of children. We needed the teacher registration criteria to 'speak' to us about Mele's own unique, creative and ethical practice. We puzzled over and eventually better understood the irony of the 'regulated' teacher registration process: that the form must *be* the function; that teacher registration is a very ethical process driven by a strong political sense of professionalism. Through critically reflective dialogue, we realised that this complex, dialectic understanding of the teacher registration process requires "teachers to engage in professional discussion, debate and critique" (Watson, 2014, p. 132), even more so when they work daily in settings that favour technical practice.

Conclusion

Mele did not want to create a 'collection of stuff'; she wanted to present a meaningful record of her sustained, linked and critically reflective professional practice. It was important that our mentoring relationship, and the learning generated by that relationship, was "realized in the lived-in world of engagement in everyday activity" (Lave & Wenger, 1991, p. 47). By examining the polarities (contradictory abstract concepts) that lie beneath the surface of Mele's practice, and by continually revisiting the complexity of quality practice, we created a mentoring relationship that is always open to new and uncertain ways of looking at children's learning, the role of the teacher and the continual exchange of ideas between people—both adults and children.

At the same time, we have reached a point, as mentee and mentor, where we are comfortable to generate certain ways of being when such processes as teacher registration call for a circumscribed response, knowing that *function* and Mele's integrity as a teacher underpin the *form*. The interrelated, connected, reflective, subjective, sometimes uncertain, value-laden and sustained nature of Mele's pedagogy and practice will always remain as important as, if not more important than, the articulated, objective process of teacher registration.

References

Claxton, G. (2002). *Building learning power: Helping young people to become better learners.* Bristol, UK: TLO.

Dahlberg, G., & Moss, P. (2005). *Ethics and politics in early childhood education.* London, UK: RoutledgeFalmer.

Greenough, H. (1947). Collected essays. In H.A. Small (Ed.), *Form and function: Remarks on art.* Berkeley, CA: University of California Press.

Lave, J., & Wenger, E. (1991, 2005). *Situated learning: Legitimate peripheral participation.* Cambridge, UK: Cambridge University Press.

NZTC. (2015). *The teacher registration process.* Retrieved from http://www.teacherscouncil.govt.nz/content/teacher-registration-process

Slattery, P. (2006). *Curriculum development in the postmodern era.* New York, NY: Routledge.

Watson, B. (2014). Mentoring provision in education and care settings: Policy and professional issues. In H. Hedges & V. Podmore (Eds), *Early childhood education: Pedagogy, professionalism and philosophy* (pp. 123–138). Auckland: Pearson.

Chapter 14
Mentoring provisionally registered teachers in neoliberal times
Bradley Hannigan

Introduction
The presence of professional mentors post-training is a key support for registering teachers entering the teaching profession (Ailwood et. al., 2006; Podmore & Wells, 2011). Mentoring, like any human endeavour, takes place within an ecology of contexts—in a physical sense, a social sense and a socio-political sense. You may have come across this idea in *Te Whāriki* (Ministry of Education, 1996), and in the work of Urie Bronfenbrenner (1979). In this chapter I will be discussing some of the consequences of a neoliberal context on mentoring provisionally registered teachers, sharing an example from the Nelson Tasman Kindergarten Association. I will be showing some of the ways in which a market-driven environment can affect decisions on the mentoring of new teachers and will comment on the devaluing effect this can have on an inherently valuable practice. My aim here is to add to the sociocultural understanding of mentoring by examining the influence of a neoliberal context on a particular mentoring programme, highlighting the need for advocating the value of mentoring programmes for provisionally registered teachers within this particular zeitgeist.

At the outset, some understanding of neoliberalism as political discourse is required. I will introduce it in a general way, and then in a rather particular sense in order to lead you into the thrust of my argument. It should be noted from the outset that there are many neoliberalisms, made up of multiple dimensions, meaning that any definition can only ever be partial. That said, according to Harvey (2005, p. 2):

> neoliberalism is in the first instance a theory of political economic practices that proposes that human well-being can best be advanced by liberating individual entrepreneurial freedoms and skills within an institutional framework characterized by strong private property rights, free markets, and free trade.

A neoliberal context

The argument I set out uses a sociocultural perspective (e.g. Bronfenbrenner, 1979; May, 2009) to highlight the insight that discourse and perspectives in the political context influence practices within various fields of application, such as early childhood education. The political context is made up of policy frameworks, the language used to construct them and the political agenda that underpins the choice of language (Foucault, 1988). This chapter uses that insight to present an argument that highlights the effect of neoliberal discourse on mentoring for registering teachers. This is based on the assertion that the contemporary political context in Aotearoa New Zealand is neoliberal in orientation.

Translated, neoliberalism involves an integration of the concepts of individual freedom, market forces and deregulation. A neoliberal context idealises the ability of individuals to choose what is right for them and trusts the market to offer goods and services designed to meet those choices. From a neoliberal perspective, the state should have only a minimal role in the distribution of resources/services, leaving it instead to individual consumers to decide on which resources/services are in demand and which are not (i.e. market forces). One key outcome of the neoliberal agenda is that those who have money have choice: money equates to personal freedom. Writers such as May (2009), Codd (2005) and Ongley (2013) have clearly marked the past two decades in Aotearoa New Zealand as a neoliberal epoch.

If fiscally based practices of individual freedom and the power of market forces in determining the shape of society convey a general understanding of what I mean by the term 'neoliberal context', then the idea of 'economic utility' (Taylor, 1991) conveys the specific sense in which I am using the term. Taylor, in his critique of Western civilisations, highlights three discontents that he believes have led the West into a moral decline: self-serving individualism, the rise of instrumental reasoning, and a stark reduction of choice as a result of the other two malaises. It is the concept of instrumental reasoning that I will draw on here.

Taylor (1991) defines instrumental reasoning as "the kind of rationality we draw on when we calculate the most economical application of a means to a given end. Maximum efficiency, the best cost-output ratio, is its measure of success" (p. 5). When the key reason for making a decision is economically based, then one is engaging in instrumental reasoning. For Taylor, "the fear is that things that ought to be determined by other criteria will be decided in terms of efficiency or 'cost-benefit' analysis" (p. 5). A neoliberal environment where market forces rule and where money talks naturally amplifies the role of instrumental reasoning in decision-making processes. This, I argue, is one of the keenest felt effects of the neoliberal context on mentoring practices in early childhood settings.

Writers like Duhn (2010) have commented on the tension between the neoliberal agenda and traditional ideas of professionalism. Brown (2014) has pointed out that successful teachers in a neoliberal environment struggle to explain and conceptualise their practice in ways that do not draw on neoliberal ideas of teaching and learning. Ritchie, Skerrett and Rau (2014) have observed that "the individualism of neoliberalism directly contravenes the collectivism of te Ao Māori" (p. 21), as well as being devoid of an ethic of care. Each line of reasoning could be applied to the subject of mentoring practices equally well. In a measurement culture professional growth is necessarily made measurable, in the way in which mentees articulate their practice, and in the way in which the journey into the profession is essentially individualised by the personal accountability of documented growth.

The remainder of this chapter shares the experience of two kindergarten teachers who developed a Teachers Registering Teachers programme in the Nelson Tasman area. These teachers offer insights into how this programme came about, the consequences of the cut to funding of mentoring for registered teachers in early childhood services, and discussion of how they met the challenges. The research for this chapter involved semi-structured interviews (Wengraf, 2001) with the two mentor teachers who initiated and implemented the Teachers Registering Teachers programme. Participants mentored registering teachers throughout the Nelson Tasman region as well as teachers in Westport and Marlborough over a 5-year period. Data were analysed using a thematic approach, and the research was carried out in accordance with the New Zealand Association of Researchers in Education ethical guidelines. In the following section the quotes are from the participants.

The Teachers Registering Teachers programme

The Teachers Registering Teachers (TRT) programme was developed in 2010 by teachers at the Nelson Tasman Kindergarten Association. The 2-year programme was offered to registering teachers in the Nelson Tasman, Marlborough and Westport areas. The TRT programme began with teachers recognising the value of mentoring as a catalyst for improving quality outcomes for children. The architects of the programme were spurred into action by the recognition that not all early childhood teachers enjoyed the quality of mentoring they deserved. After attending a workshop on the subject of registering teachers and hearing about the lack of direction among participants, a decision was made to establish a programme within the Association: "these teachers have got no support, they don't know where they are going to get support, and we should be doing something."

Alongside a personal moral impulse on the part of the mentors to ensure all teachers had access to good-quality mentoring, there was also a concern that newly registered teachers were being asked to sign off provisional registration before they themselves had become established in their craft: "how do you teach expertise when you are just at the start of your journey?" This concern led to the development of a programme that aimed to be robust in its approach, and send a clear message that the process by which new teachers gained registration, through a learning relationship with a professional and experienced mentor, was important for entry into the profession. This intention was summed up as follows:

> if you want to make teacher registration, then it must be robust, it must mean something and we must all know what it means … And going through that process you have to feel like at the end you have achieved something. Teachers Registering Teachers seemed like a good name, which actually spoke about what it was we were trying to achieve.

Contextual barriers to the roll out of the programme included a sector-wide distrust of the commercial intentions of the programme—that instead of providing a service to support new teachers, it might in fact be a money-making scheme. However, once government funding was made available "they accepted us coming into their centres, and we were very clear that this is not about commercial gain." The availability of funding targeted to registering teachers also created internal tensions in some services, where some of the funding earmarked for specific registration support was used in ways that benefited the service rather than the registering teacher, indicating that while funding enabled the TRT programme, its use was not always aligned to outcomes for new teachers:

> what happened was that you would go in and they [the registering teacher] would say they want to buy a book for teacher registration, but the centre was going to use the money to buy a whiteboard.

Despite early barriers in the form of distrust and questionable use of funding in some services, the TRT programme was successful in achieving its goal of developing a rigorous mentoring programme. As one mentor put it:

> I think the confidence that the teachers came out of it with, they said that they did not really know what they were doing as teachers until they started that programme… I think that the ability to self-reflect was created and also the ability to see what is possible, the ability for them to challenge and advocate as well. One of the successes of TRT was the unity of the teachers in the teaching team, particularly in those big centres where we were registering groups of teachers … It also brought teachers from multiple centres together.

The mentoring relationship coupled with the opportunity for

registering teachers to gather together on a regular basis for workshops and feedback sessions meant that networks of support, similar to those that many teachers would have experienced through their initial early childhood education training provider, were able to be established.

The TRT programme began at a time when many experienced, but unregistered, teachers were seeking registration, often incentivised by the then government's commitment to providing a higher level of funding for those services that employed 100 percent registered teachers. The rigour of the programme and the close professional relationship with a professional mentor meant that for some teachers—and some leaders—long-held practices were challenged and questioned as the catalyst for professional growth. As one mentor put it, "some people just assumed that they were really good teachers, and when you had a conversation with them that might challenge their thinking on that, they found it quite difficult to come to terms with." This comment points to the value of professional mentoring as a key element in raising the quality of teaching practice, and also leadership capability, because teachers in some centres:

> very quickly went to leadership positions, and sometimes you were able to guide and say 'have you really thought about that, while it's a short-term gain what is the long-term cost?' Also, for those who went straight to leadership—where are their leaders? How do they learn the craft? So again, being able to go out and have those professional conversations meant that aspects of leadership were challenged, and provocations were given.

Once funding for registering teachers was revised, with the outcome that financial support disappeared for most services almost overnight, participation in the TRT programme dropped significantly:

> the minute the funding stopped most of the services said they certainly can't afford to pay for the service any more so at that point the number shrunk, and not through the teachers' own choice, it was a management decision.

The value of the programme in terms of lifting the quality of teaching and learning outcomes for children was not questioned, but management "had to re-evaluate where the money goes. They were running on the smell of an oily rag just the same as everyone else."

The programme did not stop altogether, with some services placing high value on high-quality support for their new teachers. However, in response to the changes the programme itself had to change.

Several changes were implemented by mentors to ensure the original vision of a robust programme to support registering teachers, such as a pay-as-you-go strategy to break down the overall cost into manageable increments. Another change occurred in a shift away from a mentor–mentee relationship toward mentors supporting mentor teachers within the services themselves, especially where there were multiple registering teachers at a single site: "we are supporting the mentor and they are supporting the registering teacher." While the programme had been originally designed as a triadic relationship between mentors, internal mentors and mentees, the mentee was moved to the background as a result of contextual pressures. However, for some services and some registering teachers, mentoring support dropped off altogether.

Another change that was made allowed services to purchase elements of the programme on a user-pays basis (i.e. opting in for specific visits when required, or targeting specific group sessions). This in turn meant that the strong relationships between registering teachers, and between those teachers and the programme mentors, became loose connections that could, for some, undermine the robustness of the mentoring programme. This was seen as a great pity by both mentors interviewed. That sentiment was summed up by one mentor in the following way:

> It's about quality, that was our guide, it's about quality. It's not just about teachers being ticked off by somebody who doesn't know what they are ticking off … Often it falls down at management because they don't want to cost it out, whereas they actually can fund the money, it's about the mind-set really and understanding that mentoring is of value. If we ever get the funding again it is something worth resurrecting to the level it was.

Discussion

The example above sets out the profound effect of the neoliberal context on the TRT mentoring programme. In a neoliberal context, the power of the dollar is amplified, and with it the rhetoric of limited resources and, perhaps most powerful of all, budgets. Throughout the interview the issue of funding as an enabler and a disabler was discussed. In this case funding itself was not the only enabler, as management decisions also played their part in directing the flow of money, even in the golden years of government support. The effectiveness of the mentoring programme depended not only on the relationship between the mentor and the new teacher, but also on the management of funds, which in turn related to the degree to which those managing the funds valued the mentoring programme and were willing to support it. Even in the golden years, in some services managers were able to subvert funding away from the mentoring programme and into other elements of centre life, creating a mini marketplace within the walls of the service, where money could flow freely toward those things that were deemed to be of value.

The loss of funding affected the TRT programme overnight. Without money flowing in, money would have to be released from elsewhere in the budget to allow for the continuation of the mentoring programme. Again, in a neoliberal context, money flows to where there is the greatest demand, and for many services (if not all), a key demand is continued economic viability in a context where funding has increased only marginally over the past 5 years, and where the incentive to hire 100 percent trained and registered teachers (and therefore teachers who have learnt their craft through a mentoring relationship) has disappeared.

In a neoliberal context the flow of money greatly influences the structure of the social entity (Taylor, 1991). Changes in the flow of money affect the ecosystem of the early childhood service by prompting a reprioritisation of spending, and, for some areas of the service, a de-prioritisation of spending. While for-profit services are perhaps more susceptible to funding shifts, because they are required to provide a return to owners and/or shareholders, not-for-profit services are also susceptible because they, too, need to return a surplus in order to maintain facilities and develop their contingency funds. Given that money flows freely within a neoliberal system (meaning that there are no regulated areas for spending, such as a mandated amount that must be spent on mentoring new teachers), the most pressing and most valued aspect of the business will attract the lion's share of the available funds. It has long been noted across many sectors that when the money is tight, professional development is the first budget to be cut back.

In our contemporary context, the mentoring of new teachers is just one more line in a spreadsheet that vies for a limited resource. But it is an important line, and one that must be actively advocated by teachers—new and experienced alike. The tyranny of a neoliberal environment is that it normalises the language of business in the consideration of professional growth for beginning teachers. Cost–benefit analysis is too clumsy a tool to use in this regard, as it is easy to quantify the cost of a mentoring programme but difficult to quantify or qualify the immediate benefit of engaging in such a programme, and, indeed, the long-term and ongoing benefits of completing a rigorous 2-year programme. It is in this space that the spectre of instrumental reasoning (Taylor, 1991) raises itself, amplifying one set of values over another (or, in the words of one participant, one type of *mind set* over another). It is in the space of competing values that the effect of neoliberalism is most keenly felt; it is in this space that instrumental reasoning looks like common sense, and investment in high-quality mentoring for new teachers can look like a luxury rather than a necessity.

Conclusion

In a neoliberal context, the question is not whether the mentoring of new teachers matters; it is whether having a rigorous mentoring programme is valued and to what degree. This example has shown that as money shifts, so too does structure. For some services this meant that engaging in the mentoring programme was no longer viable; for the programme itself it meant that changes were made to make it more affordable in terms of reducing its scope, thus offering only elements of the programme, and developing internal mentoring capacity in services.

Both participants aligned teacher quality to the quality of the mentoring programme, and both participants aligned a valuing of teachers and teaching with the success of the programme. Taylor's (1991, p. 5) fear that "things that ought to be determined by other criteria will be decided in terms of efficiency or 'cost-benefit' analysis" was echoed by these teachers. In a neoliberal context, money moves to where the value lies. The task therefore is one of advocacy to ensure that a rigorous mentoring programme for registering teachers sits high in the value system of individual early childhood services, so that programmes such as TRT can be seen as a necessity rather than a luxury that can be cut at will.

References

Ailwood, J., Black, A., Ewing, B., Heirdsfield, A., Meehan, C., Thomas, L., et al. (2006). Supporting transitions from student to professional: A mentoring case study from early childhood education. In G. Rienstra & A. Gonczi (Eds), *Entry to the teaching profession: Preparation, practice, pressure and professionalism* (pp. 48–55). Deakin West, ACT: Australian College of Educators.

Bronfenbrenner, U. (1979). *The ecology of human development: Experiments in nature and design*. Cambridge, MA: Harvard University Press.

Brown, C. (2014). Conforming to reform: Teaching pre-kindergarten in a neoliberal early childhood system. *Journal of Early Childhood Research*, 1(*August*). doi: 10.1177/1476718X14538602.

Codd, J. (2005). Neoliberalism, democracy, and education for citizenship in New Zealand. In C. White & R. Openshaw (Eds), *Democracy at the crossroads: International perspectives on critical global citizenship education* (pp. 13–30). Oxford, UK: Lexington Books.

Duhn, I. (2010). 'The centre is my business': Neo-liberal politics, privatisation and discourses of professionalism in New Zealand. *Contemporary Issues in Early Childhood*, *11*(1), 49–60.

Foucault, M. (1988). *The history of sexuality: Vol. 3: The care of the self* (trans. R. Hurley). New York, NY: Vintage Books.

Harvey, D. (2005). *A brief history of neoliberalism*. Oxford, UK: Oxford University Press.

May, H. (2009). *Politics in the playground: The world of early childhood in New Zealand* (2nd ed.). Dunedin: University of Otago Press.

Ministry of Education. (1996). *Te whāriki: He whāriki mātauranga mō ngā mokopuna o Aotearoa: Early childhood curriculum*. Wellington: Learning Media.

Ongley, P. (2013). Work and inequality in neoliberal New Zealand. *New Zealand Sociology*, *28*(3), 136-163.

Podmore, V., & Wells, C. (2011). *Induction and mentoring pilot programme: Early childhood educators: By teachers, for teachers*. Wellington: NZTC.

Ritchie, J., Skerrett, M., & Rau, C. (2014). Countercolonial unveiling of neoliberal discourses in Aotearoa New Zealand. *International Review of Qualitative Research, 7*(1), 111–129.

Taylor, C. (1991). *The ethics of authenticity.* Cambridge, MA: Harvard University Press.

Wengraf, T. (2001). *Qualitative research interviewing: Biographic narrative and semi-structured methods.* Thousand Oaks, CA: Sage.

Chapter 15
Awakening beginning teachers' passion through mentoring
Celeste Harrington

"I am not a teacher, but an awakener." Robert Frost

Introduction
There are different ways of inspiring beginning teachers to remain passionate about their work. Beginning teachers often finish their teaching qualification and then feel lost as to how to continue and where to go next with their career path. The work to become fully registered can seem like yet another mountain to climb at the end of an already long road to becoming qualified. This chapter will discuss some different ways that one can work with beginning teachers in their journey to full registration. I will tell three stories about three different teachers, which will show that gaining and maintaining your full registration is a unique process, and that working closely with your mentor is something to be valued and not dreaded.

My mentoring experience
As a professional leader working for a private education and care organisation, an aspect of my job was to mentor provisionally registered teachers. It was during my work with these teachers that I found

a recurring theme among the provisionally registered teachers I mentored. I found that teachers who had been inspired and passionate during their study lost their 'spark' once faced with the day-to-day reality of teaching. This may not necessarily be true of all teachers in all teaching situations, but I encountered it often enough for it to be something that resulted in me reflecting deeply on the role of the mentor. This theme repeatedly highlighted how crucial having a good mentor is in order to continue to inspire the teacher to reach their full potential (Ingersoll & Strong, 2011).

It is known that teachers—and indeed mentors—are not always supported in the same way as graduates in other professions (Patterson & Thornton, 2014). There is also evidence that novice teachers who have recently graduated may feel overwhelmed and out of their depth upon beginning work with children (Ingersoll & Strong, 2011). Having only experienced relatively short periods of time on practicum, it is a very different feel for them to suddenly come face to face with the responsibility of being in ratio and having to be fully responsible for assessing and documenting children's learning. At the same time they know that they need to continue to provide evidence over a period of time to demonstrate that they are able to be fully registered.

The 2-year journey towards full registration for many teachers in the New Zealand context becomes a seemingly impossible hurdle, and after 3 or more years of study it can be viewed as yet another set of assignments to be completed. It is, therefore, all the more important that teacher have a mentor, who can in many ways alleviate those fears and work towards assisting a newly graduated teacher to grow in ways that not only benefit themselves but also the children they are teaching. The mentoring process thus becomes pivotal to them not only remaining in teaching but also being successful in their roles.

The ECE context

In early childhood education (ECE) and care centres the mentoring process has had to undergo transformation in order to be successful in meeting the mentoring needs of beginning teachers. Early childhood education and care centres are different to sessional, community or public kindergartens, with the centres open extended hours and with greater child-contact hours. This results in the teachers having most of their time in contact with children. Non-contact times, in which teachers have the opportunity to engage in administrative and professional tasks, may be limited to as little as 2 hours per week, time used very quickly in assessment and planning requirements. This 2-hour limitation is specific to the environment where I was working, and I accept that it is not necessarily the norm across the sector. However, several serious challenges may face both mentor and mentee in such environments. From my experience, these challenges include: being time poor; having English as a second or additional language; and, for the mentor, having a large number of mentees.

The most challenging of these challenges is time. Early childhood education and care centres are open all day, often for longer than 11 hours, and these long opening times make discussions and meetings with a mentor challenging. Rosters of teachers' non-contact time and breaks are tightly maintained. I had to think seriously about other ways to make sure that the teachers I mentor feel valued and supported. It was through a process of trial and error that different ways of connecting were found, and it was very exciting once I hit on an appropriate response to know that this was a positive one and the process could then became fun for both mentor and mentee.

Another challenge in the mentoring process as a professional leader was the large number of mentees. Working as a mentor over the past 4 years with over 40 provisionally registered teachers, I had to be creative in terms of how I worked with the teachers in order to ensure strong relationships that enabled me to be flexible and individually responsive. It could not be a 'one size fits all' type of programme, and I believe that the enjoyment, passion and success we all had was because of the individual way I approached each mentoring relationship. It became important to make sure in the first instance that the relationship was strong and supportive, and that there was a deep understanding—on both parts—to make sure that we had sufficient trust to continue the mentoring relationship. In the same way we approach working with children, I believe that getting to know the person and how they work and how they feel about feedback, and if they like to write or talk, is key to being able to know how best they will respond to the process of growing in their ability as a teacher.

I made use of both "Advice and guidance" and the more current framework of "Induction and mentoring" (NZTC, 2011). A mentoring relationship, according to Zachary (2011), "is a parallel journey for the mentor and mentee, with a focus on mutual learning. Thus, both the mentor and mentee gain from the relationship" (p. 288). In this context I gained deeper understanding of how the mentee works and how they develop in their knowledge of being a teacher. In giving advice and guidance, I, too, was growing.

Teacher journeys

Three teacher journeys will be described to provide an understanding of the rewarding and enjoyable nature of the mentoring relationship. Pseudonyms have been used and the scenarios altered to ensure anonymity, but the mentoring process of the relationship is real.

Susan

When I first met Susan she had been a provisionally registered teacher for over 5 years. She had a variety of artefacts in her registration folder, but these were filed in a haphazard way and she felt that they were meaningless to her. She put them there because she felt that she *had* to. Susan was a busy mother and also a provisionally registered teacher. She had almost adult children and a grandchild on the way. She enjoyed her teaching, but the process of gaining her full registration was daunting and scary territory to her. The first thing I did was tell her not to worry. We had a good conversation getting to know one another and I took her folder to see how I could support her. In the meantime she was to continue to teach and enjoy the children in the ways I had observed her doing during my visits to the centre.

So, in this first part of her journey with me as her mentor, my strategy was reassurance and the beginning of the establishment of a relationship. Susan had had a number of mentors over the years and she felt despondent about ever completing her journey. Each time she had a different mentor the rules seemed to change, and this disillusioned her even further. After a couple of weeks I returned and Susan and I met again; each time our meeting was never booked for more than 20 minutes as the centre was busy and Susan was needed to be in ratio. I returned her folder and gave her both written and verbal feedback: Susan was an aural learner, and hearing how she was doing was the best way to provide her with feedback. Once she had heard it, then she could 'see' it.

It seemed that Susan had indeed been collecting a good amount of evidence, but had become unsure how to link it to the 12 criteria. (In New Zealand, all qualified teachers have to meet a set of 12 criteria over a minimum period of 2 years in order to become fully registered. These criteria form the basis of the professional standards that teachers work to. They undergo a mentoring process once qualified to guide them to be able to meet the 12 criteria.) My role then became clear: I spent time (over about 6 months, at varying intervals) observing Susan with the children and colleagues, and provided her with specific feedback on the ways in which her practice was demonstrating links to the criteria. In a short time I no longer had to do this, as Susan became able to identify and articulate the links herself. We would catch up over morning tea and she would excitedly show me the various pieces of evidence she had collected during the interval between my visits and we would talk about why they linked to the criteria and how they could in some instances link to more than one. Susan enjoyed the verbal interaction and this prompted her to take more risks, and to believe that she was a good teacher, as evidenced in her daily practice. It then only took a discussion with reflective questions as prompts and she was able to articulate her practice. Her increasing confidence and ability to contribute to the centre's staff planning meetings and self-review made her a valuable member of the team, and her journey to being a fully registered teacher was no longer daunting.

Bethany

Bethany was a recently graduated teacher who was filled with enthusiasm and energy and just could not wait to get the whole registration process out of the way. She wanted to be a fully registered teacher in as little time as possible! When I met her she was already busy writing reflections and had done some of her own research on what was required and what to do. As with Susan, the aim of the first meeting was to begin to get to know each other another and establish ways of working together. Over time it was important for Bethany to grow in her ability to collaborate with her colleagues, many of whom had been in their roles for many years and appeared to resist new ideas from a new and passionate young teacher. It was our discussions about having the kind of meaningful conversations that would result in change that was the biggest focus of this mentoring journey.

At first Bethany just could not accept that others did not see the world of teaching with the same eyes as her. She and I had one-on-one discussions in order to explore ways of communicating with her colleagues. I encouraged her to make use of the open-to-learning framework, which involves

> learning about the quality of the thinking and information that we use when making judgments about what is happening, why and what to do about it. An open-to-learning conversation, therefore, is one in which this value is evident in how people think and talk. (Robinson, 2009, p.1)

This went part of the way towards being successful, and Bethany gained some valuable skills in ways of communicating. However, there remained a gap between her philosophy and the philosophies of key members of the teaching team.

Both Bethany and the team were becoming increasingly frustrated, so I arranged an evening meeting, with me as facilitator. All team members could contribute to the meeting agenda, and upon starting the meeting a group contract was established in order to ensure that everyone felt heard and safe to express their points of view. Some of the biggest challenges facing Bethany were in the ways that the daily routine was worked out and how the teacher-directed experiences were set for children. I asked her to write down what she found difficult and to bring along some readings from her recent studies to share with the team. We divided into groups and each group took part of the readings to read and then discuss with each other. The focus was not on the specific reading, but on finding a way to discuss what each person understood from the reading and then find ways this might have an impact on their own teaching.

It was the communication that was the important part of this meeting, and the coming together in a way that allowed for, and indeed encouraged, debate and discussion—consensus did not need to be the outcome. It took a while, but by the end of the session (2½ hours) there was a lot of laughter and much talking as teachers excitedly discussed their views and shared their perspectives. The teachers and Bethany found a way to communicate, and while it was by no means always easy, Bethany grew in her ability as a young teacher to work with a variety of different people.

Lee

Lee has English as a second language and a qualification from China. She completed a Graduate Diploma in Teaching in New Zealand and achieved the necessary levels in her English comprehension. For Lee, the challenge lay in putting aside her cultural differences and becoming familiar with the New Zealand way of teaching and being. At the same time, she was teaching at a centre that had a large number of children from her country and she often found herself being used as an interpreter. This was on occasion difficult for her on ethical grounds, because her deep understanding of her own culture came into conflict with what was currently expected of her in the New Zealand context.

One of the biggest challenges for her was addressing the expectation of parents that children would be taught to read and write in a formal way. This was not part of the curriculum where she worked, and Lee sometimes became quite upset at having to be the 'in between' person in these interactions. She wrote many deep and thoughtful reflections about this and wrestled with the situation during our meetings. As her mentor I wanted her to come to her own conclusions about what she believed to be the best outcomes for children. If I had just told her what to do it would not have become internalised in her own personal philosophy.

Overview

Ambrosetti, Knight and Dekkers (2014), in their article on mentoring in relation to pre-service teachers, make use of a framework in which the mentoring relationship is divided into three parts: relational, developmental and contextual. I believe this framework can support effective mentoring with provisionally registered teachers as well. The 'relational mentorship' I developed with Susan and the openness with which we were able to communicate is what enabled the mentoring journey to be one in which she, as a teacher, felt success. It was this success that encouraged her to complete that part of her teaching journey.

The importance of the relationship is discussed by Ambrosetti et al. (2014), who suggest that "The relationship can either be of a personal or professional nature and the connection made between the participants is often reliant on the willingness to engage in the mentoring relationship" (p. 225).

In Bethany's case the other two aspects—the context in which she taught and her development as a teacher—were significant in our mentoring relationship. I was able to create a place for her to make a shift in her teaching practice and reflect on different ways of being in the centre in which she was working. Instead of becoming negative in the face of views that differed from hers, Bethany was able to reflect on these and be more open and responsive, while maintaining her own philosophy and integrity as a teacher.

I believe that all of us have to know deep down that what we are doing is the best we can possibly do for children. This may look different for each teacher and yet still be acceptable. I gave Lee readings on how children learn to read and write (even though this had been an aspect of her training, it had not been covered in a way that Lee felt comfortable passing on to others). In this way I was, in view of the three mentoring aspects, growing the relationship Lee had with others and also aiding her in the context in which she was teaching in. It is imperative that cultural aspects be considered when developing and implementing mentoring programmes. Not doing so can lead to misunderstandings and conflict (Kochan, 2013).

Conclusion

I hope that the three stories above have provided some inspiration for teachers on their journey to full registration, and their mentors. Mentoring is not a 'one size fits all' process, and the roles of the mentor and mentee are not ones that can easily be defined. As Ambrosetti et al. suggest, "mentoring will always be difficult to define as it is a social event that involves interactions between individuals, those being mentors and mentees" (2014, p. 224).

It is crucial that the relationship is central to the process, because the trusted relationship allows open communication and meaningful feedback between the mentor and mentee, and this will in turn support growth. The mentor in this process also needs to be confident enough in their own teaching and mentoring ability to allow the individual nature of the teacher to lead the process. This is not to say that standards must not be met, but that the path to full registration can be as varied as the teachers.

References

Ambrosetti, A., Knight, B.A., & Dekkers, J. (2014). Maximizing the potential of mentoring: A framework for pre-service teacher education. *Central Queensland University, Mentoring & Tutoring: Partnership in Learning, 22*(3), 224–239. Retrieved from http://dx.doi.org/10.1080/13611267.2014.926662

Ingersoll, R.M., & Strong, M. (2011). The impact of induction and mentoring programs for beginning teachers: A critical review of the research. *Review of Educational Research, 81*(2), 201-233.

Kochan, F., (2013). Analyzing the relationships between culture and mentoring. *Mentoring & Tutoring: Partnership in Learning,* 21(4), 412–430. Retrieved from http://dx.doi.org/10.1080/13611267.2013.855862

NZTC. (2011). *Professional journeys: Guidelines for induction and mentoring and mentor teachers.* Retrieved from http://www.teacherscouncil.govt.nz/sites/default/files/Guidelines

Patterson, S., & Thornton, K. (2014). Challenging New Zealand mentor practice. *Journal of Educational Leadership, Policy and Practice, 29*(1), 41-55.

Robinson, V.M.J. (2009). *Open-to-learning conversations: Background paper.* Retrieved from http://www.educationalleaders.govt.nz/Problem-solving/Leadership-dilemmas/Open-to-learning-conversations

Zachary, L. (2011). *The mentor's guide: Facilitating effective learning relationships*, San Francisco, CA: Jossey-Bass.

Chapter 16

Mentoring through the appraisal cycle: How our team became intrinsically motivated professional learners

Vicky Wilson

Introduction

This chapter is about the professional learning that occurred in our teaching team when we engaged in a collaborative research project for our shared team appraisal goal. In our early childhood setting we are encouraged to work together by having a joint team appraisal goal. There are no specific guidelines for how our goal should be achieved, but there is an expectation that we will work together. As the team leader I assumed the role of mentor for this process.

After engaging in some professional learning about being 'open to learning' I felt I was better prepared to lead the learning in ways that could—and did—have better professional outcomes for all teachers. I developed an understanding that my first role as a mentor is to understand what learners want to know, or are motivated by knowing. This was a key part of understanding what opens others up to learning. The main idea is to use certain skills such as empowerment, collaboration and respectful relationships to motivate both the mentor (me) and the learners (the teachers and me) to be open to learning.

Developing an understanding of being open to learning has led to some changes in professional learning on both a personal and a team level. Using this approach as a mentor and leader, and using our individual and collective appraisal goals, teachers moved from 'having to' engage in professional learning to 'wanting to' engage. We developed a shared understanding of the value of individual and collective professional learning, both individually and as a team.

Being open to learning was a professional learning focus of the NZTC over a period of 18 months in order to assist professional leaders to carry out teacher appraisals based on the Registered Teacher Criteria (NZTC, 2010). Engaging in this series of seminars and professional learning groups led me to understand how to have conversations about learning for learning and gave me some strategies that I could use within our team. These are called 'open to learning conversations'. I pursued my interest in this and found other literature to support the development of these skills to enable me to become a more effective mentor (Dalton & Anderson, 2010; Hargreaves, 2004; Timperley, 2011).

The process

In our team we had varying levels of understanding about research. The four teachers came from very different backgrounds and had qualifications ranging from a 2-year diploma to a master's degree. After going through the inquiry process together for our annual appraisal goals, we had a positive outcome with new shared understanding and knowledge. Through developing a culture of being open to learning and change, we developed new practices that will have long-term positive impacts on the learning outcomes of children. What is even more exciting is that the disposition to be an inquiry learner will ideally remain with each teacher, and they will be intrinsically motivated and open to learning. Through becoming intrinsically motivated to be professional learners, there is more collaboration and ownership in terms of creating an environment that supports the best learning outcomes for all.

Our team appraisal goal was "to use the action research cycle to inform our practice", while my (team leader) appraisal goal was "to lead the process of research with the team". At first there was some resistance within the team to engaging with this topic. One reason for this may have derived from the perspective that this was a mandatory expectation as opposed to self-initiated change (Hargreaves, 2004). Given that our team was made up of diverse teachers with a range of experience, another may have been fear of the unknown.

To overcome these barriers, my first thoughts were related to how our inquiry might begin. Given what I had recently learnt, I knew the first step was to identify what knowledge others had. This started with collective dialogue, which was timetabled into our collective professional time set aside for appraisal work. We began by questioning what research is and then decided to investigate 'What is action research?' Action research can also be called inquiry learning and is a tool for systematic investigation that enables teachers to engage in research at a practical level. It promotes collaboration, reflection and communication as a means to solve problems and make decisions, with a focus on best practice (Rodd, 2006).

As the leader of the process, I thought the best way to begin would be to find readings that would help the team to understand what inquiry/action research was and how it was carried out. However, once we engaged in dialogue I realised that some team members did not know how to carry out a literature search. To accommodate this we used what could be termed tuakana–teina, or scaffolding, by joining a more experienced participant up with another who was less experienced. The pairs worked to gather the literature, read it and bring their findings back to the group. We continued to use this collaborative model of learning and gathering knowledge throughout the year. Hargreaves and Fullan (2012) identify this learning as collective responsibility and utilising peer coaching. I believe these two factors were instrumental in creating a change in our professional learning.

Through the process of working collaboratively we developed our shared understanding and became a "community of learners" (Wenger, 1998). We also developed our own "professional capital" (Hargreaves & Fullan, 2012). Professional capital is part of our social capital. Where social capital defines us as a whole group, professional capital defines us as a profession. This can be the "resources, assets and investments that make up, define and develop a profession and its practice" (Hargreaves & Fullan, 2012, p. 92). This is similar to the dispositions (attitudes, skills and knowledge) that we use to describe learning outcomes for children (and adults).

Further to this is the notion that the quality of the professional capital is relative to the quality of the peer interactions, mentoring and culture of our daily work place (Hargreaves & Fullan, 2012). This idea recognises the importance of valuing an inquiry model of learning, action research, and being open to learning. It also highlights how learning does not occur in isolation. Especially in early childhood, where we team teach, it follows that we are more likely to team learn and develop shared understanding over time. As Senge (1990) suggests, team learning does not occur simply because teams consist of talented individuals. Team learning is complex and involves three critical dimensions:

- to think insightfully about complex issues, which is the responsibility of each person
- to have innovative, co-ordinated action, developed through operational or relational trust
- the ability of a team to influence other teams (Senge, 1990, p. 219).

Using a collaborative approach based on an inquiry model, our team became what could be termed a "professional learning community" (Hargreaves & Fullan, 2012; Thornton & Wansbrough, 2012; Wenger, 1998). This term was developed in the 1990s and, put simply, refers to teachers inquiring together "to improve their practice in areas of importance to them" (Hargreaves & Fullan, 2012, p.127). In a professional learning community, the teachers would implement what they had learned to create change (Hargreaves & Fullan, 2012) through intentionally being collaborative (Hargreaves & Fullan, 2012; Thornton & Wansborough, 2012; Wenger, 1998).

An inquiry model of learning can also be identified as a habit of mind, or "the habit of needing to know and valuing deep learning" (Timperley, 2011, p. 40). Both professional learning communities and utilising an inquiry model of learning share similar key factors for success. Already highlighted is the importance of collaboration. Further characteristics of both professional learning communities and the inquiry model of learning are: being open to learning and change; communication; respectful and trusting relationships; and reflection.

Most cycles of inquiry appear to go one way, but I found that the process of professional inquiry learning was so intertwined it was difficult to identify one factor as more influential than another. Critical and challenging reflection does not exist without being open to learning or being in a trusting, respectful relationship, with strong communication. Similarly, being open to learning requires some form of critical reflection and open, respectful communication based on trust. Integral to all of this, as previously mentioned, is collaboration. With all of these indicators we can expect positive learning outcomes for all.

This is similar to the pedagogy of the early childhood education. *Te Whāriki* (Ministry of Education, 1996), the New Zealand early childhood curriculum, uses the metaphor of a woven mat to represent learning in early childhood. The same principle of interconnectedness can be applied to professional learning using the inquiry model. The key idea of being open to learning can also be found throughout the strands and goals in *Te Whāriki*. As a mentor in early childhood, I think it is important to remember what our curriculum and pedagogy are based on, and to make sure these are reflected in our professional learning. Among other things, we need to make sure we are empowering others, realise the importance of relationships, have strong communication skills, and see each learner holistically.

Open to learning and change

Being open to learning and change is necessary for ongoing professional learning. It can occur from one person's internal motivation, or as a dynamic collaborative process with input from both a mentor and a learner. For a joint process to be successful, the mentor needs to develop skills and strategies to elicit information from the learner and build on that knowledge base. Concurrently the learner is required to be open to change and learning. Without this dynamic there is a risk that information is shared but learning does not occur. As Timperley (2011) points out, once teachers realise the potential of inquiry learning, they move from *professional development* (which is often an external expectation) to *professional learning*, which is more likely to be a state of mind focused on being open to learning and change.

Through our appraisal process and mentoring skills we developed a culture of being open to learning and change. I believe this occurred through the intentional leadership of inspiring a team to understand not only the value of inquiry learning and being a professional learning community, but also the value of being open to change. Developing a culture of change, however, requires the ability of all teachers to have open-to-learning conversations (Dalton & Anderson, 2010; Thornton & Wansbrough, 2012). Open-to-learning conversations are similar to engaging in dialogue rather than discussion. Discussion, according to Senge (1990), is often characterised by the sharing of views, one of which must be the right one. Dialogue is more likely to have an empowering quality that is about creating collective new knowledge (Senge, 1990).

Communication

Through our dialogue and reflections, we were able to share what was important to each of us and build new understanding that allowed us to move to the next level of engagement with research. What made this step of the process more meaningful was the discovery of having conversations for learning which have the same characteristics as engaging in dialogue. The importance of this is best described by Dalton and Anderson:

> All educators need to know how to skilfully navigate important, learning focused conversations. If you can't have conversations, nothing changes. (Dalton & Anderson, 2010, p. 15)

What we found, through our professional dialogue, was that once we were all open to learning and change, then change naturally occurred without any effort. In terms of team learning, we were engaged in the process of "mastering the practices of dialogue" (Senge, 1990, p. 221).

Communication that is effective for learning and change needs to be based on trusting and respectful relationships. All literature advocating the need for collaboration, collective learning, being part of a professional learning community and change states quite clearly that relationships are a key factor in promoting learning (Hargreaves & Fullan, 2012; Rodd, 2006; Thornton & Wansborough, 2012; Timperley, 2011). Once again, the parallels between professional learners being open to learning and *Te Whāriki* (Ministry of Education, 1996) are highlighted. *Te Whāriki* clearly advocates for relationships to be at the foundation of all children's learning. Without respectful, trusting relationships, deep learning is less likely to occur.

Respectful and trusting relationships

As already discussed, relationships are critical for any learning to occur. As the mentor and leader of the appraisal process, part of my role was to facilitate an environment that was safe for learning (Rodd, 2006). This did not happen at the beginning of the process. We had already been working together for some years and our relationships had developed over that time. However, we did make time to discuss, engage in dialogue and research together. This led to a deeper understanding of our shared values and beliefs. The more we practised being respectfully critical, the more trust was developed and the relationship strengthened.

The practising of dialogue and discussion is integral to team learning (Senge, 1990). The benefits of having an open relationship based on trust and respect are that it creates a place where robust discussions can take place and where challenging and critical reflections are encouraged (Thornton & Cherrington, 2014). Although initially it was the role of the mentor/leader to develop a culture of respect and trust (Robertson & Notman, 2013), any one of the team can do this as part of a culture of shared leadership. To maintain an ethos of collaboration and team learning, each person within the team must take responsibility for maintaining trusting and respectful relationships.

Reflection

Critical reflection is a tool that has not always been used well in education. However, it has become adopted in education as a tool for challenging assumptions, beliefs, values and practices (Smyth, 1992). When used in conjunction with the action research/inquiry model, critical reflection has the potential to improve practice, challenge thinking, empower teachers and improve learning outcomes (Benade, 2014; Robertson & Notman, 2013; Rodd, 2006; Smyth, 1992). Mitchell and Cubey (2003, cited in Thornton, 2010) argue that children's learning is enhanced when teachers engage in critical reflection. In our journey we found that reflection was a factor in changing learning. Reflection as a team was highly valued, and teachers appreciated the opportunity to bounce ideas off each other, revisit what was being researched, and have conversations that challenged in a trusting and open environment.

The feedback from the team after the project finished indicated that at some point the teachers moved from the feeling of 'having to' engage to 'wanting to' engage. As one teacher stated, "We are more reflective and interested in collaborative research. We all see the value in research and how it can be positive for our learning community".

In terms of mentoring, I found the reflection process was again an area where teachers had different skills and experiences. This highlighted the importance of having strong communication skills and a trusting relationship so that we could begin the initial process of discovering what we individually knew. Then, through discussion, reflection and dialogue, we could begin to build shared understanding. Critical and challenging reflection is most beneficial when teams feel safe to share their thoughts and ideas and when they can explore new thinking and critique their practice without fear of ridicule or repercussions (Rodd, 2006; Thornton & Cherrington, 2014).

The transition to a professional learning community

As the mentor/leader of the process, I found it a challenge to achieve a balance between encouragement, setting tasks and being able to step back and allow the learning to happen. An example of this occurred right at the beginning of the process. I asked the team to research their ideas on action research without me and share their understanding of this. After this process I reflected on how they had collaborated without me and appeared to be highly engaged. I began to wonder if this deeper engagement occurred because I was not there leading the way. This may have led to the teachers feeling comfortable and empowered to get on with it. Wheatley (2002, cited in Dalton & Anderson, 2013) states:

> It is very difficult to give up our certainties—our positions, our beliefs, our explanations ... We will succeed in changing this world only if we can think and work together in new ways. (p. 8)

I noticed that the learning came to be initiated by the collaboration of the team. This event highlighted to me the importance as a leader of stepping back, leading from behind, and allowing the collective inquiry to occur. The more I reflect on this initial episode, the more I realise its significance. There is a clear difference between having expectations of professional development for teachers, and developing a professional learning community of teachers, who, both individually and collectively, have the desire to engage in self-initiated changes (Hargreaves, 2004; Hargreaves & Fullan, 2012; Thornton & Wansbrough, 2012; Timperley, 2011).

As part of being a professional learning community, the next strategy that enabled us to meet our learning goals was planning. The importance of planning has been identified through research as an integral part of supporting a professional learning community. Both Hargreaves and Fullan (2012) and Thornton and Wansbrough (2012) cite scheduled release time and planning as indicators of a professional learning community. I allocated time within our collective administration time without children where we collaboratively developed a research question; made plans for gathering data; engaged in reflections, dialogue and discussions; developed shared understanding; and, finally, evaluated the research outcomes to inform our next steps and practice. Change, whether professional or social, relies on opportunities to revisit information over time and to engage in discussions after the initial knowledge has been transmitted. This includes time to practise new skills, reflect, and once again dialogue collaboratively to develop deeper understandings of new knowledge. This is how deep learning and understanding occur (Senge, 1990; Timperley, 2011).

Conclusion

The value of the team being intrinsically motivated to achieve self-initiated changes was evident in feedback at the end of the process. One teacher stated:

> We gained some new knowledge about what research is and the process. We collaborated together, shared readings and had meaningful discussions. It brought ideas out in the open, fired up thinking and developed shared understandings. It was a team effort. Taking small steps made it meaningful and not overwhelming.

Another teacher commented, "I enjoyed the collaboration of the inquiry/research process and hearing different thoughts, it felt supported". This makes it clear to me that the process of breaking down the goal into small steps, planning to be intentional in our professional learning, and working together to develop shared understanding and be a community of professional learners is how team leaders can mentor others into being self-initiated learners.

During our final reflection, dialogue and feedback on the process, teachers identified how the process allowed them to feel they were empowered and had a leadership role. Shared leadership was a factor identified by Thornton and Wansbrough (2012) as a characteristic of a professional learning community. As we reflected, the following thought was shared: "It is about ... collaborative learning and sharing the workload, promoting leadership and empowering us all [through] promoting deeper learning". This was important to me as a leader and mentor, because it meant the teachers had become intrinsically motivated to use this knowledge, skills and attitude in their own personal appraisal goals. They had indeed moved from seeing their learning as an external expectation to us all being part of a professional learning community where showing an inquiring habit of mind was valued as much as trust and respect for each individual (Hargreaves & Fullan, 2012; Timperley, 2011).

References

Benade, L. (2014). Reflective practice and appraisal: A contradiction in terms. *Leading Lights: New Zealand Educational Administration & Leadership Society Newsletter, 4*, 11-13.

Dalton, J., & Anderson, D. (2010). *Learning talk: Build understandings.* Melbourne, VIC: Hands on Educational Consultancy.

Dalton, J., & Anderson, D. (2013). *Learning talk: Develop the art of inquiry.* Melbourne, VIC: Hands on Educational Consultancy.

Hargreaves, A. (2004). Inclusive and exclusive educational change: Emotional responses of teachers and implications for leadership. *School Leadership and Management: Formerly School Organisation, 24*(3), 287-309.

Hargreaves, A., & Fullan, M. (2012). *Professional capital: Transforming teaching in every school.* New York, NY: Teachers College Press.

Ministry of Education. (1996). *Te whāriki: He whāriki mātauranga mō ngā mokopuna o Aotearoa: Early childhood curriculum.* Wellington: Learning Media.

NZTC. (2010). *Registered teacher criteria handbook.* Wellington: Author.

Robertson, S., & Notman, R. (2013). Leadership factors that influence the development of teacher practice. *Journal of Educational Leadership, Policy and Practice, 28*(2), 57–68.

Rodd, J. (2006). *Leadership in early childhood* (3rd ed.). Crows Nest, NSW: Allen & Unwin.

Senge, P. (1990). *The fifth discipline: The art and practice of the learning organization.* New York, NY: Doubleday.

Smyth, J. (1992). Teachers' work and the politics of reflection. *American Educational Research Journal, 29,* 267–300.

Thornton, K. (2010). School leadership and student outcomes: The best evidence synthesis iteration: Relevance for early childhood education and implications for leadership practice. *Journal of Educational Leadership, Policy and Practice, 25*(1), 31–41.

Thornton, K., & Cherrington, S. (2014). Leadership in professional learning communities. *Australasian Journal of Early Childhood, 39*(3), 94–102.

Thornton, K., & Wansbrough, D. (2012). Professional learning communities in early childhood education. *Journal of Educational Leadership, Policy and Practice, 27*(2), 51–64.

Timperley, H. (2011). *Realizing the power of professional learning.* Berkshire, UK: Open University Press.

Wenger, E. (1998). *Communities of practice: Learning, meaning, and identity.* New York, NY: Cambridge University Press.

Chapter 17
Who's learning here: Mentee or mentor?
Janet Dixon and Emma Stanić

Introduction

This chapter describes a 2-year mentoring process involving a provisionally registered early childhood teacher being mentored towards full teacher registration by an independent mentor. It shows how the process facilitated the teacher's engagement in inquiry through the exploration, observation and analysis of her own practices. This led to changes in understanding, policies and practices, which enhanced the wellbeing and learning of the children in her centre and her own self-confidence as a teacher. This process helped the teacher to build her practice while increasingly demonstrating the Registered Teacher Criteria (NZTC, 2010).

The chapter draws on the mentee's experience and the mentor's strategies, voice and ideas, along with theoretical underpinnings. The content is organised under section headings taken from the characteristics of "High quality, intensive induction and mentoring" identified within the NZTC's *Guidelines for Induction and Mentoring and Mentor Teachers* (2011, p. 26). The headings are used to order the components of high-quality and educative mentoring within this chapter, and also to illustrate teacher learning and development that occurred as the mentee progressed from provisionally registered teacher to full registration. The resulting changes that occurred for the children in the centre are also embedded within this narrative.

Contextual setting

Emma started her registration while working with children under the age of 2. This was 2 years after completing a graduate early childhood education (ECE) diploma. She felt she needed strong guidance and support because of the 2-year break. An ECE teaching colleague who had been mentored by Janet recommended her as an independent mentor and spoke highly of her approach. After checking with her manager, Emma rang Janet and they set up a first meeting to ascertain whether they were suited and could work well together. Both wanted to work collaboratively, hence the importance of an initial meeting. As Bradbury (2010, p. 3) suggests, "personality compatibility" is one of "the conditions that support effective mentoring". They both signed a contract, which covered:

- dates of mentoring sessions (how long between sessions) and suitable times for professional discussions (e.g. fitting in with non-contact time)
- observations (e.g. time of day and particular things to be observed)
- an agenda, setting each time and the content (e.g. observations, discussion topics, challenges and questions)
- sharing resources (e.g. articles, books, professional development, specific places to look for information)
- goals included for the professional discussion held after Janet had observed Emma (the work to be covered before the next meeting), and Emma's overall goals for her registration.

This contract and the discussion of it formed the foundation of an open and trusting relationship between mentor and mentee. Their contract highlighted Emma (the mentee) as an active driver of this process as she made the decisions about the details in the contract on an ongoing basis (i.e. the next date, her goals, etc.). This idea of the provisionally registered teacher (PRT) determining the next steps and taking responsibility is listed in *Guidelines for Induction and Mentoring and Mentor Teachers* (2011, p. 26).

The mentoring process

ECE service structure

Emma: I was fortunate to work in an early childcare centre that was very supportive and valued the mentoring programme. Management gave me the freedom to choose a mentor who would extend and support me professionally and with whom we could set the dates for our sessions. To begin with it tended to be about every six weeks, but as I grew in confidence and professionally the time between our meetings lengthened. Also time was available away from the children to work on my mentoring programme, invite facilitators to take professional development, go to courses and visit other centres.

Links practice to a view of good teaching

Emma: Janet's first observation of my teaching practice set the precedent for one of my goals as a PRT. During our discussion I gave her a list of 17 goals. She suggested that I be more specific and emphasised the importance of keeping goals aligned with children's wellbeing and learning, which would increase through professional understanding. Also we talked about what Janet had observed. She commented about a particular child who became very upset when I left the room. She asked me what I thought the child was feeling and commented that it was good that this child was crying because this showed that she was clearly attached to me. We discussed it further and because of this I chose to focus one goal on attachment theory. I wanted to gain a deeper understanding of this topic and learn how to foster healthy attachments and further support children's learning and wellbeing in an ECE setting. This focus reflected the following Registered Teacher Criteria: 1, 2, 6, 7, 9, 11, 12 (NZTC, 2010).

Janet: I wanted to provoke Emma's thinking in a positive way to reframe the belief being used with this child (Feiman-Nemser, 2012). I asked for some background of this child's learning and what strategies were being used as a team to support the child who was crying. It then became obvious that the teaching team were not consistent with their approach towards supporting this child to deal with separation if she became too 'clingy'. Emma was feeling at a loss as to how to reassure the child so that she felt secure. I suggested that Emma might read The

Art of Being Fully Present with Young Children (Da Ros & Wong, 1996)—it had been written some years back but the theory was still current. I suggested that Emma should try to be more 'fully present' with this child when she was with her. My previous experience with this article had taught me that a stronger relationship could be formed as a result of implementing the ideas in this reading. I discussed long-term strategies to support both Emma and the children and drew up some ideas/questions for her to take back to her colleagues. I also suggested that Emma visit other under-two settings within the Wellington region to gain some further insight and understanding. Emma's personal needs were met in that she had something positive and concrete to work on with this child and she began thinking about her long-term goal learning about attachment theory. This is consistent with Bradbury (2010), who stated that "Educative mentoring seeks to meet the immediate needs of novice teachers while also focusing on long-term goals for professional development" (p. 1049).

Builds confidence by developing pedagogical expertise

Emma: Janet encouraged me to seek relevant professional development, which broadened my understanding of pedagogical theories and led me to examine current centre philosophy, policies and practices, as well as the Licensing Criteria (Ministry of Education, 2008) and Te Whāriki (Ministry of Education, 1996). Also in line with my goals I took advantage of some of the opportunities available in the broader ECE environment; e.g. started utilising the Brainwave Trust's website and presentations, finding out more about infants and toddlers (planning etc.), visiting other under two centres especially inquiring about transitions, self-review (Ministry of Education, 2006), and Pikler-based approaches (Weber, 2010).

Janet: I found that specific professional development to build on Emma's knowledge really motivated and supported her to create change in her practices with children. Feiman-Nemser (2012) terms this as "individualized professional development" and suggests that it is "crucial for beginning teachers" (p. 13).

Has a developmental (but not linear) view of learning to teach

Emma: Early on in my mentoring programme I wondered about my personal teaching philosophy and realised that it did not now sit comfortably with some of my colleagues nor was it consistent with the existing centre philosophy. The more I read articles and books lent to me by Janet about attachment theory, the more I wanted to make changes within my working environment with infants and toddlers. My aim was to change our collective practice so that it supported attachment theory principles by creating a secure learning environment by each child having a primary care giver. Janet was aware of my philosophical dilemma and was able to make suggestions, which I took back to my team. However, altering our teaching practice was slow and it was not until there was a change of staff that we were able to introduce primary care giving and strengthen attachment practices with children. I realised that in order to change centre culture or introduce new ideas I had to work very hard through discussion about theory and research on best practice and communication with all teachers so that collectively we all owned the changes we were making and were consistent as a team.

Janet: I talked with Emma about why the teaching team were resisting change. However, as they worked more on primary care-giving strategies the children themselves became more settled and engaged. I noted in one of my observations that "there seemed to be less crying and children were busy and involved" (Dixon, field notes, August 2011).

Develops teacher autonomy and agency

Emma: Initially I felt that I had not achieved much between one mentoring session and the next. I often doubted myself professionally, especially because I still had a head full of best practice and found it challenging to integrate into my work. I also realised that I needed to know more about infants and toddlers. Janet asked me to write down all the things that I had done well either professionally or personally. I found this process to be very therapeutic and a useful reflective tool as it gave me some perspective about where I was professionally and supported me to have a more positive outlook. At the end of each meeting we would write down a list of what I would work on before the next session. On the next visit Janet would observe me with that list in mind, then she would document what she saw. I found this process very useful [because] it gave me the freedom to try out different ways of being and use critical thinking. If my teaching strategy was working that was great but if it was not, why? As I developed deeper reflective practice through conversations with Janet and learned to use critical thinking as a tool and not view it as something negative, my perception began to change and I felt I started to gain deeper insights and understanding of children. I was then able to apply these skills and thinking to other scenarios. Also a question she asked is, "Who are your allies in this centre?" Through discussion I found that one of the other teachers had similar views to me about many of the issues I was thinking about. I did have an ally! Another strategy Janet used was to suggest that I ask a question of other teachers at a meeting. Ostensibly this question came from Janet; however, it came as a result of our discussion and was designed to provoke thinking and discussion for everyone. This was successful because there was no emotional ownership from me when I gave the provocation; e.g. I would say, "Janet was wondering why we do things this way?"

Janet: I believe that many things may change over time but that they don't always change in the way that we think they will. Also that it is important to take a positive approach with ourselves and notice what we have done rather than a deficit model of what we have not done. I found that I needed to balance delivery of difficult feedback with support and challenges for Emma so she would grow professionally. For example, when Emma talked about a "clingy child", I asked. "What do you think was happening for this child at this time?" The questions Janet asked Emma (and her colleagues) promoted "teacher development by cultivating a disposition of inquiry" and also fostered "disciplined talk about problems of practice" (Feiman-Nemser 2001, p. 14).

Builds knowledge by using their teaching as a site of inquiry

Emma: Our primary care-giving system and supporting children's attachment with their caregivers evolved over the next 2 years. Firstly I worked on the settling-in process. Children settling in to the infant room previously were given two settling visits and I felt that this was not enough time for teachers to initiate and build a trusting bond with the child and parent/ whānau. I instigated a self-review using Ngā

Arohaehae Whai Hua / Self Review Guidelines for Early Childhood Education (Ministry of Education, 2006) on our settling procedure and read articles from Janet on separation anxiety for both the infant and the parent and how a caregiver could support this. My next step was to visit an early childhood centre which had recently reviewed their settling policy and they kindly shared their process with me. I compiled information from my visit and the articles and then we discussed this with our team. We came up with a new policy and practices that we thought supported children's wellbeing. Once these were in place we found children settled easily when they became more familiar with the environment and staff.

Janet: One of the things that I noticed on early visits was the number of interruptions from adults who for various reasons came in and out of the children's environment requiring teacher's attention when they were settling a child. I suggested a discussion about this at a staff meeting. The next time I observed in the centre I noticed that "it is now so much more about the children rather than the day to day jobs and adults!" (Dixon, field notes, July 2012). Maybe a quieter environment supported children to settle as well.

Provides planned—and takes advantage of—incidental learning opportunities

Emma: I found the notes Janet wrote very useful to refer to and then I would voice any thoughts or reflections I had about my practice. We used Janet's observations as provocations, which proved essential to stimulate discussions. We followed the interests of children or teachers to be curious about what was happening.

Janet: We planned an agenda together at the beginning of a session, which included looking at the finishing time of this session, reflecting on the observation just done, goals from the last session, questions and any issues or particular challenges as well making new goals to work on and a next session date. I would write up these meeting notes, link them to the Registered Teacher Criteria (NZTC, 2010) and email them to Emma. Through these observations Emma became more aware of teaching strategies that she was already using; e.g. she was scaffolding a child to demonstrate pro-social behaviour, which I suggested was social coaching (Webster-Stratton, 2012). As a result of their conversation around this observation, Emma became more conscious of using social coaching as a tool consistently and purposefully. During these professional discussions we would sometimes do a role play trying out possible ways to say things, question and problem solve about how to create change. We swapped roles and words until Emma was satisfied she had a useful script to follow. Discussions about Emma's emotional wellbeing and personal life were important from time to time. This is another example of the balance that Feiman-Nemser (2012) talks about. We talked over her self-care and ability to juggle work and family commitments. Emma remembers a discussion we had about giving herself at least one compassionate moment each day—she learned to be compassionate with herself.

Engages in serious professional conversations

A prerequisite for all their conversations was trust and respect. The following discussions would not have happened if that had not been established. Professional discussions included Janet asking about theories underpinning practice (e.g. what was happening for the child? Why was she clingy? What do you know about attachment theory? How does the young child's brain develop? How do young children and babies learn? What do you know about leadership?).

For example, during one meeting Janet gave Emma feedback regarding continuity of care and settling children. They discussed the effect on the child's brain of being constantly unhappy and how it is really vital to work on wellbeing and belonging (Ministry of Education, 1996) first with new children before they can be interested in learning and engage with what is in the centre. McCaleb and Wallis (2005) state that "Children under stress are children whose brains are not able to focus on learning" (p. 6). Although Janet asked these questions of Emma, they would then be "co-thinkers" and "co-planners" (Bradbury, 2010) in gathering some thoughts together and creating strategies:

> **Emma:** I attended a leadership course, and as a result of our discussions we talked about how to create robust management systems, delegation, not taking on too much work, and knowing simply when to say NO! Janet's support helped me to regulate my working systems. In a later observation she noticed that I was doing less problem solving

for adults and therefore I was more available to be fully present with the children. Over this time I gathered articles of relevance to share with all teachers and whānau to deepen and inform the conversations about respecting young children and babies. We now have a teacher's resource reference book.

Bases feedback and assessment on evidence

Emma: Evidence was challenging to gather and file and make sure that I had covered each registered teacher criteri[on] adequately. However, professional colleagues, whānau and children proved to be valuable sources of evidence for me. When tangible evidence was not available, Janet supported me to consider creative and lateral thinking ways to accumulate suitable material as evidence for each registered teacher criteri[on]. Intangible evidence was seen in children's behaviour. Examples of this include welcoming guests and showing them around; or an older child giving toys to a younger child (unasked); and dating and documenting evidence, even if it was a little note or a short reflection show[ing] what I was doing and how I was thinking. Sometimes asking about "How are things done differently from what I did before and why did I change?" would provoke reflection and information. I was surprised as I compiled my portfolio how it highlighted my progression, understanding and changes of thinking of each [registered teacher criterion] over time.

Janet: Positive feedback and celebration of successes as I noticed them was very important. This happened when I observed these changes or they arose from talking with Emma. For example, my notes from one meeting included the following message to Emma:

Teachers are now following through with a child to feed them, change them and then settle them for a sleep. This provides continuity of care which is more secure for under twos. Great following through on your part, changes like this do not happen easily but are based on the needs and ages of the under twos and follows best practice as shown in research. The changes in primary care giving and follow through by teachers and routines are amazing. This is a huge positive step forward! WELL DONE EMMA! This is a major achievement! (Dixon, field notes, December 2012).

One of the ways for me to assess my strategies as a mentor was to ask Emma for feedback so I would keep that in mind when I worked with other PRTs in the future. We have both concluded that over time it is important to keep an open mind when gathering evidence in relation to the Registered Teacher Criteria as we have more professional conversations, and be more creative and lateral.

Conclusion

Not only have we both been learners in this educative mentoring programme, but our dispositions to learn were also strengthened. The chapter has highlighted that our respectful, open and trusting relationship was pivotal for the success of this mentoring journey. The relationship facilitated collaboration, co-thinking, critical inquiry and lateral and creative problem solving. It also gave Emma the confidence to inform, support, provoke and challenge—not only herself, but also other teachers and parents. A positive context was created through centre support and clear shared expectations, as stated and agreed to in our contract. This enabled Emma to become an active driver of the process by setting her own goals, dates and agenda for the next mentoring session. The strategy of relating theory to everyday practice motivated us to reflect, question and document to create informed practice that focused on optimal outcomes for all children.

References

Bradbury, L.U. (2010). Educative mentoring: Promoting reform-based science teaching through mentoring relationships. *Science Education, 94*(6), 1049–1071.

Da Ros, D.A., & Wong, A. (1996). The art of being fully present with young children. *Early Childhood Education Journal, 23*(4), 215–216.

Feiman-Nemser, S. (2001). Helping novices learn to teach. *Journal of Teacher Education, 52*(1), 1–17.

Feiman-Nemser, S. (2012). Beyond solo teaching. *Educational Leadership, 69*(8), 10–16.

McCaleb, M., & Mikare-Wallis, N. (2005). Relationship-reshaping: Teacher consistency and implications for brain development. *The First Years: Ngā Tau Tuatahi: New Zealand Journal of Infant and Toddler Education, 7*(2), 1–10.

Ministry of Education. (1996). *Te whāriki: He whāriki mātauranga mō ngā mokopuna o Aotearoa: Early childhood curriculum.* Wellington: Learning Media.

Ministry of Education. (2006). *Ngā arohaaehae whai hua: Self review guidelines for early childhood education.* Wellington: Learning Media.

Ministry of Education. (2008). *Licensing criteria for early childhood education and care centres 2008 and early childhood education curriculum framework.* Wellington: Learning Media.

NZTC. (2010). *Registered teacher criteria handbook.* Wellington: Author.

NZTC. (2011). *Professional learning journeys: Guidelines for induction and mentoring and mentor teachers.* Wellington: Author.

Weber, S. (2010). The work of Emmi Pikler: *Research Bulletin, 15*(2), 19–26. Retrieved from http://waldorflibrary.org/images/stpries/articles/RB15_2weber.pdf

Webster-Stratton, C. (2012). *Incredible teachers: Nurturing children's social, emotional and academic competence.* Seattle, WA: Incredible Years, Inc.

PART 5: MENTORING COMPLEXITIES AND FUTURE DIRECTIONS

Chapter 18

Politics and practices: Critical provocations for meaningful early mentoring

Andrew Gibbons, Sandy Farquhar and Marek Tesar

Introduction

The mentoring relationship is a complex and, at its best, an enduring connection between two or more teachers at different points in their professional development. The complexity of this relationship influences not only the mentoring but all of the professional practices that are the subject of the mentoring relationship. In this chapter we explore the influence of teacher education on both mentor and mentee. Our interest focuses on a set of connected experiences: how and what student teachers learn as they progress towards their qualification; the ways in which that knowledge about teaching and about being a professional are shared in a teaching team; and how the mentoring then affects the centre community. We draw on the research of scholars whose work provides a critical gaze on both the experience of being a professional and the experience of learning to be a professional.

> Teacher education is not just about the acquisition of knowledge, skills, and dispositions (qualifications) or just about doing as other teachers do (socialization) but starts from the formation and transformation of

> the person, and it is only from there that questions about knowledge, skills and dispositions, about values and traditions, about competence and evidence come in, so to speak. (Biesta, 2014, p. 135)

Key themes in this chapter include transformation, emancipation and the economic nature of educational policy. We suggest that this economic nature drives the purpose of education, where teachers must be employable, flexible and contribute to the economy. Teachers must also engage in ongoing learning, underpinned by a research culture in which universities play a strong role, and so that a nation is regarded as a leading player in the global knowledge economy. The purpose of the chapter is to open up critical thinking and talking about the economic relationships and experiences of teacher education and mentoring for both the teacher educator and the early childhood teacher. We particularly wish to encourage conversations about mentoring that recognise the often-challenging working conditions in which early childhood teachers find themselves.

Challenging teacher education

> Developing sophisticated and deep knowledge about teaching takes several years to develop ... and this is dependent both on high challenging and high quality initial teacher education, as well as continuing mentoring and professional development within schools. (Cameron, 2003, p. 25)

Does initial teacher education *make* excellent teachers who engage in continuous mentoring relationships as critical professionals? The answer to this question requires some idea of the purpose of teacher education, and the purpose of mentoring. We would like to look at teacher education first. Debates about teacher education provide evidence of the spectrum of teacher knowledge and skills that are valued (Biesta, 2014). This section engages with two views on teacher education and mentoring in early childhood education. We think these views provide a challenge to our assumptions about the very nature and purpose of education and have very important implications for the ways in which mentoring relationships are experienced by all involved. We are concerned with the impact of the teaching profession on the experience of mentoring: the rise of 'professions' has been influential in the ways that societies organise themselves and how they distribute, share or make available resources and knowledge.

Dall'Alba (2009) claims that entering into a profession necessarily involves some kind of preparation, which for a professional life tends to focus too much on knowledge and skills for effective teaching practice, and not enough on the "transformation of self that is integral to achieving such practice" (p. 34). In other words, the quality of teachers' practice is made possible by the ongoing journey of who we are. Dall'Alba summarises: "if we are fully to understand knowing within various forms of professional practice, we must understand the being of those who know" (2009, p. 35). The very purpose of studying to be a teacher "can then be conceptualised in terms of developing ways of being the professionals in question, rather than simply as a source of knowledge and skills acquisition" (2009, p. 35).

The experience of learning to be a member of the teaching profession requires a kind of being that can make sense of the incredible complexity of what knowledge and skills are and how they affect teachers. For instance, how do teachers make sense of the possibility that at all times they are both teacher and learner, which is part of a bigger question: what does it mean to be a teacher? There is, fortunately, no right answer to these questions. However, if we do not ask them, we may find ourselves engaged in mentoring that loses a sense of who we are and focuses on some kind of 'normal' teacher identity that we should all strive for.

To support the importance of these questions, Dall'Alba (2009) acknowledges Martin Heidegger, a German philosopher, and his view that the purpose of education is "transformation of the self" (p. 39), through which the constraints and expectations of the world, and a world of possibilities, are revealed. In this view, teacher education is an experience through which student teachers explore the experience of transformation as they learn about their profession. It offers both resistance and possibilities beyond thinking of education as a process in which a teacher and/or a curriculum determine and then transmit knowledge and skills to a learner, who in return uses them in appropriate and agreed contexts. This argument suggests that teacher educators concern themselves with more than efficient and linear evidence-based models of teacher education.

For Biesta (2014), education necessarily involves the transmission of valued skills and knowledge. His concern is that this purpose of education overwhelms the transformative aspects of education through which we learn about and act upon who we are, who we have been, and who we might be. He regards education as necessarily a risky experience, as education without risk is not properly education at all. Therefore, his work promotes a resistance to the idea that we can, or should, talk about education in ways that suggest that more evidence is required in order to meet predetermined outcomes. Biesta's point is to break out of docility and to get teachers *asking questions of education*, because asking questions of education *is* education. Here again, asking questions is critically valued for its ongoing influence on the experience of mentoring—long after graduation from initial teacher education.

Biesta's (2014) critique of evidence-based and competency-based training suggests that these ideas ignore teachers' values and beliefs in favour of predetermined and measureable standards, where evidence becomes more valuable than professional judgement. The idea of the competent teacher has led, as Biesta argues, to "ridiculously long checklists" (p. 120) of skills, against which the teacher must be measured as competent or otherwise. A focus on competence neglects what is not known, entrenching a teacher in available answers rather than new ideas and relationships. Biesta regards the reliance on evidence and competence in teacher education as an anxiety and "a lack of courage to think and act differently and independently" (p. 123). He argues that "if we wish to say anything *educational* about teacher education, … we need to engage with a way of speaking and thinking that is more properly educational" (Biesta, 2014, p. 127). Teacher education should then provide for the study of educational qualification (what we need to know and why), socialisation (who we need to know it for and why), and how it affects who teachers are. These concerns are very relevant to the nature, purpose and experience of mentoring in education.

Considering the mentoring relationship

Mentoring, according to Galvez-Hjornevik (1986) and Little (1990), emerged as an educational necessity during the 1980s. The considerable interest in mentoring was accompanied by little agreement on what mentoring might actually mean and just what its purpose is.

Galvez-Hjornevik (1986) claims that other professions were far clearer on the meaning of mentoring, while Little (1990) argues that the purpose of mentoring was driven by political agendas regarding the role of schools in the education of children, and in particular, the role of teachers in those schools, as opposed to the role of systems such as standardised testing.

The four decades of research on mentoring indicates that there is not enough evidence of what counts as good mentoring, and that such evidence is required because mentors seek guidelines on mentoring (Langdon, 2011; Moore, 2014). Moore (2014) notes that attempts to create unambiguous guidelines for mentors have not been realised, and that consistent national guidelines are required for "clear and specific direction" (p. 143) despite the 2011 introduction of national guidelines (NZTC, 2011). Moore (2014) also argues that while there is a lot of interest in talking about mentoring in order to make the mentoring experience better, there does not appear to be the same interest in defining mentoring. We argue that there should not be a universal or agreed definition—which is not the same as neglecting to ask questions such as 'What is mentoring', 'What does it mean to be a mentor, or to be in a mentoring relationship', 'What is the purpose of mentoring' and, indeed, 'Why is mentoring important?' The concerns about mentoring are thus closely associated with the concerns about education and teacher education discussed earlier; that is, the purposes of both mentoring and education are being overlooked in favour of systematic answers and better management. Fullan and Mascall (2000) note that an interest in the mentoring relationship is

> probably fueled by a concern on the part of a number of educational systems that they are facing a shortage of qualified teachers, and that new practices are needed to attract and retain educators. (p. 23)

The OECD's (2012) 'toolbox' for early childhood educational policy notes that mentoring is widely regarded as one of a number of mechanisms to ensure that teachers remain up to date with "scientifically based methods and curriculum subject knowledge" (p. 148). Teacher registration in New Zealand requires beginning teachers to participate in a 2-year induction and mentoring programme. At the end of this period the mentor-teacher must be satisfied that the beginning teacher meets the NZTC Registered Teacher Criteria. In this sense, the purpose of mentoring is to extend the quality assurance process beyond teacher education to provisional registration.

However, a stronger sense/purpose of mentoring, we suggest, is one more typically associated with the importance of a relationship between a senior teacher and a beginning teacher on account of the importance of early career experiences for the development and retention of teachers, the career pathways of experienced teachers, and the meeting of educational targets (see, for instance, Cameron, 2003; Galvez-Hjornevik, 1986; Little, 1990; Moore, 2014; Murray, 2006; Timperley, 2013). A focus on sharing rather than instructing or measuring the beginning teacher is justified as a constructivist approach to learning (NZTC, 2011), yet with recognition that the expert teacher shares their knowledge with the beginning teacher and, by extension, with the profession (Moore, 2014).

Cameron (2003) argues that new teachers

> learn better when those in their work environments provide leadership and support based on evidence of student learning, and when working conditions sustain ongoing reflection and professional development. (p. 41)

These conditions are intimately associated with professional knowledge, and in particular with the dynamic nature of knowledge of teaching and learning. Not only is mentoring essential to making sense of changing knowledge; it contributes to that knowledge. Cameron (2003) argues that teachers

> should have ongoing opportunities to develop their own knowledge and capabilities, based on their own scholarship and that of others. Such research should also inform programmes of teacher education. (p. 41)

The transition from teacher education to provisionally registered teacher requires that teacher educators and mentor teachers work together to understand the nature and purpose of mentoring (NZTC, 2011; Podmore, 2011). This brings together a unique inter-relationship between a new teacher, a senior teacher-mentor and the academy, and is arguably a challenge given ongoing concerns about a lack of certainty on what makes a good mentoring programme (Fullan & Mascall, 2000).

In working together and developing relationships between teachers in schools and teachers in the academy, we may attenuate the concerns we have addressed above with regard to the development of checklist evidence and guidance for mentoring and induction programmes (Langdon, 2011; NZTC, 2011; Podmore, 2011).

Mentoring as a sharing of knowledge

Biesta (2014) offers three inter-related purposes for education, which have a lot to offer mentoring: learning about how to do things, learning about the world in which we live, and learning about ourselves. The mentoring relationship is one where the individuals involved are engaged in active participation in communicating about a shared world. The ends of our communication about our teaching cannot be known or predetermined, because talk about teaching is complex. Talking about this complexity is part of what Biesta (2014) regards as the nature of education. A worrying excess of standards and measurements minimises teaching as an act of judgement and, Biesta (2014) observes, developmental thinking dominates in education. The teacher is required to fashion their identity in particular ways, and matters concerning the actual task of being a teacher are seen as simply inevitable outcomes of the mentored product.

The terms 'critical' and 'reflective' are often associated with this approach to knowledge of the learning and teaching environment. Critical reflection is not an individualised experience. It is, rather, necessarily a collective experience (MacNaughton, 2003), in which teachers have an awareness of the 'others' in their early childhood centre. Using a model such as Bronfenbrenner's ecological systems theory allows us to focus on how the experience of teacher education affects the teaching team relationships and on the teaching and learning in early childhood education. A bidirectional model explores how the children, the curriculum, the parents and community, the teaching team dynamics, as well as national policies and the general status of early childhood education and the teaching profession all affect mentoring relationships. The relationships are complex and shifting, and they are an essential part of the talk between teachers that characterises a mentoring relationship.

The nature of early childhood knowledge has a significant impact on the mentoring relationship. This includes new and old knowledge about child development and wellbeing, as well as curriculum knowledge and theories of learning. The connection between early childhood educational philosophies and curricula is an important characteristic of mentoring in early childhood education teaching teams. Scholars of professional development have asserted the importance of early childhood professional relationships in terms of requiring their own theoretical and practical grounding, arguing that effective models for working together in teaching teams should come from within the profession, grounded in the contexts and aspirations of teachers, and critically attuned to the complexities of centre communities (Dalli, Miller, & Urban, 2012; Urban, 2008). In line with this, the effectiveness of teaching teams is understood to be affected by responsive communities of support (NZTC, 2011).

This focus requires understanding that early childhood teachers regard the nature of knowledge in quite specific ways, and that this varies from centre to centre, and community to community. At the same time, there are some common 'strands', which are woven through influential academic theories and government policies. The interplay between intimate micro-knowledge and overarching macro-knowledge is evident in very different assumptions that teachers are confronted with regarding their professional roles in early childhood education. For instance, the ways in which they assess children's learning, or the ways in which they provide for transitions to primary school, reveal many contending beliefs about what teachers need to know.

So, it is possible to think about the ways in which different perspectives on the nature of a caregiver–child attachment, the merits of digital literacy, or the role of the adult in scaffolding children's knowledge affect not just the way in which we teach, but the way in which we engage in the mentoring relationship. Through sharing critical discussions and different narratives of experience, teachers enrich their teaching teams and the centre community (Dalli, Miller, & Urban, 2012). This approach to mentoring builds on the continuous development of skills, in collaboration, that are regarded as important for early childhood centre communities (Mitchell, 2006). It aligns with current research and scholarship in the field of teachers' work that calls for a rich, deep understanding of how teachers work together and share ideas about themselves and their teaching practices (see, for instance, Dalli, Miller, & Urban, 2012; Madrid, Baldwin, & Frye, 2013; Osgood, 2012).

So what might happen differently in the experience of teacher education that might have an impact on mentoring in early childhood centres? Dall'Alba (2009, p. 40) argues that "as trainee teachers learn to teach, their positive and negative experiences of being students in classrooms over several years can serve as a resource for their teaching." In what ways, then, can student teachers be prepared for the sharing of knowledge when "innovative ideas brought by trainee teachers sometimes challenge pre-conceptions about teaching among experienced teachers, or vice versa"? (Dall'Alba, 2009, p. 41.)

Teacher education is—and should be—a time in which student teachers observe and practise making judgements through asking critical questions about educational content, purposes and relationships (Biesta, 2014), rather than through showing evidence of how their practice aligns with a set of standards. Hagger and McIntyre (cited in Langdon, 2011) write that "expertise is better understood by asking questions about the appropriateness, significance, and achievement of a teacher's goals, and the attainment and learning of students" (p. 254). This kind of experience in making judgements about educational knowledge allows an entirely different kind of mentoring relationship from one that perpetuates the ticking off of standards. The lesson for mentoring seems to be that attempts to systematise and narrow down the purpose of mentoring teachers in their professional knowledge/practice is un-educational.

Conclusion

This chapter has discussed the impact of teacher education on mentoring relationships between teachers in early childhood communities. It argues that it is valuable for a teaching team to openly and critically discuss how their experiences of teacher education have affected how they feel about sharing their ideas about their own practice and the practice of others. Exploring these matters promotes a deeper understanding of the impact of teaching team dynamics on practice, and on the richness of the curriculum that is constructed within each early childhood centre. This includes the ways in which teaching networks affect learning networks, or the ways in which the openness of teachers to each other's knowledge influences their openness to the knowledge of the children with whom they work.

Opportunities to discuss, for instance, tensions between theory and practice 're-place' and value the teacher in teaching (Duncan, 2004; Osgood, 2012), and promote a critical awareness of how such debates and perspectives affect the centre's teaching and learning. Teacher education provides a space and time to focus on the ways in which teachers make complex judgements; this calls for "*judgment-based* professional formation, or *judgment-focused* professional formation", where the experiences of practice lend themselves to the experience of judging "what is educationally desirable in relation to a particular constellation of educational purposes" (Biesta, 2014, p. 136). The study of teaching involves teachers who are exemplars in practising educational judgements—in asking questions about educational purposes. Yet the purpose of mentoring seems to be increasingly guided by calls for more evidence, standards and checklists.

This chapter elevates some important questions in teacher education and in mentoring relationships: why and who are we engaged with in a mentoring relationship, and how is mentoring shaping the way we share knowledge about education? These questions lead to further questions that require significant confidence in a very political and sensitive area. If working conditions that lead to teacher attrition are indeed one of the reasons that mentoring is regarded as an important activity (more mentoring to keep teachers), should mentoring involve critical questions regarding the poor working conditions that early childhood teachers experience? So, through mentoring relationships, teachers engage in knowing about teaching, about what counts as good teaching practice, and about what the purposes of teaching are or could be. Mentoring—in the sense of sharing in the world—opens teaching up to a shared and careful inquiry that is supportive, reciprocal, and dynamic.

References

Biesta, G.J.J. (2014). *The beautiful risk of education*. London, UK: Paradigm.

Cameron, M. (2003). *Teacher status project: Stage 1 research: Identifying teacher status, its impact and recent teacher status initiatives*. Wellington: Ministry of Education.

Dall'Alba, G. (2009). Learning professional ways of being: Ambiguities of becoming. *Educational Philosophy and Theory, 41*(1), 34-45.

Dalli, C., Miller, L., & Urban, M. (2012). Early childhood grows up: Towards a critical ecology of the profession. In L. Miller, C. Dalli, & M. Urban (Eds), *Early childhood grows up: Towards a critical ecology of the profession* (pp. 3-19). London, UK: Springer.

Duncan, J. (2004). Misplacing the teacher?: New Zealand early childhood teachers and early childhood education policy reforms, 1984-96. *Contemporary Issues in Early Childhood, 5*(2), 160-177. Retrieved from http://dx.doi.org/10.2304/ciec.2004.5.2.4

Fullan, M., & Mascall, B. (2000). *Human resource issues in education: A literature review*. Wellington: Ministry of Education.

Galvez-Hjornevik, C. (1986). Mentoring among teachers: A review of the literature. *Journal of Teacher Education, 37*(1), 6-11.

Langdon, F. (2011). Shifting perception and practice: New Zealand beginning teacher induction and mentoring as a pathway to expertise. *Professional Development in Education, 37*(2), 241-258.

Little, J.W. (1990). The mentor phenomenon and the social organization of teaching. *Review of Research in Education. 16*, 297-351.

Madrid, S., Baldwin, N., & Frye, E. (2013). 'Professional feeling': One early childhood educator's emotional discomfort as a teacher and learner. *Journal of Early Childhood Research, 11*(3), 274-291.

MacNaughton, G. (2003). *Shaping early childhood*. Maidenhead, UK: McGraw-Hill.

Mitchell, L. (2006). Collaborative relationships in practice: Possibilities and challenges. *Childrenz Issues, 10*(2), 27-31.

Moore, W. (2014). *Experiences of first-time mentor teachers in New Zealand primary schools*. Unpublished doctoral thesis, Auckland University of Technology.

Murray, S. (2006). *Beginning teachers 2000-2004: Characteristics, employment trends, qualifications and subjects*. Wellington: Ministry of Education.

NZTC. (2011). *Professional learning journeys: Guidelines for induction and mentoring and mentor teachers.* Retrieved from http://www.educationcouncil.org.nz/content/guidelines-induction-and-mentoring-and-mentor-teachers-2011-englishpdf

OECD (Organisation for Economic Co-operation and Development). (2012). *Starting strong III: A quality toolbox for early childhood education and care.* OECD Publishing. Retrieved from http://dx.doi.org/10.1787/9789264123564-en

Osgood, J. (2012). *Narratives from the nursery: Negotiating professional identities in early childhood.* Abingdon, UK: Routledge.

Podmore, V., with Wells, C. (2011). *Induction and mentoring pilot programme: Early childhood education.* Wellington: NZTC.

Timperley, H. (2013). *Learning to practice: A paper for discussion.* Wellington: Ministry of Education.

Urban, M. (2008). Dealing with uncertainty: Challenges and possibilities for the early childhood profession. *European Early Childhood Education Research Journal, 16*(2), 135–152.

Chapter 19
Strengthening practice with teachers of priority learners: Mentoring and managing change

Claire McLachlan, Chrissy Lepper, Karen Mackay, Alison Arrow and Tara McLaughlin

Introduction

This chapter examines issues associated with professional learning and development (PLD) and the mentoring of early childhood teachers in relation to early literacy. It presents the theoretical underpinnings and practical implementation of the mentoring offered to early childhood teachers in the Strengthening Early Learning Opportunities (SELO) programme offered by Massey University. This programme is funded by the Ministry of Education and is based on earlier studies of literacy we conducted. The SELO programme is targeted at communities populated by 'priority learners' and now has further funding for a family literacy programme, designed to support families to help their children develop literacy at home.

The chapter discusses how to support change in teachers' beliefs and literacy practices using mentoring (McLachlan & Arrow, 2014; McLachlan, Arrow, & Watson, 2013). We provide background for the approaches to mentoring that are adopted in work with teachers in our

SELO-funded communities, and explain the importance of skilled, knowledgeable facilitators and specific feedback strategies to teachers.

Professional learning and early literacy

Our collective interest in PLD and the mentoring of teachers in relation to early literacy is longstanding. The SELO programme is based on a solid foundation of research into professional learning, including some of our own. Underpinning our efforts is research that indicates the kind of PLD that meets the eight characteristics of effective PLD identified by Mitchell and Cubey (2003) and is critical for supporting teachers' knowledge and enhancing pedagogy in ways that result in children's learning. The eight characteristics identified by Mitchell and Cubey (2003, p. xi) are as follows.

1. The professional development incorporates participants' own aspirations, skills, knowledge and understanding into the learning context.
2. The professional development provides theoretical and content knowledge and information about alternative practices.
3. Participants are involved in investigating pedagogy within their own early childhood settings.
4. Participants analyse data from their own settings. Revelation of discrepant data is a mechanism to invoke revised understanding.
5. Critical reflection enabling participants to investigate and challenge assumptions and extend their thinking is a core aspect.
6. Professional development supports educational practice that is inclusive of diverse children, families and whānau.
7. The professional development helps participants to change educational practice, beliefs, understanding and/or attitudes.
8. The professional development helps participants to gain awareness of their own thinking, actions, and influence.

Mitchell and Cubey (2003) also identified the key structural features of effective PLD: it is of the right intensity and duration to change teacher practice; researchers and advisors are involved in planning and supporting PLD; and a whole-centre/all-staff approach is considered. Other critical contextual factors include understanding the unique needs and strengths of the participants; the knowledge, skill, and expertise of the facilitators; and the organisation of the service.

Further underpinning the programme is research indicating that children who have alphabetic knowledge, phonological awareness (awareness of sounds in words) and a large vocabulary at school entry are well positioned to transition from emergent to conventional literacy (National Early Literacy Panel, 2009; Whitehurst & Lonigan, 1998). Although most children develop the requisite knowledge and skills as part of early education in Aotearoa New Zealand, about 25 percent of children do not (Nicholson, 2005) and struggle with beginning reading. One key challenge is how teachers can foster emergent literacy within a holistic early childhood curriculum such as *Te Whāriki* (Ministry of Education, 1996).

Two of our doctoral studies (Arrow, 2007; McLachlan-Smith, 1996) showed that teacher knowledge was a factor in why teachers display restricted repertoires of literacy behaviours with children, which implicated in-service PLD and mentoring. Claire's doctoral research examined the literacy policy and practices in New Zealand kindergartens prior to the advent of *Te Whāriki* and found that teachers espoused eclectic views of literacy acquisition, and that children's access to and mediation (Vygotsky, 1978) of literacy in the curriculum depended on the beliefs and practices of the teachers. Alison's doctoral research (Arrow, 2007) examined the earliest acquisition of reading and spelling through an intervention study carried out individually with kindergarten children. She found that as children transition from emergent literacy to conventional literacy, children with good alphabetic knowledge have multiple pathways to reading and spelling. Alison's research supports the importance of incorporating literacy teaching into the early childhood curriculum through increased recognition of phonological awareness, alphabetic knowledge and vocabulary development. The implications for initial teacher education, PLD and mentoring were highlighted in both studies.

More recent research (McLachlan, Carvalho, de Lautour, & Kumar, 2006) found that although most teachers reported providing literacy-rich environments, fewer than 50 percent used *Te Whāriki* to support literacy in their centres, and teachers showed a diverse understanding of literacy and how to promote it. It was also not clear that teachers were able to identify and support children who could be considered 'at risk' of reading failure, many of whom would be classed by the Ministry of Education as 'priority learners'. These findings were reinforced in studies by Hedges (2003) and Foote, Smith and Ellis (2004). A small study by Hedges (2003) found that teachers may find themselves in a dilemma when deciding whether or not it is their role to foster literacy and numeracy. Foote, Smith and Ellis (2004) found that although the teachers in their study provided rich literacy experiences, when it came to teaching literacy they used formal skills-based instruction without necessarily being able to articulate why. These studies provide further evidence that teachers may require PLD and mentoring in order to promote literacy effectively with young children.

Given the existing research, there is a clear need to mentor teachers so that they can gain the understanding and skills needed to support children's literacy learning. Our model of PLD includes processes to gain strong content knowledge and apply it in context, with the support of a mentor.

Given the complexities, it is essential that mentors have a strong knowledge and understanding of both ECE and early literacy. Teachers and mentors can jointly consider areas of literacy learning that affect all children and areas that may require special consideration or differentiated support. For example, *Te Whāriki* defines the domain of literacy as "oral, visual and written". This definition includes the following parameters:

- observing and listening
- playing with language and literacy practices
- using literacy for purpose
- critically questioning and transforming language.

Thus defined, literacy—and in particular oral literacy—is explained from the perspective of both psycholinguistics and social practice critical literacies. In *Kei Tua o te Pae*, literacy is defined as "A lens focused on the symbol systems and technologies for making meaning" (Ministry of Education, 2009, p. 5), which builds on children's literacy competencies derived from home and community and provides them with opportunities to learn about the literacies of ECE and school settings in meaningful ways. The SELO programme is based on sociocultural theorising, in which children learn within the context of their early childhood centre, home and community (Vygotsky, 1978). The role of teachers is to help children move from home concepts to schooled concepts of literacy, building on their pre-existing fund of knowledge.

Oral language and literacy are of particular significance for second-language learners in New Zealand, particularly in low-decile communities. New Zealand research that examined learning in more than one language (Mitchell, Wylie, & Carr, 2008) found that effective early childhood education can have strong benefits for the language and literacy of children. The authors argued that "good quality ECE enabled ethnic minority children, children with English as an Additional Language (EAL), and children from low-income families to develop at a faster rate" (p. 34). In the Centre of Innovation (COI) project conducted with the A'oga Fa'a Samoa in Auckland (Podmore, 2006), children's heritage language was shown to be important for literacy and successful transition to school. There is evidence that the PLD and mentoring in the COI process assisted teachers to understand language immersion and bilingual education. In the COI project at Roskill South Kindergarten (Ramsey, Breen, Sturm, Lee, & Carr, 2006), in a community where English is an additional language, innovative use of ICT provided a common language for families and children to communicate with each other and with teachers, providing a transitional or bridging language. Ramsey et al. identify the importance of teachers having access to ICT resources, and having time to reflect on existing practices with a mentor.

The Ministry of Education has funded some research into literacy and at-risk children in New Zealand. Phillips, McNaughton and McDonald (2002) found that many early childhood teachers had limited knowledge of literacy, and that PLD and mentoring improved literacy outcomes for children. Timperley and Robinson (2001) similarly found that teachers' perceptions of children's literacy on starting school changed if they had their assumptions about literacy challenged through PLD and mentoring by skilled facilitators. Research by Tagoilelagi-Leota, McNaughton, MacDonald and Ferry (2005) with Samoan and Tongan children (from 6 months before school entry until a year after school entry) indicated that children who were incipient bilinguals at the beginning of the study were supported to gain literacy skills in both their home language and in English when they experienced ECE that focused on the quality of literacy teaching. In this study, teachers had had explicit mentoring in second-language and literacy acquisition.

An Education Review Office (ERO) (2011) report on literacy highlights the current issues in literacy teaching in early childhood education in New Zealand. In the review of 353 early childhood services in the fourth quarter of 2009 it was found that although most services provided an appropriate range of literacy opportunities, concerns were identified regarding inappropriate use of commercial phonics packages with 2-year-olds, large formal mat times that did not cater to the diverse abilities of children, and formal teacher-led 'transition to school' programmes that limited children's engagement with meaningful literacy activities. ERO recommended to the Ministry of Education that written guidelines for literacy teaching in early childhood be developed, which could be used by PLD facilitators and mentors for strengthening literacy pedagogies.

As this brief review shows, early childhood teachers play a significant role supporting early literacy, but this may require explicit mentoring to strengthen their practice. In the following section we outline two studies that have underpinned our approaches to PLD and mentoring in SELO-funded centres. Note that both studies were supported by the Massey University Research Fund and had full ethics approval because of the involvement of children under the age of 7. We used written parental consent and verbal assent from children whenever we collected data from children.

Our interest, stemming from both our own research and the extant literature, stems from two aims: we aim to improve literacy learning opportunities for children, and we aim to understand the key mechanisms of change in PLD models. As noted by Sheridan, Edwards, Marvin and Knoche (2009), there is a need to examine:

> the processes underlying professional development—that is, areas in need of investigation that can inform the early childhood education field in terms of how professional development efforts exert their influence and produce meaningful change in practitioners' skills, behaviors, and dispositions—as compared to a meta-analysis or comprehensive review of the research literature on the effects of specific forms that professional development takes (p. 2).

The studies highlighted issues to be considered for mentoring in SELO 3.

Mentoring literacy pedagogies in low-decile ECE settings

The first study examined whether PLD for teachers would increase children's literacy skills in low-decile early childhood settings and lead to changes in teachers' beliefs and practices over an 8-week intervention period. A quasi-experimental QUAL-QUAN mixed-method design (Punch, 2009) was used, in which teachers' and children's knowledge was pre- and post-tested in five child-care centres. Teachers' (32) beliefs and phonemic awareness were tested using a questionnaire. A range of literacy measures, which tested alphabet knowledge, phonemic awareness, ability to recognise and write their own name, and the British Picture Vocabulary Test, were used with children aged 3 to 5 years (103 in total).

PLD was offered to teachers at the beginning of the study in four centres; the fifth centre was a control. The PLD consisted of a 2-hour workshop held at the end of the working day in each centre and based on the National Early Literacy Panel (2009) findings on the predictors of early literacy. We asked that all teachers attend the workshop: some of our previous research with teachers indicated the importance of having the whole team attend (McLachlan & Grey, 2013). In addition, we asked teachers to keep logbooks of how they promoted literacy during the 8-week intervention period.

Some changes in children's skills were found, along with some differences in teachers' beliefs and practices (see McLachlan & Arrow, 2014 for a full report). In the intervention centres we also talked to teachers about literacy whenever we were in the centre collecting data with children, and thus provided one-on-one mentoring on specific literacy pedagogies and issues. The results suggest that workshop PLD models with teachers have some effects on children's literacy outcomes and teachers' practices, but we hypothesised that PLD needs to involve more purposive mentoring. This was confirmed in discussions with teachers, who highlighted the importance of our spontaneous conversations in the centre to their changes in literacy pedagogy.

Study 2 was designed to test recent research which suggests that greater changes in teachers' beliefs and practices and children's literacy outcomes can be achieved through in-service PLD that involves intensive collaboration, coaching and mentoring (Cunningham, Zibulsky, & Callahan, 2009; Justice, Kaderavek, Fan, Sofka, & Hunt, 2009; Phillips, Clancy-Menchetti, & Lonigan, 2008; Piasta & Wagner, 2010). In this study we worked with two kindergartens for three school terms and collected data from children at three intervals (pre-, mid- and post-). We used many of the same measures as in study 1, but we used pre- and post-interviews with teachers and regular meetings at which we shared the data we had collected with children, along with the teachers' assessment and other documentation data, and we brainstormed ways in which literacy could be enhanced for children.

Our role in this study was explicitly as mentors, in which we provided resources and discussed and critiqued current practices. The mentoring process involved in-depth discussion of collected assessment data, teachers' artefacts and observations. Karen Mackay, as PLD facilitator for SELO, provided regular mentoring, and our collective discussions with teachers—as well as spontaneous discussions when we were in the kindergartens—were highlighted as key factors in teachers feeling supported as they tried out new literacy pedagogies.

In many ways we used a simple 'PDSA' planning cycle—plan, do, study, act—as part of mentoring in these kindergartens. The study or reflection component of the planning was particularly important in provoking thought and changes to pedagogies. For instance, we surveyed parents about children's home literacy practices and found that approximately half of families in one kindergarten had access to either an iPad or an iPhone which was new information for teachers about literacy in homes. This led to discussions about how to better support family literacy practices. As a consequence, teachers sent home newsletters with suggestions for free links to children's books and literacy activities and arranged two large shared lunches with families, where pictures of children engaged with literacy in the kindergarten were shared, along with preliminary analyses of children's literacy results. Parents commented that the first session was so useful that they wanted another one at the end of the year, where they wanted to discuss what it meant for their children's literacy potential at school. This notion of running a family literacy programme alongside PLD and mentoring was suggested by our findings and has underpinned our family literacy programme for the SELO contract.

Study 2 revealed greater changes in children's literacy when teachers had more information about children's specific literacy knowledge and skills, and tailored literacy opportunities in the curriculum to enhance learning (see McLachlan & Arrow, 2014; McLachlan, Arrow & Watson, 2013), which also influenced our approaches to mentoring in the SELO 3 programme. Findings suggested that, in order to make a change in their practice, teachers need a mix of content knowledge, specific assessment of children's literacy, reflection on existing practice, and mentoring to try out new approaches.

Principles underpinning SELO programmes

The delivery of the SELO programme is based on insights from our previous research, adult learning research, and considerable experience providing PLD and mentoring to the early childhood sector. The Institute of Education has a long history of providing effective PLD that is research informed. The Centre for Educational Development (CED) has held Ministry of Education early childhood contracts since their inception in the late 1990s. A number of the other contracts delivered by CED have involved ECE services such as the Teachers Council Induction and Mentoring workshops, the Ministry of Education Teen Parent Unit development contract and subsequent TPU individual contracts, and the Montessori organisation Journey to Excellence pilot programme working to develop schools and services. Currently Massey also holds the Ministry of Education contract for Māori-medium PRT and mentor development in kura kaupapa Māori in the North and Central North regions. Mentoring is a key approach used in CED programmes.

Our intention with the SELO programme was to focus on engagement, activity, fun and friendly approaches to learning, based on the considerable body of research on adult learning and diverse learners. Malcolm Knowles (1984), a pioneer in the study of adult learning, observed that adults learn best when:

- they understand *why* something is important to know or do
- they have the freedom to learn in their own way

- the learning is experiential
- the time is right for them to learn
- the process is positive and encouraging.

Knowles (p. 12) also made five assumptions about the characteristics of adult teaching and learning (andragogy) that are different from other assumptions about teaching (pedagogy): self-concept, experience, readiness, orientation, and motivation to learn. The mentoring programme involves teachers in inquiry processes to examine their literacy practices through supportive mentoring relationships and developing professional development plans based on an understanding of adult learning and development (Chu, 2012). CED mentors are aware that the learner needs a safe place to learn with other adults who respect their experience and ability to identify their own needs, interests and values. Specific processes involved in mentoring in this context involve goal setting, having a plan, observation, *in situ* support, debrief meetings, reflection and feedback. Time is obviously constrained by the Ministry budget, but the mentoring process is explicitly focused on increasing knowledge, changing practice and improving outcomes for children.

Accordingly, the programme offered is grounded in the experiences of teachers, families and whānau, and the relevance of knowledge, skills and strategies for promoting literacy are tied explicitly to learning in the centre and home environments. Because adults like to make choices about how they learn, a range of ways of learning are included, such as video clips, group work and hands-on practice in the workshops with teachers and parents, along with discussion forums/blogs, suggestions for activities, and examples of good ideas shared at workshops. Participants in workshops are encouraged to document their observations of children engaging with literacy as a way of sharing good practice and helpful ideas and documenting children's literacy outcomes. The workshops are interactive, involve lots of discussion and sharing of experiences and ideas, and use a range of visual, kinaesthetic and practical stimuli.

Previous CED work has shown that when teachers start to look for evidence of outcomes for children through their personal inquiry, they realise that their assessment and planning process is not robust enough to make these outcomes visible. Therefore it is essential that this is the focus of one of the threads of an inquiry. Teachers are mentored—at an individual and group level—through the implementation of frameworks such as the dimensions of strength, repertoires of practice and *Te Whatu Pōkeka* to strengthen their documentation and the continuity of children's learning. The ways in which mentoring is enacted differ according to the centre, its stage of development and the pressing agendas for change, and this is a collaborative process. As Chrissy Lepper was quoted as saying recently in *Hawke's Bay Today* ("Dannevirke: When Uni and Kindy Combine Knowledge", 2015):

> My role is about the strategic direction for the local association and its two kindergartens. Things don't need fixing but rather teachers feel like someone is now helping mentor them. The agenda is collaborative and I haven't come here with my own. Instead it's a continual process for teachers in all sectors who are constantly being asked to review their practices based on research and practical wisdom. I'm pumped about what I'll be doing here as I listen and help teachers to navigate through their own learning.

Conclusion

As this brief chapter has indicated, we have a growing body of evidence about how to mentor practising teachers to be more effective in supporting literacy acquisition in priority learners, who are those most likely to be struggling with beginning reading. Our experiences show that through strong mentoring, teachers are encouraged and empowered to learn new ideas from research, to try out new strategies for teaching and learning, and to use effective documentation techniques for assessing and planning for children's successful progression through the continuum of literacy development. In terms of mechanisms for change, a skilled and knowledgeable mentor is central to strengthening literacy pedagogies.

References

Arrow, A.W. (2007). *Potential precursors to the development of phonological awareness in preschool children.* Unpublished doctoral thesis, University of Auckland.

Chu, M. (2012). *Developing mentoring and coaching relationships in early childhood education: A reflective approach.* Upper Saddle River, NJ: Pearson.

Cunningham, A.E., Zibulsky, J., & Callahan, M.D. (2009). Starting small: Building preschool teacher knowledge that supports early literacy development. *Reading and Writing, 22,* 487–510.

Dannevirke: When uni and kindy combine knowledge. (2015, 5 March). *Hawkes Bay Today.* Retrieved from http://www.nzherald.co.nz/hawkes-bay-today/news/article.cfm?c_id=1503462&objectid=11412347

Education Review Office. (2011). *Literacy teaching and learning in early childhood.* Wellington: Author.

Foote, L., Smith, J., & Ellis, F. (2004). The impact of teachers' beliefs on the literacy experiences of young children: A New Zealand perspective. *Early Years: Journal of International Research and Development, 24*(2), 135–148.

Hedges, H. (2003). A response to criticism and challenge: Early literacy and numeracy in Aotearoa/New Zealand. *New Zealand Research in Early Childhood Education, 6,* 13–22.

Justice, L.M., Kaderavek, J.N., Fan, X., Sofka, A., & Hunt, A. (2009). Accelerating preschoolers' early literacy development through classroom-based teacher-child storybook reading and explicit print referencing. *Language, Speech and Hearing Services in Schools, 40,* 67–85.

Knowles, M. (1984). *Andragogy in action.* San Francisco, CA: Jossey-Bass.

McLachlan, C., & Arrow, A. (2014). Promoting alphabet knowledge and phonological awareness in low socioeconomic child care settings: A quasi experimental study in five New Zealand centers. *Reading and Writing, 27,* 819–839.

McLachlan, C., & Arrow, A. (2014). Promoting the predictors of literacy in early childhood settings: An analysis in low SES settings. In C. McLachlan & A. Arrow (Eds), *Literacy in the early years: Reflections on international research and practice.* New York, NY: Springer.

McLachlan, C.J., Arrow, A.W., & Watson, J. (2013). Partnership in promoting literacy: An exploration of two studies in low decile early childhood settings in New Zealand. In J. Duncan & L. Conner (Eds), *Research partnerships within early years education: Relational expertise and knowledge in action* (pp. 71–91). New York, NY: Palgrave Macmillan.

McLachlan, C., Carvalho, L., de Lautour, N., & Kumar, K. (2006). Literacy in early childhood settings in New Zealand: An examination of teachers' beliefs and practices. *Australian Journal of Early Childhood, 31*(2), 31–41.

McLachlan, C., & Grey, A. (2013). "It's just part of being a professional": Looking back and looking forward at self-review. *Early Education, 53*, 23–26.

McLachlan-Smith, C.J. (1996). *Emergent literacy in New Zealand kindergartens: An examination of policy and practices.* Unpublished doctoral thesis, Massey University.

Ministry of Education. (1996). *Te whāriki: He whāriki mātauranga mō ngā mokopuna o Aotearoa: Early childhood curriculum.* Wellington: Learning Media

Ministry of Education. (2009). *Kei tua o te pae: Assessment for learning: Early childhood exemplars.* Retrieved from: http://www.educate.ece.govt.nz/learning/curriculumAndLearning/ Assessmentforlearning/KeiTuaotePae/Book16.aspx

Mitchell, L. & Cubey, P.(2003). *Professional development in early childhood settings: Best evidence synthesis iteration (BES).* Retrieved from: http://www.educationcounts.govt.nz/publications/series/ 2515/5955

Mitchell, L., Wylie, C., & Carr, M. (2008). *Outcomes of early childhood education: Literature review: Report to the Ministry of Education.* Wellington: New Zealand Council for Educational Research.

National Early Literacy Panel. (2009). *Developing early literacy: Report of the National Early Literacy Panel.* Washington, DC: National Institute for Literacy.

Nicholson, T. (2005). *At the cutting edge: The importance of phonemic awareness in learning to read and spell.* Wellington: NZCER Press.

Piasta, S.B., & Wagner, R.K. (2010). Developing early literacy skills: A meta-analysis of alphabet learning and instruction. *Reading Research Quarterly, 45*(1), 8–38.

Phillips, B.M., Clancy-Menchetti, J., & Lonigan, C. (2008). Successful phonological awareness instruction with preschool children. *Topics in Early Childhood Special Education, 28*(1), 3–17.

Phillips, G., McNaughton, S., & MacDonald, S. (2002). *Picking up the pace: Effective literacy interventions for accelerated progress over the transition into decile 1 schools.* Auckland: The Child Literacy Foundation and Woolf Fisher Research Centre.

Podmore, V.N., with Wendt Samu, T., & the A'oga Fa'a Samoa o le tama ma lona fa'asinomaga. (2006). *Nurturing positive identity in children: Final research report from the A'oga Fa'a Samoa an Early Childhood Centre of Innovation*. Wellington: Ministry of Education. Retrieved from http://www.educationcounts.govt.nz/publications/ece/22551/22555

Punch, K. (2009). *Introduction to research methods in education*. Los Angeles, CA: Sage.

Ramsey, K., Breen, J., Sturm, J., Lee, W., & Carr, M. (2006). *Strengthening learning and teaching using ICT: Roskill South Kindergarten final research report*. Wellington: Ministry of Education. Retrieved from http://www.educationcounts.govt.nz/publications/ece/22551/22563

Sheridan, S.M., Edwards, C.P., Marvin, C.A, & Knoche, L.L. (2009). Professional development in early childhood programs: Process issues and research needs. *Early Education and Development, 20*(3), 377–401.

Tagoilelagi-Leota, F., McNaughton, S., MacDonald, S., & Ferry, S. (2005). Bilingual and biliteracy development over the transition to school. *International Journal of Bilingual Education and Bilingualism, 8*(5), 455–479.

Timperley, H., & Robinson, V. (2001). Achieving school improvement through challenging and changing teachers' schema. *Journal of Educational Change, 22*, 281–300.

Vygotsky, L.S. (1978). *Mind in society: The development of higher psychological processes*. Edited by M. Cole, V. John-Steiner, S. Scribner, & E. Souberman. Cambridge, MA: Harvard University Press.

Whitehurst, G.J., & Lonigan, C.J. (1998). Child development and emergent literacy. *Child Development, 69*, 848–872.

Chapter 20
Mentoring Australian early childhood teachers: Belonging, being and becoming
Andrea Nolan and Anne-Marie Morrissey

Introduction

Mentoring has been identified as playing an important role in supporting early childhood teachers new to the profession, with evidence that effective mentoring reduces teacher attrition (Smith & Ingersoll, 2004; Waterman & He, 2011) and enhances outcomes for children (Davis & Higdon, 2008; Nolan, Morrissey, & Dumenden, 2012). Much has been written on the benefits of mentoring for both mentees and mentors in terms of supporting and extending professional learning (Jacobs, 2001; Risko, Vukelich, Roskos, & Carpenter, 2002), improving reflective practice (Elliott, 2004; LoCasale-Crouch, Davis, Wiens, & Pianta, 2012) and affecting educational systems (Cummins, 2004; Howes, James, & Ritchie, 2003; Ramey & Ramey, 2006). It is now recognised that teachers can be more effective when they are supported by colleagues in a community of practice, moving mentoring from an expert–novice positioning to a more reciprocal and collaborative relationship (Wenger, McDermott, & Snyder, 2002).

In Victoria, Australia, the first state-wide mentoring programme for early childhood teachers was launched in 2011 by the then Department of Education and Early Childhood Development (DEECD). We, the authors of this chapter, were the director and deputy director of the programme. This chapter highlights the findings of this 4-year initiative in relation to outcomes for the participants. It includes case studies of professional growth, and participants' voices relating their experiences of the mentoring relationship and their professional development. In the 4 years of the programme, 316 early childhood teachers participated—236 as mentees and 80 as mentors. Ethical approval to research the mentoring programme was obtained from both supporting universities, Victoria University and Deakin University.

Birth of a state-wide mentoring programme for early childhood teachers

The State-wide Mentoring Program for Early Childhood Teachers (SWMP) (2011–2014) addressed a workforce need for new or professionally isolated early childhood teachers to access support from experienced colleagues. As well as geographical isolation, many teachers in Victoria also experience professional isolation as the only degree-qualified teacher employed in their service. The SWMP also provided an opportunity for experienced early childhood teachers to take on leadership roles as mentors, sharing their knowledge within the profession. Funding for the mentoring programme was announced in the 2010–11 Victorian Budget, and partners Victoria University and Deakin University won the tender to design, deliver and evaluate the programme.

This programme received significant government funding and was the first of its kind across the state of Victoria. It aimed to increase teachers' access to mentoring and had the goals of:

- ensuring early childhood teachers new to the profession had access to regular, targeted support from experienced colleagues
- developing a shared understanding between mentees and mentors as to the nature of good mentoring practice
- providing opportunities for experienced early childhood teachers to develop their mentoring skills and their own practice through the mentoring relationship

- encouraging teacher mentees to reflect on their pedagogical practice
- developing skills and confidence in new and professionally isolated early childhood teachers to deal with the challenges they experienced
- supporting the development of networks and leadership within the early childhood field.

The programme was designed to create strong mentor–mentee relationships and networks through a programme of mentor training, 'shared learning days' (workshops where all the participants came together), mentor visits to mentee workplaces, resources (in the form of templates, journal articles, tip sheets) and online communities. The mentees were supported and advised in developing and implementing a Reflective Practice Project, where they chose an aspect of their everyday practice as a focus for the mentoring relationship (over a 10-month period). Reflective Practice Project topics generally clustered around programme planning, professionalism/leadership, assessment for learning and documentation, collaborative and inclusive practice, connecting with families, working as a team, and managing children's behaviour.

What we learnt about mentoring

We have learnt a lot about mentors, mentees and mentoring from conducting the SWMP. Our findings are organised in relation to the national Early Years Learning Framework (EYLF): *belonging* (connecting to the profession/community), *being* (recognising knowledge, skills and capabilities), and *becoming* (professional growth).

Belonging

Mentors saw their participation in the SWMP as a way to demonstrate their commitment to their profession. Initially, mentors were excited by the networking opportunities offered by the programme. Mentees also saw participation as a way to feel part of a community, as typified in the following mentee comment:

> I think this experience has helped me to feel less alone. Although I work in a long daycare setting I still have a sense that I am somewhat on my own, as far as running the Kindergarten program. I believe this program has given me the confidence to get through this year, my first as a graduate teacher, and I am really appreciative of the support

and guidance from my mentor, but also from the other mentees. Everybody has such wonderful knowledge to share and it has been a great experience being able to share this knowledge and network with people who are in the same position and are feeling similar.

Being

Mentors' initial feelings about being part of the mentoring programme included a mix of excitement, nervousness and professional pride. Initially some mentors questioned their own capacity to mentor, noting that they felt "overwhelmed", and "concerned" that perhaps they did not have the knowledge and skills to be an effective mentor. Over time, mentors gained confidence, experiencing achievement, enjoyment, professional growth, and a sense of being valued and seen as knowledgeable.

By the end of the programme mentors were, on the whole, feeling more confident and empowered, realising they had plenty to offer from their years of experience. There was also a real sense of reward and pride for mentors in what their individual mentees had achieved. They were generally pleased with mentees' progress and enjoyed the journey of their mentees. By being valued, mentors felt they could offer something back to the profession and had a sense of being part of a community of learners.

Self-confidence was highly valued by mentees as an outcome of the programme. This related to being stronger personally and professionally. This newfound sense of confidence enabled some mentees to recognise themselves as capable and empowered: "I have learnt that I am capable of so much more than I thought. If I am confident I can do it". These sentiments were strongly associated with being self-reliant and resilient. Being self-reliant also calls on the ability to try new things and be open to different ways of working: "During this programme I have learnt that I am quite resilient and an advocate for the children I teach and their families". Another mentee commented, "I now have the power of my convictions and will question others' practice in future and be true to myself and my early childhood philosophy".

Becoming

There were many benefits reported by participants related to their own professional growth, including mentees benefiting from mentors' wisdom and experience, and mentors having opportunities to develop leadership, mentoring and communication skills. In improving their mentoring skills, mentors acted as sounding boards for their mentees rather than offering them a quick-fix solution. This approach was deliberately fostered in the mentor training as a way to empower mentees rather than make them reliant on their mentors. As one mentor explained:

> I have had to learn not to problem solve or try and fix the situation but to listen and reflect with the mentees. I have tried to be an active listener and use 'coaching' techniques in preference to directly giving advice.

Mentors also mentioned how mentoring had caused them to reflect more critically on their own practice: "I have discovered that by being asked how or why you do things within your teaching practice, allows you to critically reflect on your practice and to clearly articulate the reasons why". For some mentors there was a sense that they had learnt as much, or more, than their mentees:

> It was a very affirming experience—I was able to see how much knowledge, experience and wisdom I have accumulated as a professional. It was a real joy to support another teacher—to see them grow was inspiring.

For one mentor, participation led to new professional opportunities for leadership:

> Participating in this program has increased my confidence as a professional, so much so, that I applied for more of a leadership role within another organisation and got the position! It has also crystallised for me the direction I want to take within the profession (more in leadership), when before the program I felt I was just drifting.

For the mentees, the Reflective Practice Project provided a focus on one aspect of their practice and enabled them to implement changes, with guidance and support from their mentor. The programme reports document the changes in practice. Mentees reported improved outcomes for children and families as a result of implementing their projects with effective mentoring support. Two excerpts from mentees are included here to illustrate the learning:

> The children now are undertaking a program based on their interests, not what I thought they liked, so for them the days are more enjoyable. For the parents they can now appreciate my planning and see what their children are undertaking and achieving easier which has sparked more conversations.
>
> I am now encouraging the children to be more autonomous over their choices and encouraging self-reliance rather than giving them the answer. [I now allow] them to problem solve in challenging moments as I have learnt so much from this myself.

Mentees were assisted to think more deeply about their practice through these projects, highlighting what they already knew and could do, along with ideas for improvements. This led to mentees describing how they developed a stronger sense of professional identity. As one mentee confirmed:

> I have learnt that through reflecting on my practice, not only personally but professionally as well, I have developed a greater awareness of my own professional identity and my self-confidence is showing signs of increasing.

Important considerations for effective mentoring

There are a number of factors that affect the effectiveness of mentoring programmes. In this section we outline the factors that had the greatest impact on our programme.

Building collaborative reciprocal relationships

The mentee–mentor relationship is crucial to the success of the mentoring process (Elliott, 2004). The choice of mentors is important, because they need to be willing to share their experience and knowledge, nurture the mentees, and allow them to develop and gain confidence through their own achievements. What we quickly discovered was that feelings of isolation can become crippling to innovation. Prior to participating in the SWMP, many mentees lacked confidence in their own practice and questioned if what they were doing was 'right'. This lack of confidence can lead to stressed teachers, in turn affecting teachers' interactions with children and families.

This self-doubt, along with limited opportunity to share these feelings with a trusted colleague, left many feeling alone and timid about seeking support. Allocating a mentor for each mentee, and bringing them together through face-to-face workshops, supplemented by an online forum and centre visits, brought about a newfound confidence and a sense that they were not alone. Research suggests that developing collaborative and informal networks with peers is an effective strategy in mentoring programmes (Smith & Ingersoll, 2004; Woodrow & Newman, 2007).

To achieve the all-important trust element in the reciprocal relationship, both mentors and mentees needed to be open and willing to participate, and choose to do so of their own volition. When this was not the case (i.e. a mentee's early childhood service decided for them that they would attend the programme), mentors noticed a lack of engagement from these mentees and felt dissatisfied with their own mentoring experience. Conversely, we learnt that mentors who were time-poor and prioritised other aspects of their work over availability to mentees created dissatisfaction among mentees.

All mentees in the programme appreciated the fact that their mentors were from outside their own workplaces. This is an important point, as this professional distance allowed the mentees to be honest in their discussions about their development as professionals. Trust was built between each mentor and mentee, with mentees very much seeing mentors as 'on their side' and working in their best interests. It would be difficult for someone who was in charge of appraising staff to also act as a mentor. This could potentially affect the type of information that was shared with the mentee and the freedom of the mentee to speak candidly about their challenges or concerns (Morrissey & Nolan, 2015; Nolan & Beahan, 2014). The impartiality of an outsider as mentor can be especially vital for new graduates who have not yet established their practice.

Supporting mentors and mentees

The effective selection, training and support of mentors were all crucial factors in the success of the SWMP. For example, while all of the teachers involved in this programme were qualified to teach, this does not equate to the ability to mentor, which sits more in the domain of adult education. As Merriam (2008) acknowledges, "adult education is a complex phenomenon that can never be reduced to a single, simple explanation" (p. 94). Learning is about the construction of knowledge, and therefore some strategies lend themselves to supporting this process, such as dialogue and critical reflection (Mezirow, 1991). Mentoring is a skill that needs to be learnt, developed, practised and supported (Stanulis & Russell, 2000). This calls for training and ongoing support (Achinstein & Athanases, 2006; Holloway, 2001; Zeichner, 2004). These processes were built into the programme and delivered through an online forum and time spent in face-to-face workshops. This allowed colleagues to find support from within the field and created a community of practice culture (Wenger, McDermott, & Snyder, 2002).

Meaningful engagement
Locating the mentoring around an issue/topic identified by each mentee made the experience meaningful and did not present itself as just another task to do (Cook-Sather, 2006; Graue, 2005). This was important, because many new graduates initially thought the mentoring programme involved extra work in addition to what often felt like an overwhelming workload in their centres. Organisers realised that they needed to make clear that the Reflective Practice Project was about helping mentees to identify and achieve some of their goals and develop more efficient and effective practice—it was not about creating more work for mentees. As they developed and implemented their projects, mentees appreciated the opportunities to engage in action research on their own practice, with guidance and support from their mentor. They saw this as relevant and meaningful to them, and that it promoted their engagement (Ehrich, Hansford, & Tennent, 2004).

Conclusion

This chapter has shown how both mentors and mentees can gain in confidence and a sense of professional identity by participating in a mentoring programme. In the programme under study in this chapter, mentors expressed satisfaction at being able to contribute to the field, while many mentees described how they learned to think strategically and not get overwhelmed by the challenges they faced. Both groups talked of the importance of continual learning and reflective practice, as well as a greater sense of their own leadership capacities.

We have learnt that mentoring is important for beginning, isolated and experienced teachers, and that everyone gains from participating in mentoring if they are open to the process. Mentors can gain lots of new ideas, are prompted to reflect on their own practice, learn mentoring skills which they can transfer to their own settings, and can expand their networks. Mentees can feel part of a professional network and valued for what they know and bring to their teaching. They can gain confidence in themselves as educators, have a 'critical friend' (a trusted colleague) to share successes and disappointments with without fear of being judged, and have the opportunity to reflect on one aspect of their practice with guidance and support from a mentor and other colleagues.

It is clear to us that for effective mentoring to occur there need to be:

- clear expectations for both mentors and mentees in terms of outcomes
- time and resources dedicated to the programme
- training and support on an ongoing basis.

An effective mentoring programme can help teachers to feel that they belong, that what they bring to the mentoring relationship is acknowledged as valuable (being), and that everyone involved can experience professional growth (becoming).

Case studies

In the following case studies we hear the journeys of two mentees in the programme who agreed to share their experiences.

Case study 1: Evette's story (mentee)

When I applied for this mentor programme, I envisaged gaining skills in leadership as I began my first year teaching kindergarten. As a pedagogical leader in my workplace I started the year with trepidation, particularly when I met my strong and experienced team I would be working with. On meeting my mentor, we defined my project as 'Gaining confidence in my leadership skills'. As the year progressed, and the stresses grew, I began to have considerable self-doubt and anxiety about my knowledge and skills in early childhood teaching. I felt beaten down by behaviour guidance issues in my kinder group, team management of the educators working in my room, and in particular how to cope with a very dominant co-worker. My mentor provided me with support: not just someone to listen, but someone to tell me I have a right to be overwhelmed by this.

My project began as 'Gaining confidence in my leadership skills' but quickly turned into many rambling, yet supportive, conversations with my mentor. We nutted out that I actually do know what I'm doing and talking about, and that I need to stop second-guessing everything I say and do. Slowly I began believing that I wasn't the worst teacher ever and that I was doing the best with the situation I have. Together we worked out strategies I felt comfortable in using when approaching challenging conversations and confronting co-workers, who I felt didn't respect my ideas or decisions. This enabled me to begin to come out of the shadow of my dominating co-worker. These strategies included using a reflective journal, defining rationales behind my decisions, and personally documenting my achievements, however big or small.

On my first visit I had specific goals—to question myself less and stick to the decisions that I make. [The visits referred to in this case study are visits by the mentor to the mentee's workplace.] By the second visit I was struggling quite a lot with negative comments and constant critique from my colleague. I found it difficult to stand up for myself as I felt our approaches to early childhood education differed so dramatically. I felt she didn't listen to me anyway, so what's the point in standing up for myself as the kindergarten teacher. Looking back on my reflective journal from my third visit, I described myself as feeling like I was drowning in relation to confronting people and dealing with conflicts. However, I felt much more positive and self-assured about my kindergarten programme and my work with children. At my fourth visit I felt less stressed and anxious and I think I was back to my bubbly self again, and this was lovely to share with my mentor on this final visit. The mentoring programme allowed me space to have honest and open communication about my practice, and has been invaluable as I have grown both personally and professionally throughout this year and believe I am now a stronger person as a result.

Case study 2: Cassandra's story (mentee)
On commencement of my project, I was very unclear about what I would investigate. In the end I chose to look at 'Assessment for teaching

and learning'. I felt that my assessment of students focused around learning stories and was parent focused and didn't really mean anything to me when planning for children's learning. I was just pumping out learning stories and not considering the FOR, AS and OF of assessment. I met with my mentor, looked at a format that would guide me in assessing students and searched for ideas.

Mid-year I presented a document to parents in an exchange session that provided a guide to the five learning outcomes (Early Years Learning Framework) and each child's learning in these areas. I also sat with individual children and asked them to look through their folio and tell me about what they had learnt. I jotted notes and shared their ideas in their folio. Later in the week, the students presented their folios to their families. The parents and children drew and wrote their ideas and thoughts in the folio. In term three, I began to run small workshops, assessing students as I interacted with them. I wanted to make sure that all of the ideas of student knowledge weren't just in my head but down on paper and in the form of different assessment methods. Along the way I had many questions about my process and discovered that assessment could be quite shallow if it is not carefully planned and recorded.

I realise that I am a lifelong learner and this is only the beginning of where I am going, and next year I will be able to continue to reflect on my practice and implement new ideas and strategies in relation to assessment. I discovered that no matter how intentional our teaching, every student learns something different and we can't assume that our teaching focus will be grasped the same way.

References

Achinstein, B., & Athanases, S. Z. (2006). Mentors' knowledge of equity and diversity: Maintaining a bifocal perspective on new teachers and their students. In B. Achinstein & S. Z. Athanases (Eds), *Mentors in the making: Developing new leaders for new teachers* (pp. 38–54). New York, NY: Teachers College Press.

Cook-Sather, A. (2006). The "constant changing of myself": Revising roles in undergraduate teacher preparation. *The Teacher Educator, 41*(3), 187–206.

Cummins, L. (2004). The pot of gold at the end of the rainbow: Mentoring in early childhood education. *Childhood Education, 80*(5), 254–257.

Davis, D., & Higdon, K. (2008). The effects of mentoring/induction support on beginning teachers' practices in early elementary classrooms (K-3). *Journal of Research in Childhood Education, 22*(3), 261-274.

Ehrich, L., Hansford, B., & Tennent, L. (2004). Formal mentoring programs in education and other professions: A review of the literature. *Educational Administration Quarterly, 40*(4), 518–540.

Elliott, E. (2004). Building a partnership through collaboration, reflection, dialogue. *Journal of Early Childhood Teacher Education, 24*(4), 247-255.

Graue, E. (2005). Theorizing and describing preservice teachers' images of families and schooling. *Teachers College Record, 107*(1), 157–185.

Holloway, J.H. (2001). The benefits of mentoring. *Educational Leadership, 58*(8), 85–87.

Howes, C., James, J., & Ritchie, S. (2003). Pathways to effective teaching. *Early Childhood Research Quarterly, 18*(1), 104–120.

Jacobs, G.M. (2001). Professional development providing the scaffold: A model for early childhood/primary teacher preparation. *Early Childhood Education Journal, 29*(2), 125-130.

LoCasale-Crouch, J., Davis, E., Wiens, P., & Pianta, R. (2012). The role of the mentor in supporting new teachers: Associations with self-efficacy, reflection, and quality. *Mentoring & Tutoring: Partnership in Learning, 20*(3), 303-323.

Merriam, S.B. (2008). Adult learning theory for the twenty-first century. *New Directions for Adult and Continuing Education, 119*(Fall). Retrieved from www.interscience.wiley.com. doi: 10.1002/ace.309

Mezirow, J. (Ed.). (1991). *Transformative dimensions of adult learning.* San Francisco, CA: Jossey-Bass.

Morrissey, A., & Nolan, A. (2015). 'Just another meeting?': Investigating mentoring for early childhood teachers in Victoria. *Australasian Journal of Early Childhood, 40*(2), 40-48.

Nolan, A., & Beahan, J. (2014). *Professional mentoring program for early childhood teachers: Final report cohort 3.* Report for the Department of Education and Early Childhood Development, Victoria.

Nolan, A., Morrissey, A.M., & Dumenden, I. (2012). *Mentoring for early childhood teachers: Research report 2012.* Melbourne, VIC: Department of Education and Early Childhood Development.

Ramey, S.L., & Ramey, C.T. (2006). Creating and sustaining a high-quality workforce in child care, early intervention, and school readiness programs. In M. Zaslow & I. Martinez-Beck (Eds), *Critical issues in early childhood professional development* (pp. 355–368). Baltimore, MD: Paul H. Brookes Publishing Co.

Risko, V.J., Vukelich, C., Roskos, K., & Carpenter, M. (2002). Preparing teachers for reflective practice: Intentions, contradictions and possibilities. *Language Arts, 80*(2), 134–145.

Smith, T.M., & Ingersoll, R. (2004). What are the effects of induction and mentoring on beginning teacher turnover? *American Educational Research Journal, 41*(3), 681–714.

Stanulis, R.N., & Russell, D. (2000). 'Jumping in': Trust and communication in mentoring student teachers. *Teaching and Teacher Education, 16*, 65–80.

Waterman, S., & He, Y. (2011). Effects of mentoring programs on new teacher retention: A literature review. *Mentoring & Tutoring: Partnership in Learning, 19*(2), 139–156.

Wenger, E., McDermott, R., & Snyder, W. (Eds.). (2002). *Cultivating communities of practice: A guide to managing knowledge.* Boston, MA: Harvard Business School Press.

Woodrow, C., & Newman, L. (2007). Moving beyond 'prac': Building communities of practice. *Every Child, 13*(4), 14–15.

Zeichner, K. (2004). Becoming a teacher educator: A personal perspective. *Teaching and Teacher Education, 21*, 117–124.

Chapter 21
Relational–cultural theory: Future possibilities for mentoring in early childhood education?
Shirley Harris and Kaye Kara

Introduction

Mentoring plays a key role in early childhood education at both the practitioner and teacher–educator levels (Langdon, 2014). It is the cornerstone on which growth occurs within the sector on a daily basis, and it is therefore critical that we have an authentic way of knowing what effective mentoring relationships look like. Broadly speaking, according to Hudson (2013), effective mentoring relates to the qualities of both mentor and mentee, the attributes and practices of the mentor, and the context, selection and pairing of the mentor and mentee. This highlights the critical nature of the actual relationship within the mentoring dyad.

This chapter considers the efficacy of a feminist relational–cultural theory (RCT) framework for achieving effective, meaningful mentoring relationships for both mentor and mentee within the early childhood education sector. Previously this framework has been applied within the therapy/health sector but it has not been used with mentoring in education environments. Traditionally in education, mentoring relationships have been based on patriarchal models, whereby roles are viewed as dyadic, with the mentor as the 'expert' and the mentee as the 'learner'.

Both the health and education sectors are highly feminised professional areas in which "relationships and a relational work environment are important in women's career and development" (Hammer, Trepal, & Speedlin, 2014, p. 4), so a more empathetic approach to mentoring seems fitting. As a way of locating the potential of the RCT framework for early childhood education, it is important to briefly review the current mentoring literature, particularly as it relates to education. Not only will this contextualise the ways in which mentoring has been perceived and implemented, but it will also identify any possible gaps in the mentoring literature.

Having taken this into account, we will then draw on our own knowledge and experience to deconstruct the concepts that underpin the framework. Using Freire's dialogic methodology, we will also consider the relevance of this framework, not only for our own work within initial teacher education, but also for the wider early childhood sector.

Redefining the mentoring dyad

As mentioned above, mentoring has traditionally been embedded within a patriarchal paradigm. According to Peterson, Valk, Baker, Brugger, and Hightower (2010), "Mentoring is defined as a one-on-one long-term relationship between an expert and a novice that supports the mentee's professional, academic, or personal development" (p. 157). Similarly, within the early childhood context, the research suggests that mentoring has often been perceived as a 'peer relationship', where "a more experienced practitioner provides professional guidance to one or more novice practitioners, either on a 1:1 basis or as a group" (Wong & Waniganayake, 2013, p.164). Not surprisingly, therefore, most research in early childhood education has focused on pre-service and then induction of beginning teachers. In these cases the focus is on understanding the work environment or supporting new teachers into the profession through traditional means (Gut, Beam, Henning, Cochran, & Knight, 2014; Peterson et al., 2010; Wong & Waniganayake, 2013).

In spite of the prevalence of dyadic relationships, there is evidence within the research literature that there is growing recognition that the one-directional mentoring relationship needs to be reconceptualised. Pavia, Nissen, Hawkins, Monroe and Filimon-Demyen (2003) argue that

> although mentoring has often been viewed as a one-way process (i.e. the experienced teacher providing support to the novice), current literature highlights the need for a more reciprocal venture … A reciprocal mentoring relationship can enable both mentor and protégé to enhance their use of developmentally appropriate practices in early childhood settings. (p. 251)

Benefits for mentor and mentee

Being in a mentoring relationship can be of great benefit to the mentee. A meta-analysis conducted by Allen, Eby, Poteet, Lentz and Lima (2004) found that "mentored individuals were: more satisfied with their career, were more likely to believe that they would advance in their career, and were more likely to be committed to their career, than non-mentored individuals were" (cited in Denmark & Williams, 2012, pp. 263–264). More recently, evidence is appearing on the benefits of mentoring for improving the early educator practices of mentees (Peterson et al., 2010). Langdon's (2014) recent research in the primary sector on the benefits to mentees through analysis of the professional conversations that occur between mentors and mentees also supports this finding. Conversely, Langdon's research found that there is little evidence on how mentoring relationships add to the growth or development of the mentor.

With regard to the mentor's role, the need for ongoing training as a way to avoid the traditional one-directional dyadic relationship from forming and being maintained is well defined in the research literature (Cohen, 2003; Denmark & Williams, 2012; Hudson, 2013). Nasser-Abu Alhija and Fresko (2014) recognise that being an expert teacher in itself is not sufficient, and that "In order to perform their role effectively, mentors require preparation beforehand and continuing professional development and support throughout" (p. 164). Cohen (2003) reiterates this by asserting, "Certainly, the more aware and knowledgeable both mentors and mentees are about mentoring as a developmental process of learning, the more they can jointly contribute as practitioners to the final benefit of the outcomes" (p. 5).

Mentoring relationships

Irby (2014) conducted a content review of research on developmental mentoring relationships spanning the last 20 years. This identified three key dimensions for the development of mentoring relationships: recognition that the mentor–mentee dyad is an evolutionary process of growing awareness between both parties; the mentor understands both their role and the process required to scaffold the mentee towards 'independence' and 'transformation'; and mentoring programmes need to be custom designed to enhance the development of positive relationships between mentor and mentee.

There still appears to be a paucity of research on the type and ongoing development of mentoring relationships that will best support women within the early childhood sector. Little is written about forming, developing, and growing the mentoring relationship itself, and for this reason an alternative framework is worth considering. Moss et al. (1999) presented the concept of feminist praxis as an alternative approach for mentoring within a higher education context, and this approach is still relevant today, especially for a highly feminised early childhood sector. Moss et al. (1999) assert that "integrating feminist values into the specific acts of mentoring can benefit not only ourselves as women, but also other persons marginalised by similar social and political processes" (p. 416). It is within a feminist paradigm that RCT sits, with an underlying premise being the importance of relationships and a relational work environment for growth and development (Hammer et al., 2014).

Relational-cultural theory framework

The relational–cultural framework provides an alternative model for mentoring in the early childhood sector, at both a philosophical and a practical level. RCT has as its core concept 'mutual empathy', which in turn acts as the prerequisite for growing and fostering relationships. This occurs within an authentic relationship that openly gives attention to power and marginalisation issues that may be inherent within the mentoring relationship (Hammer et al., 2014).

When the prospect of a mentoring chapter highlighting the potential of RCT with regard to early childhood arose, it seemed entirely appropriate that we would use a dialogic method to inform both our thinking and our writing process. Freire (1998) considers dialogue to be one of the key aspects of any pedagogical relationship, particularly a mentoring one, and comments that "both participants bring knowledge to the relationship, and one of the objects of the pedagogical process is to explore what each other knows and what they can teach each other" (p. 8). Within our own multifaceted roles as leaders, teachers and researchers, we find ourselves applying the relational–cultural framework as colleagues, resulting in a constant fluidity between the roles of mentor and mentee. This juxtaposition has enabled us to engage in a conversational dialogue, linked to our own practice and experiences, thus forming the basis of this chapter.

RCT is a theoretical approach to professional interactions with strong links to feminist theory, taking into consideration the importance of relationships and mutuality. While traditional, patriarchal theories place importance on the notion of the individual, or the concept of self, RCT places the focus on the establishment and development of relationships and connections (Deanow, 2011; Hammer et al., 2014). RCT is a model that "sees mutual empathy and mutual empowerment as the basis for development" (West, 2005, p. 102). In the highly feminised early childhood sector where communication, and reciprocal, responsive relationships are particularly valued as integral to the lived curriculum *Te Whāriki* (Ministry of Education, 1996), links to the themes and concepts of the RCT framework are particularly strong. The concepts that make up a relational–cultural framework have been identified as mutual empathy, authenticity, and growth fostering while working against power/marginalisation. These concepts working in unison are evident when operating in an authentic relational environment.

Relational-cultural theory in action

The central concept of mutual empathy is described by Walker (2006) as "influencing another person through one's thoughts, feelings, and actions while also remaining open to his or her influence" (p. 62). In addition, Jordan (1991) suggests that "while some mutual empathy involves an acknowledgement of sameness in the other, an appreciation of the differentness of the other's experience is also vital" (cited in Walker, 2006, p. 62). In our multiple roles as mentor and mentee we will now take the concept of mutual empathy and from our perspectives explore what it could mean for early childhood education. (Note: SH refers to Shirley and KK refers to Kaye.)

> **SH 1:** The thing I find interesting about the way mutual empathy is being defined, is the *mutual* part of the concept, the idea that while as a mentor you influence others, you need to also remain open to the mentee's influence, it means that it works both ways. So rather than someone being an expert influencing someone else's knowledge and practices, using mutual empathy means you are actually constantly going through a cycle influencing each other.
>
> **KK 2:** I like the idea of the word *mutual* too; it implies you have an equal balance of power, there is an acknowledgement of the skills and knowledge that each of you brings to a mentoring relationship. As mature practitioners we do both have different skills that we bring and mutual empathy gives you a way of negotiating your way through using each of your skills to the best advantage in any situation.
>
> **KK 3:** Drawing on our own experience building our mentoring relationship, one of the things we made a conscious decision [about was] to slowly get to know each other, and part of that was building confidence and trust in each other, finding out the ways we could work together. So in effect we took a relational approach to it.
>
> **SH 4:** RCT is underpinned by a willingness to be vulnerable and [set] aside the role of the expert, that unless you can do that in a mentoring relationship then mutual empathy is never going to occur. So how do you do that? By establishing the ground rules, being open hearted, being willing to learn, recognising you are not the all knower, but you are actually in an equal learning relationship.

Duffey (2006/2007) comments that authenticity helps create a "place of genuineness, realness" (p. 52), and creates opportunities for meaningful connections. Miller and Striver (1997, cited in Duffey, 2006/2007) believe that being able to represent our true selves and our experiences to others is one of the most challenging developmental processes. The potential outcome of not being authentic is disconnectedness and a lack of mutual empathy. Being genuine and real is of critical importance in any relationship, and in the following dialogue we consider the role of authenticity within the mentoring partnership.

> **KK 1:** Authenticity is about trust, from a relational perspective being honest with yourself and others is the crux of being authentic. For me it is at the base of all relationships because if you are not honest what is the point?
>
> **SH 2:** …to me authenticity is about being true to yourself and being who you are, but it is also about knowing yourself. Only through critical reflection and constant reflection can you really get to know yourself
>
> **KK3:** Some things people say can cause you to learn something about yourself … it is about an ongoing relationship with yourself that can be prompted from the outside by interactions with other people
>
> **SH 4:** I don't think it matters what other people say unless it challenges you or gives rise to something you have not thought about before—then it's the process of making you reflect on your own thinking or practice again.
>
> **KK 5:** The critical aspect of questioning yourself—why you think and do that—and getting to the bottom of where you are coming from and understanding yourself is part of the work you have to do to even begin to be authentic.
>
> **SH 6:** Yes, you talked about having an authentic relationship…unless you are authentic with yourself, I don't see how you can have an authentic relationship with someone else.

Growth-fostering relationships are the result of engaging in mutual empathy. These relationships are defined as "a fundamental and complex process of active participation in the development and growth of other people and the relationship that results in mutual development" (Miller & Stiver, 1997, cited in Hammer et al., 2014, p. 6). Working in a relational early childhood environment fosters growth by generating five dynamic experiences, originally referred to by Miller (1986) as the '5 good things'. They are identified as zest or an increased energy for the work we are doing, empowerment or becoming agentic, clarity and knowledge of self and others, an increased sense of worth, and a desire for more connection to others (cited in Hartling & Sparks, 2008). Consideration is given to the five good things in our next dialogue.

> **SH 1**: I wonder whether there is often an assumption that the mentor is not in the relationship to grow—that often mentoring is the traditional one-directional model. Instead of when you look at RCT it is about a win, win—it's about how both people grow in different ways, and it doesn't have to be in the same way. The 5 good things reminds me of how I feel watching someone else learn and grow—there is nothing better! That is the excitement, the zest and energy they refer to—being able to share your own learning. Isn't that what being a teacher is all about? Isn't that what we want to see in children?

> **KK 2**: Yes and how through this process you can rediscover the love for your job, rediscovering things through other people, through those discussions and the different ideas they come up with. I firmly believe there should be time allocated each day, to share your ideas and learning—some days would be shorter, other days the discussion would be more in depth and longer …but it would become part of the organisational culture at both the tertiary and centre levels and the discussions would just depend [on] what you had come up against that day, within your practice.

> **SH 3**: I also think that you should never reach a point where you stop growing so mentoring is something that needs to be redefined as an ongoing process, and I think that is what 'growth fostering relationships' is all about.

> **KK 4**: Because what we are talking about is also the mentors having that ongoing mutual mentoring, so it is supporting them in their role of supporting other people. Yes, I definitely agree that there has got to be that forward movement for everybody, so there is not those sitting at the top of the knowledge chain, because they need to be moving forward as well in order that others can move forward.

Power is defined by Miller and Stiver (cited in West, 2005, p. 103) as "the capacity to produce a change". West (2005) continues:

> It is not the denial of power differences, but the recognition of them,

the mindful attempt to minimise differentials and to, within the context of relationship, be empowered and to empower another that creates the change inherent in growth and development. (p. 103)

Giving power a 'voice' within the RCT framework provides the space and the means for both mentor and mentee to be heard equally. So in the following dialogue we consider power with regard to the mentoring relationship in early childhood.

SH 1: In terms of the role of the mentor, one of the things that is really helpful in relation to RCT is this idea of using one's own power to empower others, so not only recognising that as the mentor you are in a position of power, but it is what you do with your power.

KK 2: I have to say that the way I was thinking about the power was more the power over, and I guess that relates more to the traditional role of mentoring somebody: it is a person in a more powerful position working with someone who is just beginning or coming through.

SH 3: Miller talks about power being defined as the 'capacity to produce a change', which is a really nice positive way of thinking about power: that you are in a position to help enable that change and facilitate that change and rather than it be power over someone else. I thought that was a really helpful way of looking at power.

KK 4: But if you think about it in those terms, surely by bringing together the mentor/mentee and the fluidity of that relationship under RCT, power has to increase for both, I would have thought, because you have two people working towards a shared vision, if you like.

KK 5: The power balance or imbalance at times is something, too, that does need to be considered, because to be completely honest it is very difficult if you feel that a person has power over you, but if you are talking to that person as your mentor/mentee and you are talking to them as an equal, you are more likely to speak honestly and actually consider you own failings without feeling like you are a bad person or a bad educator or in some way doing wrong rather than being able to explore your ideas or thoughts.

SH 6: Absolutely, I think it is imperative you have those hard conversations right from the beginning. I remember when I was a student, discussing organisational matters, but never really talking about the mentoring relationship or what to expect. You need to confront the elephant in the room in terms of power—just put it out there right from the start, being brave enough to talk about that stuff so that when there is conflict or disconnects you have actually got the structure in place to be able to talk about it and do it in a safe way for all.

Mentoring possibilities for early childhood

By reflecting on our own values, beliefs and practices when working together in a mentoring dyad, we have been able to align our relationship with the concepts that form the RCT framework. So what are the possibilities for an early childhood centre environment?

KK 1: If you were to implement an RCT mentoring programme in a centre, you would start with your management—especially getting your head teachers talking to each other, so they then could mentor a member of their team. With them working with each other already, they will know who they have a relationship with and who they haven't. I know sometimes that mistrust and conflict occur across different rooms and so targeting the head teachers would be a good place to start because you are building the environment and the expectation that this is the way we work, we work together.

SH 2: I agree this would create important role models and simultaneously staff could learn about the RCT model throughout the whole centre using a self-review process focusing on relationships. This could be led by the head teachers together and would also provide the opportunity to cross-pollinate the ideas and practices that are working in areas of the centre. It's about embracing the framework and taking the risk to make it happen together.

KK 3: Absolutely because it's about talking about ideas, it's not about "Oh I'm in the under 2s" it's ultimately about things that impact on children. Or about things that impact on our Centre or about the pedagogy, and everybody has got to have buy in to that, everybody has got to be clear about the goals and expectations.

SH 4: I think sometimes it is also about not being too over ambitious but rather recognising it takes time, and by taking small steps you can start to feel as though you are making a shift towards a more trusting and relational environment.

KK 5: I like the way RCT gives you a venue for talking about it, and acknowledges that everything isn't all glossy and fluffy, that actually as people we do have problems from time to time that we need to iron out, so I see it as a very healthy way of working together.

SH: We are only beginning to grapple with the possibilities this may have for early childhood.

KK: But we have made a start…

Conclusion

By viewing mentoring relationships between women in early childhood education through a feminist praxis lens, we have been able to focus our gaze on the relational dimensions of the mentoring dyad. This has led us to be able to consider the alternative relational–cultural theory framework as a more effective mentoring model for the early childhood context.

By taking the time to embrace the framework ourselves in our own work, RCT has provided us with the knowledge, the time and the space to be critically aware of our own mentoring relationships. This has resulted in recognition of the true potential RCT holds—its reciprocal nature, the fluidity of learning within the mentoring dyad, and its value as an ongoing form of professional learning, not only for all early childhood educators, but also for practitioners across the sectors.

References

Cohen, N.H. (2003). The journey of the principles of adult mentoring inventory. *Adult Learning, 14*(1), 4-7. doi: 10.1177/104515950301400102

Deanow, C.G. (2011). Relational development through the life cycle: Capacities, opportunities, challenges, and obstacles. *Journal of Women and Social Work, 26*(2), 125-138.

Denmark, F.L., & Williams, D.A. (2012). The older woman as sage: The satisfaction of mentoring. *Women & Therapy, 35,* 261-278.

Duffey, T. (2006/2007). Promoting relational competencies in counselor education through creativity and relational-cultural theory. *Journal of Creativity in Mental Health, 2*(1), 47-59.

Friere, P. (1998). *Pedagogy of freedom: Ethics, democracy, and civic courage.* Lanham, MD: Rowman & Littlefield.

Gut, D.M., Beam, P.C., Henning, J.E., Cochran, D.C., & Knight, R.T. (2014). Teachers' perceptions of their mentoring role in three different clinical settings: Student teaching, early field experiences, and entry year teaching. *Mentoring & Tutoring: Partnership in Learning, 22*(3), 240-263.

Hammer,T., Trepal, H., & Speedlin, S. (2014). Five relational strategies for mentoring female faculty. *Adultspan Journal, 13*(1), 4-14.

Hartling, L., Sparks, E. (2008). Relational–cultural practice: Working in a non-relational world. *Women & Therapy, 31*(2-4), 165-188.

Hudson, P. (2013). Mentoring as professional development: 'Growth for both' mentor and mentee. *Professional Development in Education, 39*(5), 771-783.

Irby, B.J. (2014). Editor's overview: A 20-year content review of research on the topic of developmental mentoring relationships published in the mentoring and tutoring journal. *Mentoring & Tutoring: Partnership in Learning, 22*(3), 181-189.

Langdon, F. (2014). Evidence of mentor learning and development: An analysis of New Zealand mentor/mentee professional conversations. *Professional Development in Education, 40*(1), 36-55.

Ministry of Education. (1996). *Te whāriki: He whāriki mātauranga mō ngā mokopuna o Aotearoa: Early childhood curriculum.* Wellington: Learning Media.

Moss, P., Debres, K.J., Cravey, A., Hyndman, J., Hirschboeck, K.K., & Masucci, M. (1999). Toward mentoring as feminist praxis: Strategies for ourselves and others. *Journal of Geography in Higher Education, 23*(3), 413-427.

Nasser-Abu Alhija, F., & Fresko, B. (2014). An exploration of the relationships between mentor recruitment, the implementation of mentoring, and mentors' attitudes. *Mentoring & Tutoring: Partnership in Learning*, *22*(2),162-180.

Pavia, L., Nissen, H., Hawkins, C., Monroe, M., & Filimon-Demyen, D. (2003). Mentoring early childhood professionals. *Journal of Research in Early Childhood Education*, *17*(2), 250-260.

Peterson, S.M., Valk, C., Baker, A.C., Brugger, L., & Hightower, A.D. (2010). We're not just interested in the work: Social and emotional aspects of early educator mentoring relationships. *Mentoring & Tutoring: Partnership in Learning*, *18*(2), 155-175.

Walker, J.A. (2006). A reconceptualization of mentoring in counselor education: Using a relational model to promote mutuality and embrace differences. *Journal of Humanistic Counselling, Education and Development*, *45*, 60-69.

West, C.K. (2005). The map of relational-cultural theory. *Women & Therapy*, *28*(3-4), 93-110.

Wong, D., & Waniganayake, M. (2013). Mentoring as a leadership development strategy in early childhood education. In E. Hujala, M. Waniganayake, & J. Rodd (Eds), *Researching leadership in early childhood education* (pp.163-180). Pirkanmaa, Finland: Tampere University Press.

Chapter 22

Mentoring as a navigational change compass: Attending to the personal transition process

Michele Morrison and Jenny Ferrier-Kerr

Introduction

Change is one of the few constants in early childhood settings. It occurs at the individual and organisational level and varies in form, duration and effect. Change can be initiated or imposed, enabling and limiting, invigorating and enervating. The affective and often profoundly challenging nature of change requires new learning, insight and action. Research suggests that when mentoring forms an integral component of change initiatives, people are more attentive to it; like coaches, mentors are "midwives for change: they know when change is coming, when it's here, when it needs a nudge, and when it's happening too fast" (Rock & Donde, 2007, p. 5).

Mentoring thus offers a powerful navigational compass that informs and guides educators as they embark on change journeys and encounter the personal transition phases that accompany these. In this chapter we focus on an often-neglected aspect of the change process: mentoring for transition. We distinguish between change and transition, introduce four transition models, connect mentee dispositions and the transition process, highlight mentoring strategies that address the internal dimensions of change (with a particular emphasis on questioning), and sound important cautionary notes.

Change versus transition

In order to provide mentoring that is appropriate in both nature and substance, mentors must be knowledgeable and skilful (de Vries, 2011). They must attend equally to psychosocial and performance needs, be attuned to the manner in which mentees adjust to change, and respond accordingly using strategies that enhance mentee efficacy and resilience in traversing multiple change initiatives. Personal change theories help mentors to focus on mentee needs at an individual rather than an organisational level, and to distinguish between external and internal dimensions of the change process (Adams, Hayes, & Hopson, 1977; Bridges, 1980; Fisher, 2012; Kubler-Ross, 1969; Schein, 1965, 1996).

Whereas 'change' refers to an event and an outwardly observable empirical shift in behaviour and practice, 'transition' refers to the "discontinuity in a person's life space" (Hopson & Adams, 1977, p. 5), generated by the change event and the largely hidden psychological shifts that accompany reorientation from one relatively stable state to another. Schein (1996) contends that transition requires "painful unlearning without loss of ego identity and difficult relearning as one cognitively attempt[s] to restructure one's thoughts, perceptions, feelings, and attitude" (p. 6). Transition is thus a profound, dynamic and uncertain internal process.

Those of you who have moved house will recall the period of transition that follows relocation to a new physical address (the change event). While the furniture removal truck signals the arrival of new occupants, what isn't so obvious is the dislocation experienced as you: decide which room, wall space or cupboard will house your possessions; get up in the middle of the night and walk into a wall; find your nearest supermarket and familiarise yourself with shelf layout; enlist new health professionals; adjust to a higher, lower or no mortgage; and, if this also involves moving town, not only get to know new neighbours, but form entirely new support networks. Change involves myriad emotions, which range from reluctance to enthusiasm, excitement to dread, buoyancy to despair, anxiety to confidence. It involves uncertainty and requires conscious effort to resist old habits and form new ones. Have you ever driven home from work only to discover that you're heading towards your old address?

The same is true in the workplace and applies equally to longstanding and new staff. It could be the centre teacher who becomes centre manager, the primary-trained teacher who accepts a position in a kindergarten, the over-twos teacher who joins the under-twos team, or the teachers who trial new pedagogical strategies and implement new systems. Each and every employee experiences crucial transitions.

Taking the first example as an illustration, the internally appointed centre manager will be easily recognised by the physical manifestations of formal position: title, badge and office. What is less obvious is the manner in which she (or he) manages the psychological stress inevitably generated by having to accept that she is no longer "one of the girls" and to form new functional relationships, cope with self-doubt and keep the imposter syndrome (Clance, 1978; Kets de Vries, 1990) at bay. She or he will also need to master new responsibilities and intensified workload, take on the burden of legal and financial liability, and decide how to allocate all that additional personal disposable income! The latter serves to illustrate that while stressors are often perceived to be negative and to have a detrimental impact on the transition process, they can also be positive and beneficial. And the list is by no means exhaustive. Readers will undoubtedly add to this example in the light of their own transition experiences, and identify other examples of change and transition within their ECE context.

As we can see, transition is much more than the time lapse between the introduction, implementation and institutionalisation of organisational change. It involves a period of turmoil as people relinquish old ways of seeing and doing and adopt new ones. In the workplace this requires employees to reframe their psychological contract (Schein, 1965). Building on the work of Rousseau (1995), Freese, Schalk and Croon (2010) define this as the "employee's belief of mutual obligations that arise in the context of [their] relationship with the organization, which shape this relationship and govern the employee's behaviour" (p. 405). When proposed or imposed organisational changes are consistent with an employee's psychological contract, that person will most likely advocate for change and experience a rapid, smooth transition process. Conversely, dissonance between organisational change and an employee's psychological contract serves to intensify personal stress levels, heighten resistance, and lower individual commitment to performance, team and organisation.

Transition models

There are a number of models that mentors may find useful in identifying and sequencing the transition stages that people typically experience when responding to organisational change. Seminal to these is psychologist Kurt Lewin's three-step planned-change model (as published by Cartwright, 1951), a visual representation of which is shown in Figure 2 below. People progress through each step at different rates. As the diagram shows, the majority will be in a state of *unfreezing* during the first phase of organisational change, *moving* during the second phase, and *refreezing* during the final phase.

Figure 2: Lewin's organisational change model

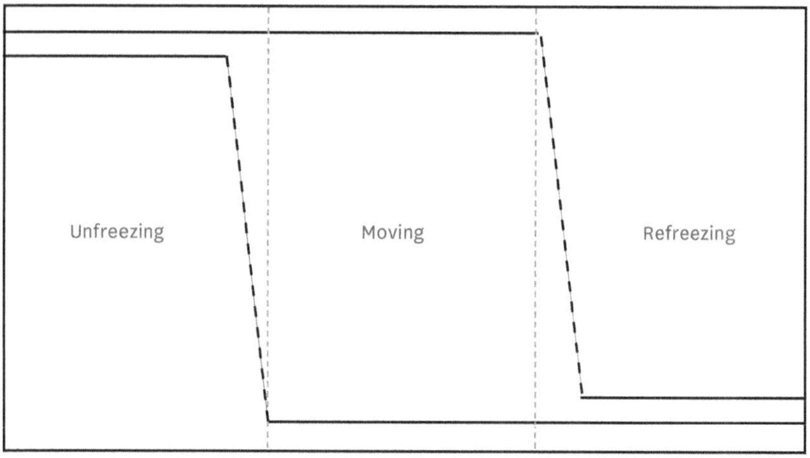

Unfreezing | Moving | Refreezing

Source: Based on Cartwright, 1951

While Lewin did not distinguish between external change and internal transition, he was one of the first theorists to suggest that change is a process rather than a single event. Lewin (1997) contended that people remain in "quasi-stationary equilibrium" until "an emotional stir up" or disconfirming evidence "break[s] open the shell of complacency and self-righteousness" (p. 330) and causes an *unfreezing* of established thinking and behaviour. It is at this point that the transition process begins. Unfreezing will not, in itself, lead to new learning and growth however. As Schein (1996) comments, we can easily

> ignore the information, dismiss it as irrelevant, blame the undesired outcome on others or fate, or ... simply deny its validity. To become motivated to change, we must accept the information and connect it to something we care about. (p. 60)

In Lewin's model, disruption of the status quo and subsequent emotional connection prompt people to experiment with new approaches and engage in a period of action research. The second stage, *moving*, comprises a complex, iterative learning process that is unsettling for all those involved. Even when change is intentional and to some extent planned, the fluid nature of relationships, organisational forces and other contextual factors, both enabling and constraining, typically means that precise "outcomes cannot be predicted but emerge on a trial and error basis" (Burnes, 2004, p. 993). When preferred outcomes become part of the cultural norm (the way we do things around here), change is institutionalised at the organisational level and *refreezing* occurs. At the individual level, this third and final stage signals the alignment of new ways of thinking and behaving with one's self-concept and marks the end of the transition process. Refreezing reflects new levels of confidence and comfort that prevent us regressing to previous ways of being. Using our newly appointed centre manager as an example, consciousness of the separation between management responsibility and team membership constitutes *unfreezing* at the personal level, acceptance of the need to maintain a professional distance constitutes *moving*, and confidence in asserting professional boundaries with colleagues constitutes a *re-freezing*.

Although Lewin's model has at times been dismissed as one-dimensional and mechanistic, *unfreezing-moving-refreezing* antecedents can be discerned in the transition models that followed (Burnes, 2004; Hendry, 1996). While limited space precludes in-depth analysis here, three classic transition models are summarised in Table 5 below, and references are included at the end of the chapter.

Table 5: A comparison of personal transition models

Author/s	Transition phases		
Hopson & Adams, 1977	Immobilisation Minimisation Depression	Acceptance of reality (letting go) Testing Searching for meaning	Internalisation
Bridges, 1980	Endings (losing and letting go, fear, denial, anger, sadness, disorientation, frustration, uncertainty, sense of loss)	Neutral zone (resentment, low morale/productivity, anxiety, scepticism)	New beginnings (acceptance, high energy, openness to learning, renewed commitment)
Fisher, 2005, 2012	Anxiety Happiness/ denial Anger Fear Threat Guilt Disillusionment Depression Hostility	Gradual acceptance (experimentation)	Moving forward (rationalisation, incorporation, comfort zone, complacency)

Hopson and Adams (1977) suggest that all change—whether intentional or unintentional, sudden or gradual—triggers a seven-phase cycle of predictable reactions and feelings that have an impact on one's self-esteem. They further suggest that while each transition phase involves discrete actions, the phases themselves overlap and movement from one phase to the next is seldom neat: "any given individual's progressions and regressions are unique to his or her unique circumstances" (p. 13). For example, a senior teacher nearing retirement may deny or minimise the need to adopt new pedagogical approaches. Conversely, that very same teacher may readily embrace new learning. To fully support her or him to navigate the change process, the mentor needs to establish which transition stage the mentee is currently experiencing and the emotions this evokes.

Bridges (1980) and Fisher (2012) similarly depict the transition process as curvilinear, the latter animating his model with cartoon figures and thought bubbles representing each phase. While concurring that people move along the curve in either direction in response to contextual factors, Fisher nonetheless concludes that transition is for the most part a sequential and linear process.

Mentee dispositions and the transition process

The ease with which people master transitions appears to be determined by their dispositions towards and previous experiences of change. Fisher (2005) thus bemoans the failure of organisational change models to adequately recognise the "influence and impact of the past, and the importance of positioning the past in the context of the actual timeline for the desired change (i.e. we are where we are today due to our actions and activities in the past)" (p. 258).

On the one hand, when experiences of change are positive, a mentor's and a mentee's sense of agency and control are greater, and their resilience in persevering with and overcoming challenge higher. It is more likely that mentees will initiate change and have a voice in the decision-making process. From an organisational perspective, the rationale for change and the mechanics of change will have been negotiated, and during the change process everyone involved will have been well informed. It is more likely, too, that resources—both human and physical—will have been designated in support of the desired change and the transition process. Moreover, research that focused on adults who remain healthy in spite of high stress levels during the transition process has found that "'hardy' executive characteristics include: clear sense of personal values, goals and capabilities; use of inner resources; positive reinterpretation of the transition; and internal belief that the effects depend upon how one handles the change" (Lewandowski, 1989, as cited in Fletsch, 2011, p. 2). For these people, while there may be rough water along the way, it is more likely that both short- and long-term benefits will result.

On the other hand, changes experienced as negative, distressing and detrimental to people's professional wellbeing are more likely to have been imposed on, or 'done to', people without the prior involvement or knowledge of those most affected. These changes are more likely to have been poorly communicated and poorly resourced, leaving people confused over the rationale and process, and feeling that they are either alone and adrift, paddling in the wrong direction, or capsized. As a result, they are likely to be complacent and reluctant to actively engage with new things.

Bridges's (2004) research demonstrates that the locus of control determines the speed of the transition process and the time spent in each transition phase. When people initiate the changes that trigger the transition process, they tend to minimise the importance of endings and deny any sense of loss or distress. An overriding optimism that new patterns of thinking and behaving will preserve, if not enhance, their self-esteem means that the first phases of transition are fleeting and often subconscious. In addition, these people are generally more open to experimenting with new approaches and more likely to embrace the uncertainty they generate. Conversely, people who enter transition unwillingly or unwittingly are more likely to resent change and to cling to the status quo. Fearful that new patterns of thinking and behaving will undermine their sense of wellbeing, they experience loss and distress more keenly and tend to linger in the early transition phases. Not only will their slow acceptance of the need to change be infused with reluctance and pessimism, but the uncertainty generated in the experimentation phase will more likely engender paralysis and low productivity.

Mentoring to support transition

Not surprisingly, the literature on mentoring to support change is extensive, but despite mentoring for transition being critical to successful change outcomes, researchers have devoted little direct attention to the latter. Alternatively, it could be argued that some authors implicitly address mentoring for transition. Rhodes, Stokes and Hampton (2004), for instance, suggest that two key activities contribute to a mentee's development. First is the development of self-awareness. According to these authors, the mentor's role in generating self-awareness is to be "sensitive to and supportive of all the circumstances in which the learner is operating" (p. 27). Further to this, Osterman and Kottkamp (1993) point out that awareness is essential for change and that to "achieve it individuals must come to an understanding of their own behavior; they must develop a conscious awareness of their own actions and effects, and the ideas or theories-in-use that shape their action strategies" (p. 2). Hence mentors must exercise discernment in applying strategies likely to build self-awareness. These include focused questioning and profound listening, guided reflection, going on retreat, and setting short- and long-term goals.

The second key activity is supporting the mentee to manage their learning. Learning needs are typically intensified when early childhood educators take on new roles, including the induction of beginning teachers, team leadership and centre management. In addition, mentors play a vital role in supporting teachers to hone their practice. In this context, mentors draw on their more significant experience to support the mentee to "think ahead in an atmosphere of trust and confidentiality" (Rhodes, et al, 2004, p. 27). The strategies employed should help the mentee to uncover their own answers to challenges, discover new perspectives and gain clarity. They should comprise listening, restatement, summary, questioning and feedback, challenge and confrontation (Brockbank & McGill, 2006).

Importantly, these kinds of activities are likely to reveal a mentee's dispositions for change and 'where they are' in the transition process. The role of the mentor is an integral part of supporting a mentee through the transition process: the mentor must be attuned to a mentee's dispositions and needs, and be cognisant of their own experiences of change and transition (Greyling, 2006). Whether mentors are members of staff or external to the organisation, the most important criterion is that a supportive relationship enables the mentee to attend to the transition process (Cranwell-Ward, Bossons, & Gover, 2004). The mentor's responsibility is considerable, but so too is the mentee's, and requires that both know about and develop their understanding of transition.

Salzman (2002) suggests that the mentoring relationship involves sharing that leads to the development of not just the mentee but also the mentor, and that the most effective mentors are co-learners with their mentees. This strategy of co-learning can rekindle motivation and reduce the "anxiety or burnout that prevents thinking and imagining new actions" (Chu, 2012, p. 21). Skilled mentors will resist solving problems, what Rogers (2012) calls "advice in disguise" (p. 76), and will instead emphasise identifying issues and questions. By asking genuine questions and listening empathically, mentors create a safe learning environment in which the mentor and mentee can work appreciatively and inquiringly (Pask & Joy, 2007) to better understand and manage the transition process. Chu (2012) cites the example of an early childhood teacher who, in addition to journaling her interactions with a preschooler, felt overwhelmed by the additional expectation that she utilise a teacher–child interaction assessment tool. Her mentor helped her, in a timely fashion, to see that the assessment tool generated new data that supported her original learning goal. As a consequence, her willingness to exercise agency and explore new ways of interacting in the classroom grew.

An inquiry-oriented mentoring approach thus makes good sense (Yendol-Hoppey & Dana, 2007). Research shows that when the principles and phases of inquiry are applied to the mentoring process, the mentee is placed at the centre of an intentional, active and enabling learning process (Awaya et al., 2003). As with transition, mentoring also comprises distinct developmental phases that are useful in establishing and maintaining the mentoring relationship. In Kram's (1983) career development and psychosocial mentoring functions, the four phases of initiation, cultivation, separation, and redefinition suggest a cycle of inquiry. Positioning mentoring as inquiry ensures the process is owned by the mentee, with questioning and action-taking centremost. Moreover, "inquiry and change are not truly separate moments, but are simultaneous" (Cooperrider & Whitney, 1999, p. 8). An inquiry-oriented mentoring approach has the potential to support the "inner-reorientation and meaning-redefinition" (Quick, Fletsch, & Rupured, 2011, para. 2) needed to incorporate personal and organisational changes. It allows both mentor and mentee to intentionally take a stance that enables them to understand and engage with the transition process by implementing a range of inquiry and reflective strategies (Pask & Joy, 2007). How this could be implemented in an early childhood education service is discussed in the next section.

Questioning: A critical mentoring strategy

Of the abovementioned strategies, questioning is essential to successful mentoring and inquiry processes. Perceiving questioning as the twin of listening, Pask and Joy (2007) claim that "genuine questioning is liberating" (p. 241). Carefully constructed questions prompt the communication of intentions, the articulation of meaning, and the creation of shared understanding. Examples of questions that draw attention to the transition process are given below.

Prior experiences
- Think about a positive change experience: what made it positive?
- What did you gain?
- What did you have to give up?
- What were you able to hold on to?
- What emotions did you experience throughout the transition process?
- How did these feelings affect your self-esteem at the time? Subsequently?
- What helped you through the transition process?
- What stumbling blocks did you experience, and how did you overcome these?
- What does this experience tell you about the way in which you approach change?
- How might this knowledge smooth the transition process that you're about to go through?

The transition process is rarely smooth, but reflection on a positive change experience is more likely to reinforce for the mentee a belief in their ability to overcome hurdles and successfully navigate new change initiatives.

The mentor's next task is to provide a catalyst for the mentee's forward movement. To support the newly appointed centre manager to establish a degree of professional distance, the reluctant senior teacher to trial a new pedagogical approach, or the shy, newly qualified early childhood teacher to communicate with parents and contribute to team meetings, wise mentors ask questions that have the power to ignite mentee agency. By deliberately focusing on the transition process, mentors communicate both an awareness of and a concern for the emotions that determine mentee behaviour. Far from constituting an exhaustive list, the questions below help the mentee to surface, reconcile and consciously shape their transition responses.

Moving along the transition curve
- How does this particular change situation resemble or differ from changes you've tackled before?

- Where do you currently sit on the transition curve?
- What are the benefits and costs of remaining where you are?
- What is stopping you from moving along the continuum?
- How motivated are you to move to the next transition phase?
- What are you going to have to let go of (relationships, skills, identity, employment)?
- What is it time to let go of?
- What will you miss most?
- What do you fear or resent most?
- From your perspective, what is over and what isn't?
- What remains the same?
- What is it about this particular change that makes you feel vulnerable?
- How might you take care of yourself during this period of vulnerability?
- What need are you addressing when you behave in this way?
- What kind of role model do you present here?
- How does your current transition phase affect the children, team, clients and organisation?
- What two or three things would make a difference to how you feel if you focused on doing these? What would put you back in control?
- What new relationships might you need to develop?
- What kind of support do you need right now?
- How might you manage or minimise the multiple transitions you are currently experiencing (queuing)?
- How could you find the courage to do what you think is right?
- What do you want the outcome to be?
- How will this align with centre goals and objectives?
- How will you know when you are on the right track?
- What will it look like when you have successfully negotiated the transition period and made the required or desired change?
- How is your understanding of the transition process developing?

Complexity and caution

Trust is an important facet of a successful mentoring relationship. At any one time people experience multiple and simultaneous transitions that cannot be differentiated from the context of their everyday lives (Meleis, Sawyer, Im, Hilfinger Messias, & Schumacher, 2000). For example, a teacher may have finally, and a little grudgingly, accepted the need to adopt a new teaching strategy when a change in reporting expectations undermines their professional self-confidence and generates new resentment. This makes the formulaic and sequential application of the above questions simplistic and potentially damaging. For these questions to elicit powerful insights for the mentee—insights that help them identify what to relinquish, retain and hopefully gain—the mentor must have established a relationship of trust that allows them to surface and probe deeply personal emotions.

Mentors play a vital role in helping mentees not only to prioritise change imperatives but to understand transition processes in ways that enable them to survive and thrive during the process of change. While there is considerable potential for growth and development, for mentor and mentee, realising new learning is a challenging undertaking. Because the transition process also engenders psychological and physiological discomfort (Hopson & Adams, 1977), mentors must be alert to the fine line between mentoring and counselling. Skilful, ethical and empathic mentors realise the limits of their expertise and, where necessary, broker the involvement of other specialists. They are particularly mindful of the fine line between mentoring and the reporting complexities in early childhood services, tensions that occur regardless of whether mentoring is an internal or an external undertaking.

Conclusion

This chapter has highlighted the internal dimensions of change and the power of mentoring to help mentees navigate the multiple and almost daily transitions that continuous change brings in early childhood education. Fisher (2005) reminds us that

> for an organization to change, individuals within that organization must change. We need to ensure that we do not lose sight of those individuals within the process, and that we focus on what the change means to each individual and its impact on their psychological

contract with the organization at a team and organizational level. (pp. 257–258)

Mentors who focus exclusively on performance risk ignoring the psychosocial dimensions of transition. Given that teachers' previous change experiences shape their dispositions towards change and help frame psychological contracts, savvy mentors endeavour to understand what lies within. This is critical to improved performance, because "unless [mentees] can make the transitions that the changes require, those changes will simply not work" (Bridges, 2006, p. 4).

References

Adams, J., Hayes, J., & Hopson, B. (Eds). (1977). *Transition: Understanding and managing personal change.* Montclair, NJ: Allanheld, Osmund & Co.

Awaya, A., McEwan, H., Heylen, D., Linsky, S., Lum, D., & Wakukawa, P. (2003). Mentoring as a journey. *Teaching and Teacher Education, 19*(1), 45–56. doi:10.1016/S0742-051X(02)00093-8

Bridges, W. (1980). *Transitions: Making sense of life's changes.* Reading, MA: Addison-Wesley.

Bridges, W. (2004). *Transitions: Making sense of life's changes* (2nd ed.). New York, NY: Addison-Wesley.

Bridges, W. (2006). *Getting them through the wilderness: A leader's guide to transition.* Retrieved from http://www.wmbridges.com/pdf/getting-thru-wilderness-2006-v2.pdf

Brockbank, A., & McGill, I. (2006). *Facilitating reflective learning through coaching and mentoring.* London, UK: Kogan Page.

Burnes, B. (2004). Kurt Lewin and the planned approach to change: A re-appraisal. *Journal of Management Studies, 41*(6), 977–1002.

Cartwright, D. (Ed.). (1951). *Field theory in social science.* New York, NY: Harper & Brothers.

Chu, M. (2012). Observe, reflect, and apply: Ways to successfully mentor early childhood educators. *Dimensions of Early Childhood, 40*(3), 20–28. Retrieved from http://www.southernearlychildhood.org/upload/pdf/Dimensions_Vol40_3_Chu.pdf.

Clance, P., & Imes, S. (1978). The impostor phenomenon among high achieving women: Dynamics and therapeutic intervention. *Psychotherapy Theory, Research and Practice, 15*(3), 241–247. doi: 10.1037/h0086006

Cooperrider, D.L., & Whitney, D. (1999). *Appreciative inquiry*. San Francisco, CA: Berret-Koehler.

Cranwell-Ward, J., Bossons, P., & Gover, S. (2004). *Mentoring: A Henley review of best practice*. Basingstoke, UK: Palgrave Macmillan.

de Vries, J. (2011). *Mentoring for change*. Melbourne, VIC: Universities Australia Executive Women and LH Martin Institute for Higher Education Leadership and Management.

Fisher, J.M. (2005). A time for change? *Human Resource Development International*, 8(2), 257-263. doi: 10.1080/13678860500100665

Fisher, J.M. (2012). *John Fisher's process of transition diagram*. Retrieved from http://www.businessballs.com/freepdfmaterials/fisher-transition-curve-2012bb.pdf

Fletsch, R.J. (2011). *Transitions and changes: Who copes well?* Retrieved from http://www.ext.colostate.edu/pubs/consumer/10215.html.

Freese, C., Schalk, R., & Croon, M. (2010). The impact of organizational changes on psychological contracts: A longitudinal study. *Personnel Review*, 40(4), 404-422. doi:10.1108/00483481111133318

Greyling, J. (2006). Managing people through transition. *Accountancy SA*, 6, 22-23. Retrieved from http://ezproxy.waikato.ac.nz/login?url=http://search.proquest.com/docview/215228590?accountid=17287.

Hendry, C. (1996). Understanding and creating whole organizational change through learning theory. *Human Relations*, 49(5), 621-641.

Hopson, B., & Adams, J. (1977). Towards an understanding of transition: Defining some boundaries of transition dynamics. In J. Adams, J. Hayes, & B. Hopson (Eds), *Transition: Understanding and managing personal change* (pp. 3-25). Montclair, NJ: Allanheld, Osmund & Co.

Kets de Vries, M.F.R. (1990). The impostor syndrome: Developmental and societal issues. *Human Relations*, 43(7), 667-686. doi: 10.1177/001872679004300704

Kram, K. (1983). Phases of the mentor relationship. *Academy of Management Journal*, 26(4), 608-625. Retrieved from http://www.jstor.org/stable/255910.

Kubler-Ross, E. (1969). *On death and dying*. New York, NY: Macmillan.

Lewin, K. (1997). *Resolving social conflicts and field theory in social science*. Washington, DC: American Psychological Association.

Meleis, A.I., Sawyer, L.M., Im, E.O., Hilfinger Messias, D.K., & Schumacher, K. (2000). Experiencing transitions: An emerging middle-range theory. *ANS Advances in Nursing Science*, 23(1), 12-28.

Osterman, K., & Kottkamp, R. (1993). *Reflective practice for educators: Improving schooling through professional development.* Newbury Park, CA: Corwin.

Pask, R., & Joy, B. (2007). *Mentoring-coaching: A guide for education professionals.* Berkshire, UK: Open University Press.

Quick, S., Fletsch, R.J., & Rupured, M. (2011). *Transitions and changes: Practical strategies.* Retrieved from http://www.ext.colostate.edu/pubs/consumer/10214.html

Rhodes, C., Stokes, M., & Hampton, G. (2004). *A practical guide to mentoring, coaching and peer-networking: Teacher professional development in schools and colleges.* Abingdon, UK: Routledge.

Rock, D., & Donde, R. (2007). *Driving organisational change with internal coaching programs.* Retrieved from http://neuroleadershipgroup.co.za/wp/wp-content/uploads/Whitepaper OnInternalCoaching.pdf.

Rogers, J. (2012). *Coaching skills: A handbook* (3rd ed.). Maidenhead, UK: Open University Press.

Rousseau, D.M. (1995). *Psychological contracts in organisations: Understanding written and unwritten agreements.* Thousand Oaks, CA: Sage.

Salzman, J. (2002). *The promise of mentoring: The challenge of professional development.* Cheltenham, UK: Hawker Brownlow Education.

Schein, E. (1965). *Organisational psychology.* Englewood Cliffs, NJ: Prentice-Hall.

Schein, E. (1996). Kurt Lewin's change theory in the field and in the classroom: Notes towards a model of management learning. *Reflections, 1*(1), 59–72.

Yendol-Hoppey, D., & Dana, N. (2007). *The reflective educator's guide to mentoring: Strengthening practice through knowledge, story, and metaphor.* Thousand Oaks, CA: Corwin.

Index

A

accountability in teacher education 112
action learning 7–8, 57
action research 188–89, 193, 196, 244, 267
active listening 92, 241
adult learning xxi–xxii, 231–32, 244
agency 57–58, 61, 257
    provisionally registered teachers 202–03
    student teachers 126
    in transition process 269, 272
āheinga kōrero, āheinga whakaaro (free to speak, free to think) 70–71
āhuatanga Māori (Māori practices) 82, 83, 85
ako 75, 82, 91
ākonga (teachers and learners) 90, 92, 93–94, 97
Aʻoga Faʻa Samoa 227
appraisal cycle, and professional learning 187–96
Appraisal for Teachers workshops (NZTC) 22
aroha ki te tangata (reciprocal obligation to care for others) 70, 71, 75
assessment in the practicum 105, 128, 247
    associate teacher role 120
    dual mentoring and assessment responsibilities 112–15
    e-portfolios 136
    teacher educator role 110
assimilation 84
associate teachers, practicum role and perspectives 109–10, 111–12, 113–14, 115, 120
assumptions 31, 32, 33–34, 36
attachment, theory and nature of 200–01, 202, 203–04, 205, 218
Australian National Quality Framework for Early Childhood Education and Care (NQF) 25
    National Quality Standard (NQS) 26
authentic relationships 41, 90, 92, 94, 120, 124–27, 129, 253, 254, 255–56
autonomy, provisionally registered teachers 202–03
āwhina (to assist, benefit, befriend) 147

B

beginning teachers *see* provisionally registered teachers; registration requirements and process
belonging
    children in early childhood centres 205
    in mentor–mentee relationship 44, 47, 120, 121–23, 127, 128–29, 146, 148, 239–40
    participation in mentoring project 239–40, 245
    Te Whāriki strand 44, 47, 49, 74, 121
biculturalism 73, 80, 85, 87
blended action learning 7–8, 57

Brainwave Trust 201
Bridges, personal transition
	model 268, 269–70
British Picture Vocabulary Test 229
Bronfenbrenner's ecological systems
	theory xxii, 217

C

Centres of Innovation programme
	A'oga Fa'a Samoa 227
	establishment xxi
	external mentors 7
	mentoring as a leadership
		development strategy 5
	Roskill South Kindergarten 227
change *see also* transition
	Lewin's organisational change
		model 266–67
	mentoring as component of change
		initiatives 263
	openness to 191–92
	versus transition 264–66
Chinese, effect of cultural
	differences 184
coaching
	definition 2
	distinguished from mentoring
		2, 94
	future practices 9–10
	practices 4–5, 241
	purpose 2
	skills required 3, 10
co-constructivist approach 30, 34,
	133, 142
co-inquiry 146, 271–72
co-learning 271–72
collaboration
	beginning and experienced
		teachers 182–84, 202, 203

and distributed leadership 6, 9–10
leadership practices 9–10, 96
in Māori-medium settings 83, 84
mentoring teacher-researchers 149
mentor–mentee 199, 205, 207, 216,
	217–19, 220, 237, 239, 240–41,
	242–43
in peer mentoring 56–57, 61
during practicum 125, 127, 135,
	139, 142
Te Rito Maioha Early Childhood
	New Zealand mentors 150
team appraisal cycle 187–96
colleagues
	communicating with 182–84
	mentoring 152–54
collective responsibility and processes
	see also inclusion
	critical reflection 217
	versus individualism 169
	Kidsfirst Kindergarten value 62
	knowledge 153
	in Māori-medium settings 70, 71,
		72, 83, 85–86, 147
	in a mentoring programme 93, 147
	peer mentoring 55–57
	team appraisal cycle 189, 192, 195
colonisation 150, 152, 153
communication
	in Māori-medium settings 70–71
	in mentoring of colleagues 154
	and mentoring relationship 127,
		217, 241, 246
	Te Whāriki strand, application to
		mentoring 44, 48, 254
	in team appraisal cycle 192–93, 194
communities
	Māori 71
	relationships with 40, 41, 43, 51

community of practice *see* professional learning communities
community plane, understanding knowledge and practice 33, 34
competency-based training 214
contextual mentorship 184, 185
contribution (*Te Whariki* strand), application to mentoring 44, 48
cost–benefit analysis 169, 175
critical friends 4, 5, 6, 245
   in communities of practice 34
   similarity of facilitators/researchers to 8
critical reflection xxi, 8, 10, 16, 17, 21, 35, 36, 165, 191, 193–94, 217, 224, 241, 244, 256 *see also* reflective practice
critical thinking 39, 92, 93, 203, 219
cultural deprivation theory 78
curriculum 162
   Te Whariki applied as 40, 80, 85, 254

D

Declaration on the Rights of Indigenous Peoples 86–87
developmental mentorship 184, 185
Dewey, John 27
dialogue
   collaborative 32
   collective 189, 192, 193, 194, 195, 196
   and effectiveness of mentoring 91, 92, 94
   in e-portfolios 135, 139, 140, 141, 142
   head teachers 52, 59
   in mentoring training 244
   power and cultural considerations 150, 152, 153
   in the practicum 124, 128, 132
   professional, in mentoring relationship 159, 160, 161, 162, 163, 165
   and relational–cultural theory framework 254–60
digital literacy 138, 218
dispositions 190
   of inquiry 203, 207
   mentee, and transition process 269–70, 271
   mentors 16, 19, 146
distance mentoring 97–98
distributed leadership 5–6, 9–10
diversity 41, 96, 151–53, 165, 224

E

ea (satisfaction) 148
early childhood centres *see also* kōhanga reo
   contextual challenges 19–20, 179–81, 184, 185, 212, 275
   funding for services employing registered teachers 172–76
   lack of fully registered teachers 20
   Licensing Criteria (Ministry of Education, 2008) 201
   owner–manager's experience of mentoring 160–66
   self-review 93–94, 182, 201, 203–04, 259
   staff lack of time for mentoring 180
   support for mentoring 200
   teaching team dynamics and knowledge 217–20
   team appraisal cycle, and professional learning 187–96

early childhood centre (*continued*)
    trainee and provisionally registered teachers' ideas 182–84, 202, 203–04, 205–06, 219
    transition of teacher to centre manager 265, 267
    under-valuing and under-resourcing of mentoring 20, 172–76
Eastern Institute of Technology (EIT) 121
ecological systems theory xxii, 217
economic utility 169
Education Amendment Act 2015 xx
Education Council of Aotearoa New Zealand (EDUCANZ) xx–xxi, xxiii *see also* New Zealand Teachers Council (NZTC)
Education Review Office (ERO) xx, 93, 228
educational policy, economic nature 212
email, use in mentoring 160, 161, 162–63, 204
emotional intelligence 29
empathy 8, 16, 132, 150, 152, 154
    mutual 253, 254–55, 256
empowerment 40, 43, 45, 48, 96, 108, 126, 187, 191, 192, 194, 196, 240, 241, 254, 257, 258
enablement 62, 272
engagement of mentees 244
e-portfolios 133, 134–35, 141–42
    challenges 137–38
    feedback about use of e-portfolios 138–41
    increasing connections in practicum setting 135–36
    looking forward 141
    security and privacy 137
    understanding the technology 138
    user training 138, 141
ethics 94, 95, 107, 154, 165, 170, 184, 228
evidence
    critique of evidence-based training 214
    registration requirements and process 73, 87, 179, 182, 206, 207
expert–novice approach 29, 30, 237, 251–52
exploration (*Te Whariki* strand), application to mentoring 44, 48

F

families/whānau
    literacy programmes 230–31
    Māori-medium settings 68–70, 73, 85, 147
    online communication 59
    paramount in child's life and experience 46
    relationships with 40, 41, 43, 45, 46, 47, 51, 239, 241, 242, 247
feedback
    constructive 29, 68, 122
    in leaderless peer groups 53, 57, 58
    for mentors 207
    personal type of mentor relationship 30
    during practicum 107–08, 109, 110, 112, 114, 122, 125, 134, 136, 137
    for provisionally registered teachers 180, 181–82, 203, 205, 206
feminist theory and values 253, 254, 260

field-based teacher education (FBTE) *see* practicum
Fisher, personal transition model 268, 269

G

Guidelines for Induction and Mentoring and Mentor Teachers (NZTC) xx, 3, 15, 17, 18, 20, 75, 180–81, 198, 199, 215

H

hā (essence) 73
heterarchical leadership model 92
hinengaro (mind, body, spirit) 80
hoa mahi (colleagues) 73
holistic development 40, 41, 43, 46, 141, 164, 191
Hopson & Adams, personal transition model 268
hui (meeting) 73
humanistic approach to mentoring 15, 20

I

ICT, use as a common language 227
inclusion 57, 70, 74, 85, 90, 93, 95–96, 122–23, 128, 129 *see also* collective responsibility and processes
indigenous peoples
  rights 86–87
  world views 153
individualism 168, 169, 254
  knowledge 153
induction programmes
  benefits 3
  lack of financial support 14, 19
  in Māori-medium settings 70, 78–79, 80, 81–83, 84–86
New Zealand Teachers Council (NZTC) pilot projects 80, 82
initial teacher education (ITE) 105, 106–07, 225
inquiry
  learning 188, 189, 190–91, 193, 196
  mentoring approach 146, 271–72
  teacher inquiry xxi–xxii
instrumental reasoning 169, 175
intellectual property, Māori 148
intergenerational learning 85
International Labour Organisation, Convention 169 86
Internet access and use 137, 141
interpersonal plane, understanding knowledge and practice 33–34

J

journal writing 33, 35–36, 246

K

kaiako (beginning teacher) 85 *see also* provisionally registered teachers (PRTs)
kaiārahi piri (mentor) 145, 147–48, 149, 152
kaitiakitanga 83
kaiwhakahaere (leader, mentor, coach, teacher) 72
kanohi ki te kanohi (face-to-face) 70, 73
kaupapa Māori (focuses) 72, 73, 74
Kei Tua o te Pae 226
kia tiaho Tamanuiterā metaphor for mentoring 89, 90–95, 97, 98–99
Kidsfirst Kindergartens 51–52, 54–61, 62

knowledge *see also* ways of knowing
   individual *versus* collective 153
   local applications 154
   mentors 16, 17, 19, 21, 240, 244, 255, 264
   sharing of, in mentoring 199, 216, 217–19, 240, 255
   teachers 213–14, 216, 217–20, 225, 241, 246
   transferring from mentor to mentee 133, 135, 139–40
kōhanga reo
   establishment 78–79
   Te Hāpai Ō 84–86
   Te Iti Rearea pedagogy 80–81
   whānau support 69
kōtahitanga (unity) 72, 83
kura kaupapa Māori 69–70, 79, 231
   Te Hāpai Ō 84–86
   Te Iti Rearea pedagogy 80–81

L

'leaderful practice' 56–57
leaderless groups
   benefits 53–54
   challenges 54
leadership
   difference between leaders and managers 92
   distributed 5–6, 9–10
   heterarchy of 92
   newly registered teachers 172
   shared 96, 196
leadership development
   coaching as a strategy 4–7, 9–10
   lack of financial support 9
   mentoring as a strategy 4, 5–8, 9–10, 91–92, 239, 241, 245–46
   peer mentoring group influence 57, 58, 61, 62
   provisionally registered teachers 205–06
   self assessment 61
   student teachers 125–26
   University of Auckland Centre for Educational Leadership, First Time Principals Programme 18
learning communities *see* professional learning communities
Lewin's organisational change model 266–67
Licensing Criteria (Ministry of Education, 2008) 201
listening 2, 8, 9, 60, 71, 75, 94, 270, 271, 272
   active 92, 241
literacy 223, 225–33
   digital 138, 218
   second-language learners 227
locus of control 269–70

M

mai rā nō (handed down from generation to generation) 86
mana (prestige) 148
manaakitanga (caring, generosity, hospitality) 70, 75, 83, 148
managers, difference from leaders 92
mangō ururoa (hammerhead shark) 89, 90, 98–99
Māori education
   educational research 149–50
   performance rates, 1960s–80s 84
Māori-medium settings
   context of induction and mentoring 78–79
   effective mentoring of provisionally registered teachers 68–70

key considerations in mentoring 70–72, 74–75, 80, 81–86, 87, 147
outcomes of a Māori perspective on early childhood education 86–87
registration requirements and process 69–70, 71–72, 79–80, 81–82, 83–86, 87
and wānanga sector approaches to teacher education 80
whānau support of provisionally registered teachers 68–69
Māoritanga (Māoriness) 72
marae 71, 77, 86, 147–48, 149
market forces 168, 169, 174
Massey University 228 *see also* Strengthening Early Learning Opportunities (SELO) programme
   Centre for Educational Development 231
   Institute of Education 231
mātauranga Māori (Māori knowledge and values) 81, 83
mentees *see also* mentor–mentee relationship; provisionally registered teachers; student teachers
   belonging and wellbeing 47, 239–40, 245
   dispositions and transition process 269–70, 271
   engagement 244
   management of learning 271
   overall benefits of mentoring 244–45, 252–53
   professional growth 240–41, 244, 245
   relationships with colleagues 47–48
   self-awareness 270
   self-confidence and self-reliance 240, 241, 242–43, 246
   work–life context 41, 205
mentor–mentee relationship 16, 27–28, 29–30, 146–47 *see also* reciprocity in mentoring relationship; respect in mentoring relationship; trust in mentoring relationship
   associate teacher perspectives 109–10, 113, 115
   belonging 44, 47, 120, 121–23, 127, 128–29, 146, 148, 239–40
   collaboration 199, 205, 207, 216, 217–19, 220, 237, 239, 240–41, 242–43
   communication 127, 217, 246
   complexity 211, 217–18, 275
   critical to effectiveness of mentoring 91–92, 242–44, 245, 250
   in distance mentoring 97–98
   effect of assessment requirements in practicum 112–13, 115
   enabling 42, 272
   expectations and attitudes 127–29
   independent mentor perspectives 200–01, 202, 203, 204–05, 206
   key dimensions 253
   Māori perspectives 68–69, 70–72, 75, 147
   mentoring a teacher renewing her registration 159–66
   nurturing 68, 145, 146, 148, 154, 242

mentor–mentee relationship (*continued*)
    participation 120, 123, 124–27, 128, 239–40, 256
    Pasifika perspectives 147
    power dynamics 29, 30, 73, 96, 150, 153, 253, 257–59
    provisionally registered teacher perspectives 181–86, 200, 201–04, 205–06
    reflexivity 30–32, 35
    relational–cultural theory framework 250–51, 253–60
    student teacher perspectives 108–09, 113–15, 120–29, 219
    and teacher education 211–12, 215–20
    teacher educator perspectives 111–12, 115, 122
    technology as a tool 133–42
    types 29–30
mentoring *see also* kia tiaho Tamanuiterā metaphor for mentoring; Māori-medium settings; peer mentoring; practicum; Victoria, State-wide Mentoring Program for Early Childhood Teachers (SWMP)
    appraisal cycle, and professional learning 187–96
    benefits 3, 7, 244–45, 252–53
    of colleagues 152–54
    definitions and description 146–47, 214–17
    developmental phases 272
    distance mentoring 97–98
    distinguished from coaching 2, 94
    formal programmes 2, 3, 4
    funding 19, 170, 171, 172–76
    future practices 9–10
    informal relationships 2, 4
    key aspects of a successful programme 95–98
    lack of financial support 14, 19
    New Zealand Teachers Council expectation 15–16
    New Zealand Teachers Council (NZTC) pilot projects 80, 82
    NZTC effective mentoring study 68–70
    practices 3–4
    questioning as a strategy 8, 10, 16, 19, 94, 264, 270, 271, 272–74
    self-review 93–95, 140, 259
    Strengthening Early Learning Opportunities (SELO) programme 223–33
    te ao Māori considerations 70–72, 74–75, 81, 82, 86, 97, 147–49, 169
    Te Whāriki framework 39, 41–49
    of teacher-researchers 144–45, 149–50
    teachers preparing for registration 159–66, 169–76, 198–207
    transition support 270–72
    voluntary nature 2
mentoring conversations 3, 16, 17, 21, 34, 41, 42, 47, 83, 125, 127, 128, 129, 165
    e-portfolio use 134–35
    in peer mentoring 57–58, 61
mentoring development and support 16–20, 243–44, 252
    contextual challenges xxii–xxiii, 19–20
    gap in provision of further education xxii–xxiv

mentor development
programme 18–19
mentors of registering teachers 173
programme review and
refinement 20–22
skill requirements and building 3,
10, 16, 17, 19, 238, 241, 244
style modelled on own
experience xxii, 14
Te Hāpai Ō 79–80, 81–82, 83–86
training xxiii, 17–18, 243–44, 245
mentors 3 *see also* associate teachers;
teacher educators
characteristics of a successful
mentor 94
confidence 185–86, 239, 240, 244
dispositions 16, 19, 146
external/independent 7–9, 200–01,
202, 203, 204–05, 206, 243
internal 7, 8
kaiārahi piri 145, 147–48, 149, 152
knowledge and skills 16, 17, 19, 21,
240, 244, 255, 264
'mentor teacher,' introduction of
term 3
overall benefits of mentoring 7, 25,
244, 245, 252–53
pou tautoko 79–80, 81–85, 87
professional growth 25, 240–41,
245, 252, 256–57
role 29–30, 179, 182
strengthening of practicum role by
e-portfolio use 138–40, 141
Te Rito Maioha Early Childhood
New Zealand 71, 144–54
Ministry of Education 9, 10, 226 *see
also Te Whariki*
Licensing Criteria 201
and literacy development 223,
227–28, 231, 232
Ngā Arohaehae Whai Hua / Self
Review Guidelines 204
professional development
contracts xxi–xxii
Tātaiako 75, 91
Te Aho Matua 69–70, 71
Teen Parent Unit 231
mobile devices 137

N

National Aspiring Principals
programme 9
Ndugore people, Solomon
Islands 151
'negotiated space' concept 153
Nelson Tasman Kindergarten
Association 167, 169–76
neoliberalism
definition 168
mentoring context 167–76
networking *see also* collaboration
and distributed leadership 6
Māori-medium settings 83
New Teachers Centre, Santa Cruz,
mentoring programme 18
New Zealand Association of
Researchers in Education 170
New Zealand Coaching and
Mentoring Sector (NZCMC) 52,
53, 54, 62
*New Zealand Code of Ethics for
Registered Teachers* (NZTC,
2004) 95
New Zealand Educational
Institute 71
New Zealand Leadership in Early
Childhood Education for '5 out
of 5' Children 60–61

New Zealand Teachers Council
(NZTC) *see also* Education
Council of Aotearoa New
Zealand (EDUCANZ)
  Appraisal for Teachers
    workshops 22
  conference on mentoring (2013) 93
  effective mentoring study 68–70
  expectation for educative
    mentoring 15–16, 22
  *Guidelines for Induction and
    Mentoring and Mentor
    Teachers* xx, 3, 15, 17, 18, 20, 75,
    180–81, 198, 199, 215
  Induction and Mentoring Pilot
    projects 80, 82, 84–86
  *New Zealand Code of Ethics for
    Registered Teachers* (2004) 95
  open-to-learning focus 188
  Registered Teacher Criteria xxiii,
    10, 20, 22, 73, 83, 87, 159, 163,
    182, 188, 198, 200, 204, 206,
    207, 216
  Tātaiako xxiii, 75, 91
  Te Hāpai Ō (2012) 79, 83–84, 85
  workshops on mentoring 17–18
Ngā Arohaehae Whai Hua / Self
  Review Guidelines (Ministry of
  Education, 2006) 204
novice–expert relationship 29, 30,
  237, 251–52
nurturing 68, 145, 146, 148, 154, 242

O

OECD 215
open-to-learning conversations 96,
  183, 187–88, 191–93

P

papa (foundation) 73
participation, in mentor–mentee
  relationship 120, 123, 124–27,
  128, 239–40, 256
Pasifika *see also* Samoan children;
  Tonga and Tongans
  collective knowledge 153
  educational research 149–50,
    151–52
  world views 145, 147, 153–54
peer coaching 189
peer mentoring 53–54
  benefits of leaderless groups 53–54,
    56–58
  challenges of leaderless groups 54,
    60
  collective responsibility 55–57
  head teachers' perspectives 55–56
  implementing head teacher
    leaderless groups 54–55
  link between individual learner and
    groups 61
  opportunities and potential 60–61
  peer influence in shifting thinking
    and changing practice 58–59
  personal growth 57–58
  progressing pedagogical
    leadership 61
peer relationship, mentoring as 251
peer supervision 52–53
personal mentoring relationship 29–30
personal plane, understanding
  knowledge and practice 32–33
pia (beginning teachers) 79, 81–85, 87
pono (honourable, true) 73
pou tautoko (mentors) 79–80,
  81–85, 87
pouako 147, 148

power relationships *see also* empowerment
  mentor–mentee 29–30, 73, 75, 96, 150, 153, 253, 257–59
  in peer groups 60
pōwhiri 69, 70
practical level of reflective practice 35
practicum
  assessment 105, 110, 112–15, 120
  associate teacher role and perspectives 109–10, 111–12, 113–14, 115, 120
  dual mentoring and assessment responsibilities 112–15
  e-portfolios 133–42
  mentoring and support 105, 107–12
  research studies 106–07, 119, 120–21
  student-teacher perspectives 107–09, 113–15, 120–29
  teacher educator roles and perspectives 110–12, 113–14, 115, 122–23
Practising Teacher Criteria (EDUCANZ) xx *see also* Registered Teacher Criteria (NZTC)
pre-service teachers *see* student teachers
principals
  mentoring of 9
    University of Auckland Centre for Educational Leadership, First Time Principals Programme 18
priority learners 223, 226
proactivity 94
procedural mentoring relationship 29
professional capital 189–90
professional development *see also* leadership development; mentoring development
  characteristics and structural features 224–25
  financial support 9, 14
  for literacy teaching 225–33
  Maori-medium settings 71, 81, 82–83
  move to professional learning community 191, 195
  for provisionally registered teachers 201
  recent approaches xx–xxii
  self-funded 19
professional inquiry
  mentoring 21
  teaching 21
professional learning communities 6, 8, 9, 10, 40, 48, 92, 237
  definition 6
  e-portfolio use 134–35
  peer groups 52, 58, 60, 62
  student teacher participation 124–27, 129, 134–35, 139–40
  team appraisal cycle 187–93, 194–95
provisionally registered teachers (PRTs) *see also* mentor–mentee relationship; registration requirements and process
  agency and autonomy 202–03
  coaching, induction and mentoring 6, 15, 178–86, 198–207, 215–17
  first experiences of teaching 179
  in Māori-medium settings 68–70, 72–74, 79, 81–85, 87
  mentoring development programme 18–22

provisionally registered teachers (*continued*)
   need for professional learning 17–18
   neoliberal context of mentoring 167–76
   NZTC effective mentoring study 68–70
   self funding of induction and mentoring programmes 19, 173
   taking responsibility in mentoring relationship 199, 207
   three teachers' mentoring experiences 181–85
   trial and error method of learning 17
psychological contract 265–66, 276

Q

questioning
   in coaching 2–3, 8, 10
   in leadership development 57
   in mentoring 8, 10, 16, 19, 94, 264, 270, 271, 272–74

R

rangatiratanga (self-determination) 72, 83
reciprocity
   aroha ki te tangata (reciprocal obligation to care for others) 70, 71
   and children's learning 40, 43
   effect of assessment requirements in practicum 112
   manaakitanga 83
   reflections 36
   ways of knowing 33, 35
reciprocity in mentoring
   relationship 25, 35, 37, 67, 74, 85, 91, 93, 94, 237, 252
   Australian SWMP findings 237, 242–43
   external mentors 7
   journaling 36
   Māori perspective 147
   mentoring of colleagues 153
   mentoring to support transition 271
   mutual empathy 253, 254–55, 256
   in the practicum 112, 120, 122, 123–24, 125, 127, 129
   and social justice 96
   whanaungatanga model 86
reflection-for-action 28–29, 30
reflection-in-action 27–28
reflection-on-action 27–28
reflective practice 7, 8, 15, 237 *see also* critical reflection
   action research 189
   Australian National Quality Standard 1.2 26
   Australian Reflective Practice Project 239, 241–42, 244
   in contrast to technical practice 165
   description 27–29
   developing in others 34–36
   mentoring 21–22, 26–27, 40, 91, 161, 237
   peer group influence 58–59
   during practicum 128, 129, 139
   professional learning and development 224
   provisionally registered teachers 182, 184, 185, 202, 203, 204
   Te Aho Matua requirement 71

team appraisal cycle 189, 191, 193–94
three levels 35
reflexivity 30–32
developing in mentoring 32–33
Registered Teacher Criteria (NZTC) xxiii, 10, 20, 22, 73, 83, 87, 159, 163, 182, 188, 198, 200, 204, 206, 207, 216 *see also Practising Teacher Criteria* (EDUCANZ)
registration requirements and process
discrete criteria 163
evidence 73, 87, 179, 182, 206, 207
form and function 164, 165, 166
funding for mentoring support 170, 171, 172–76
and kaupapa Māori situations 69–70
mentoring a teacher renewing her registration 159–66
provisionally registered teachers mentored to full registration 181–86, 198–207
Te Amorangi ki Mua model 81, 82–83, 85, 87
Te Hāpai Ō 79–80, 81–82, 83–86, 87
teachers in Māori-medium settings 71–72, 79
Teachers Registering Teachers (TRT) programme 169–76
technical practice *versus* critically reflective practice 165
relational mentorship 184–85
relational–cultural theory
framework 250–51, 253–54, 259–60
in action 254–59

relationships *see also* mentor–mentee relationship
reciprocal and responsive 39, 40, 43, 45–46
research
action research 188–89, 193, 196, 244, 267
Māori 149–50
Pasifika 149–50, 151–52
teacher-researchers 144–45, 149–50
universities' role 212
respect in mentoring relationship 5, 29, 67, 69, 94
appraisal cycle 188, 191, 193
communities of practice 34
maintaining 154
Māori perspective 70, 73, 74, 75, 149
mentoring of colleagues 153
mentoring of provisionally registered teachers 205
Pasifika perspective 154
in the practicum 121, 123–24, 126, 127, 129
Rodd, Jillian, *Leadership in Early Childhood* xxv–xxvi
Roskill South Kindergarten 227

S

Samoan children, literacy skills 227–28
scaffolding 189, 204, 218, 253
Schön, Donald 27–28
second-language learners 227–28
self-actualization 73
self-awareness 7, 270
self-efficacy 4, 29, 58, 94
self-examination 31, 32, 33, 35

self-review 93–95, 140, 182, 201, 203–04, 259
   Ngā Arohaehae Whai Hua / Self Review Guidelines (Ministry of Education, 2006) 204
'situated apprentice' approach to mentoring 15, 20
skills
   coaching 3, 10
   mentoring 3, 10, 16, 17, 19, 238, 241, 244, 255, 264
   teaching 213–14, 218, 246
Smith, Linda Tuhiwai 150, 152, 153
social capital 189
social coaching 204–05
social constructivism 30, 34, 133, 142, 216
social justice 67, 90, 93, 96
sociocultural perspective 167, 168, 226–27
Socrates xxv
storytelling 97, 150–52
Strengthening Early Learning Opportunities (SELO) programme 223–31
   underpinning principles 231–33
student teachers
   employed *versus* voluntary status 120, 121, 122, 123, 124, 126, 127–29
   leadership development 125–26
   learning to make judgements 219, 220
   need to please 113–14
   participation in learning communities 124–27, 129, 134–35, 138–39
   perspectives on mentor–mentee relationship 108–09, 113–15, 120–29, 219
   perspectives on practicum 108–09, 113–15
supervision 53
   peer supervision 52–53

T

take (cause) 148
tamariki (children) 73, 74, 85, 90
tangata whenuatanga 75
tapu (state of being set apart) 148
Tātaiako (Ministry of Education & New Zealand Teachers Council) 75, 91
Te Aho Matua (Ministry of Education) 69–70, 71
Te Amorangi ki Mua model 81, 82–83, 85, 87
te ao Māori 70–72, 74–75, 81, 82, 86, 97, 147–49, 169
te ao māramatanga (the world of light) 145, 149, 151
Te Hāpai Ō (New Zealand Teachers Council, 2012) 79, 83–84, 85
Te Hāpai Ō strategy 79, 87
   as induction and mentoring initiative 84–86
   and Te Amorangi ki Mua model 81–84, 87
te reo Māori 74, 77, 78–79, 80–81, 84, 86, 147
Te Rito Maioha Early Childhood New Zealand 71, 144–54
Te Riu Roa 71
Te Tari Puna Ora o Aotearoa / New Zealand Childcare Association 71 *see also* Te Rito Maioha Early Childhood New Zealand

Te Tiriti o Waitangi (Treaty of
    Waitangi) 74, 90
Te Whare Wānanga a Awanuiārangi
    (TWWoA) 77, 79, 80, 86, 87
    Te Iti Rearea pedagogy 80–81
Te Whariki
    applied as curriculum 40, 80,
        85, 254
    commitment to Te Tiriti o
        Waitangi 74, 80
    and contexts 167
    framework applied in
        mentoring 39, 41–49
    and literacy development 225, 226
    and openness to learning 191, 193
    practice in Māori-medium
        settings 70
    principles 40, 45–46
    strands 45, 47–48, 74, 121, 191
    and Te Hāpai Ō 85
Te Whatu Pōkeka 233
teacher education 211–12 *see
    also* practicum; professional
    development; provisionally
    registered teachers (PRTs);
    registration requirements and
    process; student teachers
    challenges to assumptions 212–14
    Māori perspective on wānanga
        sector approaches 80
teacher educators
    communication 127
    expectations of student teachers in
        field-based teacher education 120
    perspectives on mentor–mentee
        relationship 111–12, 115, 122
    practicum role and
        perspectives 110–12, 113–14,
        115, 122–23

teacher inquiry xxi–xxii
teacher-researchers 144–45, 149–50
Teachers Registering Teachers (TRT)
    programme 169–76
team learning 190
technical level of reflective practice
    35, 36
technology *see also* e-portfolios
    email use in mentoring 160, 161,
        162–63, 204
    to support literacy teaching 227, 230
teu le va (to value, cherish, nurture
    and take care of the *va*) 145, 147,
    152, 154
'through-the-mirror writing' 33
tika (correct, valid) 73
tikanga Māori (Māori cultural values
    and practices) 81, 82, 86, 147,
    148, 149
tino rangatiratanga (absolute sovereign
    right) 79, 80–81
tīpuna (ancestors) 86
Tomorrow's Schools reforms 80
Tonga and Tongans 160
    children's literacy skills 227–28
    research 150
training, mentoring xxiii, 17–18,
    243–44, 245
transformational leadership 48
transformational learning 48, 61,
    62, 108
transformative aspects of
    education 213–14
transition *see also* change
    versus change 264–66
    comparison of personal transition
        models 268
    Lewin's organisational change
        model 266–67

transition (*continued*)
   and mentee dispositions 269–70
   psychosocial dimensions 265–66, 275–76
   questioning as a mentoring strategy 272–74
   supportive mentoring 270–72
trial and error method of learning 17
trust
   in assessment 110
   in coaching 8
   in critical reflection 193, 194
   in learning 191
   in peer groups 55, 57, 60, 61, 62
   in relationships generally 45–46
   te ao Māori considerations 73
   in team/collective learning 190, 191, 192, 193, 196
trust in mentoring relationship 5, 7, 29, 35, 41, 42, 180, 193, 194, 199, 205, 243, 255, 275
   communities of practice 34
   dialogue 32, 33
   and effectiveness of mentoring 91, 94, 95, 96, 98, 185, 207
   in the practicum 110, 112, 126, 129
'trusted inquisitor' 7–8
tuakana–teina relationships 153, 189

U

United Nations Declaration on the Rights of Indigenous Peoples 86–87
University of Auckland Centre for Educational Leadership, First Time Principals Programme 18
user-pays basis for mentoring 19, 173
utu (reciprocation) 148

V

Victoria, State-wide Mentoring Program for Early Childhood Teachers (SWMP)
   case studies 245–47
   considerations for effective mentoring 242–44, 245
   establishment and goals 238–39
   findings 239–42
vivinei soloso bangara (children's stories) 151
voluntary nature of mentoring 2

W

wairuatanga (spiritual interconnectedness) 69, 70, 71, 73, 75, 80, 83
Waitangi Tribunal (Te Rōpū Whakamana i te Tiriti) 78
waka Māori (Māori canoe) 73
wānanga 75
ways of knowing
   challenging 32
   diversity of 151
   influence of assumptions 35
   Māori 72, 74, 81, 82, 98
   openness to different ways 41, 152
   personal exploration 33
   reciprocal 33, 35
wellbeing (*Te Whāriki* strand), application to mentoring 44, 47
Whaea 67
whakapapa 71
whakataukī Māori (Māori metaphor and symbolism) 81
kia tiaho Tamanuiterā 89, 90–95, 97, 98–99
whakawhanaungatanga (relationship building) 72

whanaungatanga (interconnected
    relationships) 70, 71, 72, 73, 83,
    85, 86, 147, 154
work–life context 41, 205
World Indigenous Peoples Conference
    in Education (2009) 80

www.ingramcontent.com/pod-product-compliance
Lightning Source LLC
Chambersburg PA
CBHW080759300426
44114CB00020B/2757